CHILDREN'S TELEVISION IN BRITAIN

CHILDREN'S TELEVISION IN BRITAIN

History, Discourse and Policy

David Buckingham
Hannah Davies
Ken Jones
Peter Kelley

 Publishing

First published in 1999 by the
British Film Institute
21 Stephen Street, London W1P 2LN

The British Film Institute is the UK national agency with responsibility for encouraging
the arts of film and television and conserving them in the national interest.

Cover design: Squid Inc.

Set in Minion by Fakenham Photosetting Limited, Fakenham, Norfolk
Printed in Great Britain by St Edmundsbury Press, Bury St Edmunds

British Library Cataloguing-in-Publication Data
A catalogue record for this book is available from the British Library
ISBN 0–85170–686–X (hbk)
ISBN 0–85170–685–1 (pbk)

Contents

Acknowledgments

The research reported in this book was funded by the Economic and Social Research Council, as part of its 'Media Economics and Media Culture' programme (grant number: L126251026). We would like to thank Professor Simon Frith, the director of the programme, for his support and encouragement.

At the Institute of Education, we would particularly like to thank Betty Mitchell for her sterling work in transcribing and managing much of the data, and for sharing the gossip with us. We are grateful to Kate Mitchell for keeping us supplied with copies of the trade papers. Thanks also to Professor Gunther Kress, who worked with us on other aspects of the project and discussed some of this material with us.

We have relied heavily on the staff of specialist libraries, particularly the British Film Institute and Independent Television Commission libraries in London and the BBC Written Archive Centre in Caversham. We would like to thank them for their help and hospitality. Thanks also to Lyn Eryl-Jones and Maggie Brown for supplying us with additional material.

We conducted several interviews with key individuals in the television industry. For the most part, we have decided to keep their contributions here anonymous, but we would particularly like to thank Janie Grace, Isobel Reid, Steven Andrew and Shari Donnenfeld for their additional support. We would also like to thank our colleagues in the Children and Media Network for their input, particularly David Oswell, Jim Barratt, Maire Davies, Martin Barker, Sonia Livingstone and Lewis Rudd.

Introduction
Defining the Child Viewer

Kids' TV 'dumbing down'

Come back *Play School*, all is forgiven. The BBC and ITV were facing criticism last night after one of the most detailed reports on children's programmes revealed a huge increase in the number of cartoons and repeats.

The report by the Broadcasting Standards Commission said factual and drama programmes for children were becoming an 'endangered species', and that all channels were guilty of a 'creeping erosion' of standards.

Old favourites like *Play Away* and *Play School* were being replaced by *Teletubbies*, *The Simpsons* and cheap animated series, it said . . .

Commission members, including Lady Howe, the chairwoman, said they were concerned that children's programmes had been 'dumbed down' in an effort to attract more viewers.

Lack of money had also forced television channels to buy more cheap American cartoons and imported dramas, to the detriment of home-grown drama series.

'The broadcast media form an integral part of the social development of today's child,' said Lady Howe. 'Quality programming for children should encourage the child's development as a good citizen, with critical abilities and an interest in a wide range of issues.'

She deplored 'the relentless growth of the cartoon genre' and, in a veiled threat, said it might be necessary to legislate to ensure that the BBC stuck to a specific level of diversity of children's programming.[1]

Thus began a recent report in Britain's leading liberal newspaper, the *Guardian*. Alongside a large spread of images from current and past animated successes *The Wombles*, *Rugrats* and *Hey Arnold!*, the report included a schedule of one 'animated day', showing that children with access to satellite television could effectively watch cartoons for most of their waking hours.

Stories about children and the media always make good copy, particularly if (as in this case) they appear to bring bad news. Concerns about the influence of *adult* media on children are, of course, rarely absent from the headlines: the media are regularly accused of encouraging violence, precocious sexuality and other forms of moral decay among the young. Yet the concern about *children's* media – and specifically children's television – is relatively new.

The *Guardian*'s report is just one instance of a growing number of such stories. A few months earlier, the incoming Labour government's schools minister Stephen Byers had singled out the BBC's new pre-school series *Teletubbies* as an example of the 'dumbing down' of British children – although it subsequently emerged that he had never in fact seen the programme.[2] Three months later, the publication of another study of changes in children's provision (also distributed by the Broadcasting Standards Commission [BSC]) was yet again heralded with the headline 'Children's TV "dumbed down" '. The report argued that children were being 'corrupted with mental bubblegum', and that 'public service traditions of trying to turn children into well-adjusted citizens were crumbling under a barrage of American programmes more interested in selling toys and pleasing advertisers'.[3]

We will have more to say in due course about the research on which these stories are based. In fact, the BSC study is rather more equivocal in its conclusions than Lady Howe's statements would suggest; and there are significant methodological problems which somewhat undermine the claim that British children's television is being swamped by American cartoons.[4] While there may indeed be reasons for concern about the future of children's television, the account contained in these and similar stories is one we intend to question on several grounds.

And yet in some respects, this debate seems to be about something *more* than children's television. Why should a government minister be so critical of a children's television programme he has not even seen? Why should a body like the BSC – whose remit covers issues of privacy, taste and decency – be so concerned about quality and diversity in children's programmes? And why should changes in children's television be seen as indicative of a much broader series of cultural changes, epitomised in the notion of 'dumbing down'?

Our answer to these questions is twofold, and it points directly to the central themes of this book. On the one hand, the concern about children's television reflects much broader anxieties about the changing nature of *childhood* – anxieties that are increasingly apparent in so many areas of contemporary society. On the other hand, changes in children's television are also taken as an index of changes within *broadcasting* more generally, and particularly of the apparent decline in its public service role. In both respects, therefore, children's television has come to symbolise something much broader, to the extent that it is becoming difficult to see it for what it is. The debate about children's television is increasingly used as a vehicle for these more wide-ranging concerns, often by people who have very little knowledge of the actual programmes they praise or condemn, not to mention the views of children themselves. And the loudest voices in this debate currently belong to those who wish to sustain traditional conceptions both of childhood and of broadcasting.

In studying children's television, we are thus inevitably raising questions about how childhood is defined and constructed; and about the social and cultural functions of television as a medium. There have been significant changes in both areas in the past fifty years, since television began to be widely available; and the pace of change has accelerated significantly in the past decade. We need to begin, therefore, with a brief sketch of each in turn.

Changing childhoods

The very notion of 'dumbing down' – ironically, a phrase that is itself an American import – is part of a much broader contemporary debate about children's edu-

2

cation. Concern about the 'erosion of standards' is of course perennial, but it has dramatically intensified in recent years. The Conservative government's introduction of a National Curriculum, backed up by an extensive apparatus of testing, marked a significant extension in the centralised control of education; yet it was also justified by appealing to notions of 'parental choice', whereby parents would be able to identify and select the 'best' schools for their children. It has led to an atmosphere of growing competition, not only between schools but also among children themselves. New Labour's much-vaunted emphasis on 'education, education and education' has intensified this pressure, with its insistence on national targets for schools, homework clubs and the need to call failing parents to account. Parents are increasingly urged to invest in their children's education by providing extra coaching at home; and there is currently a massive boom in the publication of books and CD-ROMS designed to 'help your child' with the tests at various Key Stages of the curriculum. Education, it would seem, is the *work* of childhood, and it cannot be allowed to stop once children walk out of the classroom door.

In this context, the status of leisure and entertainment for children is an uneasy one. The only justification for children's television, it would seem, is that it should encourage 'the child's development as a good citizen', to quote Lady Howe's words. From this perspective, children have to be 'well-adjusted' – as the *Guardian* report puts it – before they are entitled to attain the status of citizenship. To suggest that children have a right to be entertained – or even to enjoy 'mental bubblegum' – seems positively irresponsible.

In fact, historians have argued that children's leisure time has been increasingly privatised and subjected to adult supervision over the past fifty years. Broadly speaking, the location of children's leisure has moved from public spaces (such as the street) to family spaces (the domestic living room) to private spaces (the bedroom). Similarly, in the case of the media, public entertainment (the cinema) has given way to domestic entertainment (family television) and thence to individualised entertainment (the TV, computer or games console in the child's bedroom). Of course, this picture is unduly schematic: among other things, it tends to underestimate the social dimensions of contemporary media use (computer games, for instance, are a major focus of peer-group interaction); and it may also neglect the survival of more traditional forms of play and oral culture among children. Nevertheless, growing anxiety about 'stranger danger', traffic and other threats to children has led many parents to furnish the home (and particularly the child's bedroom) as a diverting, technologically rich alternative to the perceived risks of the outside world. Children's autonomy has in some respects been restricted, as more of their leisure time has come under the surveillance of parents; and yet the economic resources devoted to it have also substantially increased relative to other categories of household expenditure.[5] In this move, there is a paradoxical alliance between the traditional desire to protect and control children and the more recent notion of the child as a sovereign consumer.

These concerns about children's education and leisure time can in turn be seen as part of a broader anxiety about the fate of childhood in the closing years of the twentieth century.[6] Of course, concerns about 'the younger generation' are timeless: children and young people have always served as a focus for broader anxieties

3

about social change, indiscipline and moral collapse. In recent years, however, this concern has intensified. In the wake of events like the murder of two-year-old James Bulger by two ten-year-old boys, childhood is frequently seen to be 'in crisis'. There is growing concern right across the political spectrum about the decline in conventional nuclear families, the problem of child abuse, the increase in drug-taking and under-age sex and the need to stem what is seen as a rising tide of violent crime among the young. Children's apparently premature experience of aspects of 'adult' life – sex, drugs and violence – is seen as symptomatic of wider failures in the social and moral order.

In practice, however, these concerns are quite double-edged: children are seen here both as threatened and as threatening. Thus, in debates about child abuse, children are constructed as helpless victims in need of special protection by adults – even though it is adults (and indeed family members) who represent the primary cause of risk. On the other hand, as in debates around child crime, children are explicitly identified as a danger to the rest of us, and hence in need of stricter discipline and control.

Sociologists traditionally dismiss such concerns as 'moral panics'; and in some instances here, there are good grounds for doing so. The murder of James Bulger, for example, was widely seen as an indication of wholesale social and moral collapse among young people; and yet the incidence of child killers has actually remained constant for several decades. Far from being part of a massive increase in child crime, the Bulger case was an isolated incident; yet it provided much-needed justification for harsher approaches to youth justice that were felt to be politically necessary at the time.[7] Here again, the notion of 'childhood' is one that is frequently mobilised in support of much broader initiatives in social policy.

At the same time, one might interpret recent changes in childhood in a very different way, as a kind of extension of the rights of citizenship to children. In this sense, children could be seen as one of a number of social groups (such as women, ethnic minorities or the disabled), previously excluded from the exercise of social power, who are now being given access to it. Children are now enjoying rights to education, legal representation and welfare provision hitherto denied them. Following the UN Convention on the Rights of the Child (1989), many countries have passed new legislation to protect children's rights, both in the family and in their dealings with state agencies. Meanwhile, as we have noted, significantly greater resources are also being devoted to children's upbringing and their leisure pursuits. If capitalism can be said to have created 'the teenager' in the 1950s, children are now increasingly addressed directly as a consumer market in their own right, rather than simply as a means of reaching parents. It could well be argued that children have gained power, not merely as *citizens* but also as *consumers*; and that the two may have become impossible to separate.

However one interprets these changes, it is clear that children are increasingly experiencing aspects of what was formerly seen as 'adult' life, whether or not these remain legally forbidden. Thus, it has been argued that the boundaries between childhood and adulthood have become blurred – and that the *end* of childhood is arriving much earlier than it used to. For some, this is a positive development, a matter of the 'empowerment' of children; while for others, it provokes calls for children's 'freedom' from adult control to be restricted rather than enhanced.

4

Certainly, the 'generation gap' between children and their elders does appear to be growing rather than diminishing. Press reports regularly suggest that children and parents now live separate lives, and rarely converse or spend leisure time together;[8] while it could be argued that a great deal of 'children's culture' – not least as defined by the media – is deliberately incomprehensible to the majority of adults.

Of course, all such generalisations are highly problematic. 'Children' do not represent a singular or homogeneous category: what childhood means, and how it is experienced, obviously depend upon other social factors, such as gender, 'race' or ethnicity, social class, geographical location, and so on. Normative assumptions about children's 'social development' – not to mention their potential status as 'good citizens' – of the kind invoked above have been widely challenged within the social and human sciences over the past twenty years.[9] Certainly in terms of their access to media, children are increasingly being grouped and addressed in ever more differentiated ways. Indeed, it could be argued that we are witnessing a growing polarisation among children – not only between rich and poor but also between those who are living what might be termed 'technological' and 'traditional' childhoods.

At the risk of oversimplifying, it is nonetheless reasonable to conclude that the status of children *as a distinct social group* has altered significantly over this century, and particularly in the fifty years that have elapsed since the widespread advent of television. Traditional patterns of 'social development' – particularly in institutions such as the family – have certainly changed, albeit in complex and contradictory ways; and the pattern of children's leisure time has also been transformed, not least in relation to their use of media. While these changes may in fact be far from sudden or dramatic, they have precipitated a widespread uncertainty about the definition of childhood, and about the nature of children's distinctive characteristics and needs.

Changing media

As Lady Howe's comments imply, children have traditionally been seen as a special audience in British broadcasting. The public service ethos, guaranteed by restrictions on competition and strong government regulation, has ensured that children are to some degree protected from the consequences of 'pure' market forces. Current legislation requires that children be provided with a diverse range of high-quality programmes specifically designed to meet their developmental needs, broadcast at times when they are available to view. While the BBC is often seen as the primary upholder and guarantee of this tradition, similar imperatives continue to govern the work of commercial terrestrial broadcasters.

To risk stating the obvious, the past decade has been a period of massive change within the media industries. Thus, we can point to the increasing convergence of information and communications technologies which has been brought about by digitisation; the increase in commercialism and the relative decline of public service; and the move towards a deregulated, global media system dominated by a small number of large transnational corporations. Meanwhile, the move towards multi-channel systems may be bringing about the decline of broadcasting (and the 'common culture' it makes possible) in favour of narrowcasting, as texts are increasingly targeted at (and marketed to) specialised audiences. Audiences are gradually fragmenting – although announcements of the death of the 'mass audience' are almost certainly premature.

These changes have particular implications for children, and many of them are invoked in the press reports quoted above – although, again, those implications will depend upon *which* children we are talking about. Thus, there have been significant changes in children's *access* to media. The take-up of satellite and cable television, video and home computers is proportionately much higher in households with children. Indeed, children and parents are probably the most significant target market for these new media; and much of the advertising and promotion trades in a popular mystique about children's natural affinity with technology. In the UK, a majority of teenagers now have televisions in their bedrooms, and a significant proportion have VCRs – although in this respect, the gap between the 'technology rich' and the 'technology poor' may be widening. Nevertheless, these economic and technological developments raise the spectre of children having unsupervised access to 'adult' media, and are increasingly leading to calls for stricter control.

Meanwhile, children have effectively been 'discovered' as a new target market in the past few decades. In the case of commercial television, for example, children were not initially seen as an especially valuable audience. In the US commercial system, programmes would only be provided for children at minimum cost, and at times when other audiences were not available to view; and even in the UK, where the public service tradition has been much stronger, children's television has been comparatively underfunded. In the contemporary era of niche marketing, however, children seem to have become much more valuable: they are seen to have significant influence on parents' purchasing decisions, as well as substantial disposable income of their own. In the UK, we now have five specialist cable channels competing to attract the younger audience; and there has been a significant increase in the *amount* of provision for children, if not necessarily in its quality or diversity. At the same time, the fragmentation of the audience is evident in children's declining interest in television, and their enthusiasm for new media.

Changes are also apparent in the kinds of material aimed at children and young people. The rise of horizontally integrated, global media corporations means that children's culture is increasingly characterised by what Marsha Kinder[10] has called 'trans-media intertextuality'. The 'same' stories and characters are recycled between movies, TV shows, videos, computer games, advertisements and printed media; and they also serve as the basis for merchandising toys, clothes, food and a seemingly endless range of other commodities. On the face of it, contemporary children's television also appears to differ greatly from that of previous generations: it makes very different assumptions about how children watch or read, and about what they already understand about the medium. Comparing current animation series with those of thirty years ago, for example, one is struck by their rapid pace, their allusiveness and intertextuality, their complex play with reality and fantasy, their irony and self-referentiality: these are, one might say, quintessentially post-modern texts. Many of the most innovative new textual forms – such as 'interactive' computer games – were initially targeted at children, and only

6

later began to reach out to the adult market. Yet for many critics, these new forms and genres represent an abandonment – even a betrayal – of the cultural and educational values which 'classic' children's television of the *Play School* generation used to embody.

As the press reports above clearly indicate, children's television has become a key site in the struggle to preserve public service broadcasting; and the wider symbolic importance and emotional force of childhood makes it a particularly valuable focus in this respect. The notion that commercial competition is 'eroding standards' and that children's television is inexorably 'dumbing down' appears to confirm many adults' intuitive judgments – judgments which, it must be said, are often based on a limited acquaintance with the kinds of material (such as cartoons) that are so readily condemned. This account also has an obvious appeal right across the political spectrum, from nostalgic conservatives to leftist critics of the capitalist culture industries.

To be sure, there is an undeniable economic logic here. On the one hand, there is increasing competition to attract the child audience; yet on the other, there is a downward pressure on production budgets. There are more slots to fill in the schedules, but less money with which to do so. Inevitably, much of this new provision has been accomplished 'on the cheap', by means of an increase in the number of imported cartoons and sitcoms, and of repeats – although it is important to take account of *where* in the schedules these changes have occurred. Meanwhile, Lady Howe's 'veiled threat' about the need to 'legislate' reflects the weakness of established forms of regulation in this more commercial broadcasting environment.

Nevertheless, we would argue that – like most analyses of 'cultural decline' – this account tends to overemphasise the extent of change, and to neglect its positive potential. The public service ethos guaranteed by the regulated duopoly in British broadcasting may well be threatened, but it is very far from extinct. As we shall indicate, there are considerable continuities in terms of the kinds of television programmes most children are watching, and how they are watching them. More controversially, we would argue that the existence of commercial competition has brought particular benefits for children – in terms of both quantity *and* quality – that cannot be ignored.

More fundamentally, we would argue that this account of the apparent decline of children's television is based upon an essentially conservative analysis of the social and cultural functions of broadcasting. For instance, the concerns about the 'barrage' of 'cheap American cartoons' voiced in these reports, and in the broader debate about children's television, involve some quite dubious assumptions about cultural value and cultural identity. Animation in particular is typically regarded as homogeneous and uniformly 'bad' for children: its very presence is taken as symptomatic of 'dumbing down' and an 'erosion of standards'. In contrast, factual and drama programmes, which are more popular with older children, seem to be automatically perceived as 'quality programming'; while home-produced dramas are implicitly adjudged to be better for 'the child's development as a good citizen' than imported ones. Finally, there is an underlying concern about children's vulnerability to commercial exploitation by programmes that are apparently 'more interested in selling toys and pleasing advertisers' than in turning them into 'well-adjusted citizens'.

These judgments clearly reflect some of the traditional assumptions that continue to dominate contemporary debates about cultural policy in Britain. These are, most obviously, to do with distinctions between 'high culture' and 'popular culture', and with the fear of 'Americanisation'. Cultural identity is necessarily defined here in terms of the nation; and the nation is implicitly regarded as socially and ethnically homogeneous, rather than diverse. Likewise, cultural value is defined here in terms of settled hierarchies of taste, in which popularity is often seen as incompatible with 'quality', and culture and commerce are fundamentally opposed. The market, it is argued, simply caters to 'the lowest common denominator' and is thereby bound to neglect the audience's true cultural and educational needs. And, as in so many debates about the negative effects of the media, it is children who are seen to be particularly at risk.

The disappearance of childhood?

Thus far, we have provided two brief sketches – one outlining changes in perceptions of childhood, the other of changes in the media. How might we understand the relationships between them? One influential account can be found in Neil Postman's 'disappearance of childhood' thesis. [11] Essentially, Postman argues that the creation of our modern conception of childhood was only made possible by the emergence of print literacy; and that the demise of print literacy at the hand of the electronic media will lead to the disappearance of childhood as we know it. In a more nuanced account of the argument, Joshua Meyrowitz[12] argues that there has at least been a 'blurring of boundaries' between children and adults, as a consequence of changes in the dominant media of communications. Children and adults, he suggests, no longer have separate 'information systems': television and other electronic media allow children to witness rituals and experiences previously confined to adults.

There are several obvious problems with this argument, not least to do with the lack of evidence to support it. Announcements of the death of the book are certainly premature; and evidence that standards of print literacy have dropped over the past few decades is very questionable. Like many popular accounts of childhood and the media, this argument seems to hark back to an illusory golden age. Furthermore, it reflects a kind of technological determinism: while there clearly are connections between media such as print or television and broader developments in society, those connections are much more complex, and much less one-directional, than this analysis suggests.

Yet however overstated it may be, this argument does point to some very fundamental changes that have occurred in our conceptions of childhood; and it raises important questions about the role of communications media in producing and reflecting them. Here again, it is possible to see these developments in different ways, and to propose very different responses to them. For his part, Postman espouses a kind of anguished conservatism, which is concerned not to empower children, but to instruct them once more to know their place: the only solution is to throw out the TV, and to reassert traditional family values. By contrast, Meyrowitz is much more agnostic: he implicitly sees these developments as a form of democratisation, albeit one that may have unsettling consequences in terms of children's future socialisation. Meanwhile, other writers have chosen to celebrate this 'blurring of boundaries' between adults and children, and the role of the media in bringing it about: digital technology in particular is seen here as a means of bringing about a 'children's revolution'. [13]

The concerns voiced by Postman, Meyrowitz and others apply primarily to children's experience of 'adult' television: the problem is precisely that both groups are watching the same things. Yet similar concerns have also been raised in relation to children's television over the years. At least in its early days, the BBC's *Grange Hill* was regularly criticised in the press for its treatment of sexual relationships, and of issues such as drugs and child abuse; while more recently, London Weekend Television's sex education series *Love Bites* attracted predictable complaints from moral watchdogs. Similarly, it is not unusual to encounter parental criticism of the explicit sensuality of some of the pop performers featured on programmes like *Live and Kicking*.

Nevertheless, when one looks specifically at children's television, it would be equally possible to argue the opposite case. Far from boundaries between adults and children becoming blurred, it appears that children are increasingly being defined and addressed as a group that is quite distinct from adults, with its own unique characteristics and vulnerabilities. As in some areas of social policy, the separation between adults and children is being *reinforced*, both as a result of the increasing fragmentation of the audience and through the emergence of new and distinctive modes of address in children's programmes. With a proliferation of technology and a growing range of channels, children no longer have to watch the same things as their parents. Indeed, media addressed to children – both 'old' media such as television and new ones such as computer games – have increasingly sought to establish their appeal on the grounds that they *exclude* adults and everything they are seen to represent. Much children's culture is deliberately inaccessible and incomprehensible to many adults – a phenomenon that is only confirmed by the tone (and indeed the ignorance) of much adult criticism. In this respect, criticisms of the media's role in the 'disappearance of childhood' can be set against a growing concern about the 'generation gap' in media use – a concern that young people's experience of new technologies and of global media is driving a wedge between their culture and that of their parents' generation. [14]

Of course, such grand narratives of historical change tend to underemphasise the continuities in children's experiences. As we shall indicate, children have *always* preferred 'adult' programmes to those which are specifically designed for them; and they have always resisted the attempts of broadcasters to give them what they believe will do them good. Much of what children watch today – and the way in which they watch it – is very similar to what their parents watched twenty or thirty years ago. Indeed, much of it is identical. Furthermore, many of the anxieties which surface in contemporary debates about children's television have always been with us: the advent of commercial television in the mid-1950s provoked very similar concerns about 'Americanisation' and the need to sustain the educational functions of children's television.

Ultimately, then, there are elements of truth in both positions. In some respects, the media are contributing to a blurring of boundaries between children and adults; while in others, they appear to be reinforcing them. The half-century that we consider in this book has witnessed a continuing struggle to define childhood and the child audience. In a sense, 'the child' only comes into existence through this process: it is defined largely by distinguishing it from what it is not – that is, 'the adult'. The boundaries, in other words, have to be perpetually drawn and redrawn: they are subject to a constant process of negotiation. What unites the apparently contrary perspectives outlined here is the recognition that this process of drawing and policing those boundaries has itself become much more problematic. The status of the child audience – and broadcasters' assumptions about it – have become increasingly unstable, particularly over the past decade. Children are now perceived to be more valuable, but also much harder to reach. The distinctions between children and other audiences – 'youth' or 'family' audiences, for example – are more difficult to sustain, but they are also increasingly significant, not least in commercial terms. The stable routines established in the era of the 'regulated duopoly' in British broadcasting have given way to a much more competitive, uncertain environment, in which the audience seems to be much more powerful but also much harder to reach and to control.

In this context, some quite fundamental questions are beginning to be asked. If children's television were simply to disappear, or to degenerate into wall-to-wall 'mental bubblegum' (whatever that may be), what difference would this make? Do children in fact have distinctive *needs* or *characteristics* as viewers, and in what ways can television meet or reflect them? What can we learn in this respect from children's apparent interest in 'adult' television, or at least in certain *types* of adult television? To what extent, for example, do children need programmes that reflect their everyday lives and experiences – and do domestically produced programmes necessarily guarantee this? Will the global television marketplace result in a homogenising of cultures, or can it sustain a diverse range of cultural identities? How far can the market guarantee quality and diversity more generally in children's programming – and how are these things to be measured or evaluated? In what ways should the state continue to regulate or support children's television, and which methods are likely to prove most effective in doing so? To what extent can – or should – television address children as citizens or as consumers, or indeed as both? What, ultimately, *are* the social, educational and cultural functions of television for children?

This book sets out to trace the different ways in which these questions have been addressed by those who work in and around the children's television industry. Yet they are, as Lady Howe's comments suggest, not simply questions about television: they are also about citizenship and 'social development' – and indeed about the meaning of childhood itself. And, as we hope to indicate, they cannot be answered simply by appeals to the traditional *status quo* of public service broadcasting – nor indeed on the basis of nostalgic reminiscences about the 'old favourites' of a bygone era.

A case in point

Our analysis of children's television in Britain can therefore be seen as a case study, both of the changing nature of broadcasting and of changing assumptions about childhood itself. For the reasons we have outlined, children's television has attained a symbolic importance in debates about the future of broadcasting; and it therefore provides a useful lens through which these broader debates can be viewed and evaluated. At the same time, television remains the central preoccupation of children's leisure culture; and it therefore serves as an important index of the changing experiences and meanings of contemporary childhood.

However, this book is not about *real* child viewers. It does not seek to engage directly with debates about the 'effects' of television on children, or about their everyday experiences of the medium. On the contrary, our central concern is to trace the changing ways in which the child audience for television has been defined – not so much within television programmes themselves, as by the individuals and institutions that broadcast, produce, schedule and research them. These definitions of the child audience have an undeniable power. They construct and regulate the audience, effectively imagining particular kinds of child viewers into existence. Yet ultimately they cannot control that audience. As we shall indicate, real child viewers often remain elusive. In different ways, they are seen to resist and evade the definitions that are imposed upon them: they have to be constantly sought, and at times they can appear to be at risk of being lost for ever. Our aim, however, is not to assess whether or not television's imaginations of the child viewer are accurate – as compared, perhaps, with some higher truth about children to which we might have privileged access. As we shall indicate, imagining or defining the audience necessarily entails a debate about much broader values and assumptions, a debate which is unlikely ever to be settled or agreed.

Inevitably, much is missing from our account here. Undertaking this research has involved the collection and analysis of a great deal of data of very different kinds, only a part of which can possibly be represented in this book. Other aspects of the research – particularly qualitative work on specific programmes, and some research on audiences – will be published elsewhere. [15]

We begin in Chapter One with an account of the early history of children's television, from the 1950s to the late 1970s. Our aim here is not to provide a comprehensive history, but to focus on particular moments of tension between the broadcasting institutions and the child audience. Chapter Two takes the analysis forward from the 1980s to the present, and attempts to provide a 'political economy' of contemporary children's television. In some respects, Chapter Three recapitulates this history, looking not at the institutions but at scheduling and programming. Here we present the results of an extensive 'audit' of changes in children's programming over the past four decades. Chapter Four looks at the ways in which the industry conducts research on the child audience, again beginning with early work conducted in the 1950s before moving on to the present. Our concern here is not only with the 'findings' of such research but also with the implicit assumptions about the audience that frame and inform it. Chapter Five looks more directly at how the child audience is defined by contemporary broadcasters, regulators, lobbyists and others. Drawing on extensive interview material, we trace the shifting balance between 'paternalistic' and 'child-centred' approaches, and the more recent move towards a view of the child as both a consumer and a social actor. Finally, Chapter Six draws out some of the broader implications for future policy, both in the form of general principles and specific recommendations.

As this implies, the book is structured more like a mosaic than a sequential narrative: each chapter has a rather different emphasis, although together they should provide at least the suggestion of a more complete picture. Nevertheless, there is an argument that motivates each of the chapters, and the book as a whole. We want to challenge the idea – which implicitly informs much of the contemporary debate about children's television – that the present can only be understood in terms of a decline from the greatness of the past. As we will show, this notion of a past 'golden age' – or a 'Great Tradition' – is distinctly questionable, as is the idea that increasing commercialism will *necessarily* result in a 'dumbing down' of children's programming. Insisting on narrow conceptions of national identity, or on received definitions of 'quality programming', will not help us to devise cultural policies that reflect the diverse and changing realities of children's lives.

This is not to sanction a form of complacency about the future, however. As we shall indicate, the economic, political and technological developments that began in the 1980s have led to a new conceptualisation of the child audience that takes us beyond conventional ideas about producing 'well-adjusted citizens'. The child audience is, on one level, more powerful than it has ever been; but that power is expressed and experienced primarily through consumption. The contemporary media are now thoroughly dominated by commercial imperatives; and even public broadcasting has been transformed into a 'mixed economy'.

In this situation, we cannot afford to fall back on conservative assumptions about the social and cultural functions of broadcasting. While we need to preserve what is of value in current arrangements, it will be impossible simply to return to the status quo of the regulated duopoly. We need a coherent and principled sense of what the state should provide that the market cannot, and vice versa. Yet we also need to redefine the notion of public service in a way that builds upon the diversity and the democratising forces within contemporary culture. Public broadcasting will not survive very far into the next century if it fails to become more accountable and more responsive to the audiences it purports to serve – and that includes the television viewers of tomorrow.

Notes

1 'Kids' TV "dumbing down" ', *Guardian,* 5 November 1997. The report referred to here, Davies and Corbett (1997), is considered in more detail in Chapter Three.
2 'Parents told to sign reading pledge', *Guardian,* 29 July 1997.
3 'Children's TV "dumbed down" ', *Guardian,* 16 February 1998. The report referred to here is by Blumler and Biltereyst (1998). Some days later, the paper was obliged to publish a correction from the report's co-author, Jay Blumler, pointing out that it had been misrepresented.
4 This is discussed more fully in Chapter Three.
5 On the reduction in children's mobility, see Ward (1994); and on broader changes in leisure time, see Hendrick (1997). These issues are currently being explored in the

'Himmelweit 2' project, 'Children, Young People and the Changing Media Environment', based at the London School of Economics.

6 For discussions of the recent social history of childhood, see Pilcher and Wagg (1996) and Scraton (1997).

7 For discussions of the politics of 'child crime' in the 1990s, see Newburn (1996) and Scraton (1997).

8 This argument is typically related to the increase in working hours among certain sectors of the workforce: see, for example, 'Long hours put strain on family', *Daily Telegraph*, 4 November 1996.

9 For representative summaries of such arguments, see Burman (1994) and Jenks (1996).

10 Kinder (1991).

11 Postman (1983). For a more hysterical recent example of the same argument, see Sanders (1995).

12 Meyrowitz (1985).

13 This phrase is taken from Jon Katz (1997). Similar arguments are made by Douglas Rushkoff (1996).

14 For example, see Ohmae (1995).

15 Buckingham (1998) and Buckingham (forthcoming a) focus on texts. Davies, Buckingham and Kelley (1999, forthcoming) and Kelley, Buckingham and Davies (1999) present material on audiences.

1 For the Children
Children's Television 1946–80

In this chapter, we sketch the history of the most important institution in children's television in Britain – the BBC Children's Programmes Department. We trace this history from its earliest days in the late 1940s to the beginnings of intensified, market-driven change in the 1980s. In doing so, we describe how the Department has debated questions of childhood, children's needs and cultural change in the course of developing its policies, programmes and schedules. We argue that the work of the Department has reflected a continuing tension between educational and entertainment-based aims; and that these aims relate in turn to an unresolved conflict between a 'paternalist' model of television and one which is more attuned to the cultures of childhood. We show the different ways in which this tension has manifested itself in the Department and how it has been interpreted by some of its critics, especially within the BBC as a whole.

Before such a long and tortuous journey, it is best to start with a drink...

> Now McGivern poured me a very stiff gin and I said to him, 'What is my brief from you?' He said, 'It's very simple. You have got to recover the lost child audience without sacrificing standards'.[1]

Thus, in the summer of 1956, Owen Reed, once a British intelligence officer in wartime Yugoslavia, now the new Head of Children's Programmes, BBC Television, was set by Cecil McGivern his mission impossible – the 'frightful problem' which he could not resolve and which eventually blighted his career.[2] McGivern, Controller of Television, was asking Reed to rescue for the Corporation the child audience which the first ITV transmissions in autumn 1955 had spirited away to a commercial Neverland. In the process, the Controller was demanding – perhaps unknowingly – something more. Requiring attention to 'standards' and popularity alike, Reed's job description amounted to the reinvention of public service children's television. Ratings success without merely imitating ITV's output involved comprehensive change – in scheduling, in technology and aesthetics, in the range of the BBC's programmes for children, and in the ways in which it defined and addressed its audience. It meant disturbing settled values and working practices, and engaging with wider patterns of contemporary cultural change. The very stiff gin was more than called for.

It was a set of tasks which Reed, with terminal consequences for the Department, was not able to accomplish. Under Reed's sometimes perceptive, sometimes baffled management, the Department attempted to turn from one, tried and tested, kind of children's television to another, whose outlines it was ultimately unable to sketch. The fundamental problem was McGivern's 'lost audience'. As soon as they were given the chance, children had deserted the BBC. In doing so, they had called into question the ways in which the BBC Children's Department had interpreted and responded to their needs and interests. Winning them back involved an effort of cultural understanding, formal experimentation and internal reorganisation which stretched the Department beyond its limits. But the eight-year effort Reed made to fulfil his mission and the debates which he helped to generate have enduring interest, and explain why his dilemmas can serve as an introduction to a larger history.

Like any transitional regime, the 'Reed period' (1956–64) points both forward and back. Tracking its difficulties allows us to grasp more clearly both the conditions from which it was moving away and the ways in which the problems it grappled with were eventually – albeit only partially – resolved. The period thus provides a vantage-point from which it is possible to understand the overall development of children's television in the post-war, pre-Thatcher years. But the debates of the 1950s and 1960s also raised issues – about the meanings of 'childhood', the 'needs' of children, the nature of 'quality' television, and the role of public service television in a commercially-driven broadcasting environment – which still have resonance today. Revisiting them is less an exercise in condescension to a naive past than an experience that highlights what has been at stake in subsequent arguments and conflicts around the future of children's television. For the tensions in Reed's thinking, between the obligation of paternalism and the necessity of engaging with the growing autonomy of children's culture, eloquently signal the conflicts of later periods – from the troubled musings of Reed's successors about the effects of the pop music programmes they increasingly screened, right through to the terms of contemporary debate outlined in our introduction.

In this chapter, we chart the ways in which television 'producers' – we use the term loosely – implemented the idea of public service television for children over the thirty-year period after 1946, when the first TV broadcasts for children began.[3] We concentrate on the working of the BBC Children's Department in this period: its status within the BBC, its resources, its cultural and aesthetic values and its understanding of childhood. Our focus is thus in some ways selective – a selectiveness determined in large part by the availability of archive material. However, although the events relate specifically to the BBC, the context encompasses both the emergence of commercial television and the cultural history of post-war Britain. To this extent, we are using the richly documented and satisfyingly dramatic unfolding of the rise, decline and rebirth of BBC children's television to tell a wider story.

Our aim here, therefore, is to approach complex issues concerning childhood, public service, commerce and cultural change via an encounter with the ideas and arguments of one particular group of broadcasters. This group is cohesive enough to be thought of in terms of what the American literary critic Stanley Fish once called an 'interpretive community' – a group of people who, on the basis of particular traditions, career histories, intellectual resources, patterns of debate and working practices arrive at a more or less shared way of understanding, responding to and representing the world.[4] These meanings endure over time. In the fifty-year span of material which we have used to compose this chapter – the BBC's internal archives and public documents, our own contemporary interviews with producers, newspaper and magazine articles – we are struck by how the terms of the debates in which this 'interpretive community' engaged remained constant.

This is not to claim, however, that public service children's television has been organised around rock-solid certainties of purpose; nor that debates have ever been conclusively settled. Rather, it is to highlight the existence of persistent patterns of *un*certainty – in relation to the preferences of audiences, to the means by which they can be discovered and served, and to the effects that result from doing so. Thus, producers' forms of understanding are never stable, nor are they completely confident of their own explanatory powers and social authority, even if some accounts of children's television suggest that they are. David Oswell, for instance, has written a comprehensive, Foucauldian history of television and the child audience which considerably overestimates both the social capability of public service television and the cohesiveness of its project; in doing so, in our view he exaggerates television's effect on the subjectivities of its audience, and correspondingly overlooks what we judge to be compelling evidence about the uncertainties of broadcasters.[5] Stephen Wagg, likewise, has written a stimulating article that contrasts the consumer-centred television of the 1980s with an earlier period in which the child audience was addressed in anti-commercial and educationally inflected terms. This juxtaposition turns, however, on the suggestion that children's television was motivated in the 1950s by a 'stable and well-defined' understanding of 'childhood'.[6] As our analysis will show, producers did not in fact possess such a conception. On the contrary, by the mid-1950s, the nature of childhood had become a topic around which there was constant, uneasy and ultimately unresolved discussion.

Thus, for many who worked at the BBC, the child audience was less an object available to the shaping strategies of power than an elusive and recalcitrant set of groupings, to whose shifting preferences broadcasters were permanently subject. Discussion took this form partly because cultural changes were taking place – especially among 'adolescents' – that the BBC's traditional conceptions of childhood, described as 'middle class' by its own producers, could not explain; and partly, also, because after the founding of ITV the child audience was able to assert its own preferences more forcefully. The 'interpretive community' had to chase this audience – to research and speculate about its interests and tastes, to argue with rival conceptions of it, and to attempt to cater for its needs. Faced with evidence of their own competitive failure, producers were forced to give some account of the preferences of their desired audience and to change aspects of their own practice in order to attract it. The ways in which they discussed childhood were thus affected not just by their own professional formation but by the evident workings of popular taste; their deliberations, their experiments in programme-making and scheduling, the arguments they had with each other and with other sections of the BBC were all marked by the agency of their audience. As we shall see, the relationship between producers and audiences – never direct, and always a matter of speculation and

16

construction on the part of producers – lay at the heart of significant changes in children's television from the 1950s onwards.

1946–56

The first television programme for children – *For the Children* – was screened in September 1946. In 1948, a regular weekly service began, under the same generic heading. Overall BBC output at this time was restricted to late afternoons and evenings, and the amount of time available for children's programmes was strictly limited. Unable to take up its obvious place on Saturday afternoons because of the BBC's commitment to sport, *For the Children* found a home between 4 and 5 p.m. on Sunday afternoons, though even here it faced complaints from churchpeople that it would deter children from attending Sunday school.[7]

If time was in short supply and subject to competing, adult demands, then so was money. The BBC's files for these years are filled with the complaints of children's producers about the underfunding of their Department. In particular, they felt, they lacked access to resources – film and outside broadcasts – which would raise the status and quality of their programmes. Richmond Postgate, acting Head of Children's Programmes in 1950, sought to delay a proposed expansion in the output of children's programmes because he thought his Department was not yet ready to meet the demands of a 'national' service.[8] One of Postgate's successors, Freda Lingstrom, found herself arguing in 1953 that children's services should be 'equal to adults' and not a 'charity adjunct to the BBC'. She complained about the 'atmosphere which pervaded the whole service, best summed up by ... the most frequently heard comment, "it's only children" '.[9]

From these early days, then, children's producers were made aware of the marginal nature of their work, and the resource problems that surrounded it. The subordinate status of children's programmes was offset, however, by a kind of symbolic primacy. Public service broadcasting was meant to be an instrument of the public good. In as much as it was public, the service had to be universal, addressing all sections of its potential audience, children as well as adults. In as much as it was a force for good, it needed to have higher goals than those of entertainment. It had a duty to help form its audience as educated citizens; in the classic terms of John Reith, its mission involved education and information, as well as entertainment. The Reithian trinity of entertainment–education–information acquired a particular intensity in relation to children's programming. Children's television provided a litmus test of public service broadcasting; the BBC would be failing in its mission if it did not attend to children's developmental needs, and thus prioritise its educational role.

These needs, moreover, were deemed to be *comprehensive*. The schedule of children's television, it was argued, should mirror that of the service as a whole. Mary Adams, described by Oswell as the 'driving force' behind the establishment of children's television, envisaged it in the broadest terms. She wanted the schedule to include plays, how-to series, storytelling, a collectors' corner, programmes on pets, tales of travel, outside broadcasts from museums and factories, informational films, quizzes and encyclopaedia programmes.[10] This idea of children's television as public service broadcasting in miniature was a concept to which discussion in the Children's Department often returned. Its persistence explains the shock that greeted the reorganisation of the Department in the 1960s, as well as the fears aroused much later by the emergence of cable and satellite channels that displayed no such broad commitment.

The acceptance of a public service mission for children's television was emphatically affirmed by the appointment of Freda Lingstrom in 1951. Lingstrom replaced Cecil Madden, who had been acting Head of Children's Television for eight months. Madden had both expanded the service and centred its output more on popular entertainment; yet he was viewed with suspicion by the BBC hierarchy as someone with too great a leaning towards 'theatre people' and a drama-centred 'repertory company' approach.[11] Lingstrom's commitments were different and – as newspaper columnists complained – oriented towards 'enlightenment' as much as entertainment.[12] Under her leadership (1951–6), children's producers began to offset their lowly status by elaborating a sense of their own high calling. However much it was starved of resources, working in children's television was seen as a noble occupation, with strong moral and educative responsibilities. These responsibilities were exhaustively discussed by producers, as they reflected on the nature of the new technology at their disposal ('this powerful, intrusive invention'), and its potential effects on children.[13] The conclusions they drew affected not just their conceptions of programme content but also their views on scheduling.

Producers' early writings are marked by a pervasive sense of moral restraint and cultural austerity. Television, wrote the programme-maker Naomi Capon in 1952, was a 'dragon', a force both magical and – quite literally – enthralling.[14] Children's encounters with it had to be both rationed and planned, and the metaphors of wartime were deployed against surfeit and indulgence. 'Excess of viewing', wrote Mary Adams in 1950, 'must be reckoned with and combated with whatever weapons seem most effective ... The knob is very easy to turn on; the spell fatally strong ... Parental control is not fully mobilised.'[15] She went on to express the consensus position of broadcasters that children's viewing of television should be guided and restricted:

> By suitable signposting in billing and announcements, children will be urged to view what suits them best. Thus, restraint in viewing will be encouraged in the interests of programme quality... It will take some time to make this policy effective; it will need the co-operation of parents, and consistency in planning over a period of time.[16]

Even more emphatically, Lingstrom herself wrote in 1953 that it was the 'business' of broadcasters 'to see that as far as children are concerned the force of television shall be carefully controlled'.[17]

The forms of careful control were many. Chief among them was 'specialisation'. During the early post-war period, children were subject to several kinds of regulative division, and to forms of care in which welfare and surveillance were combined. Schools divided children on the basis of age (after 1944 the number of mixed-age classes fell considerably), ability and gender,[18] while the new Health Service watched over patterns of mothering in the name of new norms of child development.[19] The policy of specialisation is best understood in such a context. Believing, like the influential Hadow Report on primary education, that 'life is a process of growth in which there are successive stages, each with its own character and mind',[20] producers sought to make a version of this developmental principle the basis of their work. *'Benefit to child development'* reads the heading of part of a 1947 memorandum advocating the encouragement in children of a 'selective sense': 'it is bad for a child to look at a programme which he cannot understand ... Unconscious viewing is bad for a child.'[21]

To prevent the growth of the unconscious 'viewing habit', producers tried to draw strong age-related boundaries between programmes, and to enlist the support of parents in ensuring that children only watched television at the times which had been designated for them. Such responsible scheduling was perceived as the hallmark of quality. 'Freda has very strict standards,' noted Owen Reed; 'always start with the youngest, then go on to the next age group and then end with the oldest with *Jane Eyre* or whatever you want to do. Never start with the oldest.'[22] For children to stray outside their allotted time slot was a bad thing for both producers and children. If the under-fives migrated to programmes intended for older viewers, 'they would be a hindrance to the producer'.[23] If 'the adolescent' watched evening television, 'he' would experience 'programmes that would interest him technically but were likely to be unfitted to his moral judgment'.[24] In this respect, television had to act as a moral and developmental guide, roping off the dangerous areas and signposting those that suited children best. Continuity and scheduling were central to the guiding process, and the clearest signpost was built into the fundamental structure of the schedule. Under-fives were given their own separate mid-afternoon slot. An hour of children's programmes was scheduled between 5 and 6 p.m., to be followed immediately by a shutdown of an hour or more's duration. The 'toddlers' truce' between 6 and 7 p.m. was what Reed called an 'hour of protective silence', a period of non-transmission that served as a sort of moat between children's and adults' viewing, the strongest commandment that television could give that children were to view no further. (See Figure 1.)

Figure 1:   BBC Programme Schedule 20 January 1954

4.00– 4.15   Watch with Mother: The Flowerpot Men
4.15   Closedown
5.00– 5.40   CHILDREN'S TELEVISION
Bits and Pieces
William Aspden Talks about the Outdoors
Stories of the Piano
5.40   Closedown
6.55   Weather Chart

As this implies, television's developmental role was regarded by producers as one that consisted of bans and prescriptions: 'a little piece of time' was all that was allowed to children.[25] But this negative emphasis is only part of the story. The children's producer also had the job of leading children on from one developmental stage to the next. Drama, especially the 'classic serial' – the adaptation, for instance, of a nineteenth-century novel – was central to this process. Through what Reed called 'very careful, accurate planning', it could build a 'bridge' between 'child' viewing and 'adult' viewing. 'Classic serials like *Jane Eyre* of very great depth and intensity' were aimed at children 'who were really growing up and were reachable in adult terms at the right time and with the right juxtapositions'.[26] In this way, producers saw their work in strongly maturational terms. Unlike their counterparts in television for schools, they tried to avoid a specific 'curricular' content; but they nonetheless imagined their audience in terms of its capacity to learn and to grow. Thus, for Freda Lingstrom, children were active learners, 'alert and eager'. They, the future weavers of the social fabric, spent their days 'developing the habit of constructive thought' in which they 'resolved in their minds the conclusions they had drawn from the world around them'.[27] According to Richmond Postgate, television could speed this development along without the need for strained and intrusive didacticism; by seeking out 'children's real interests and values', programmes would naturally assume both an entertaining and an educative role.[28]

This invocation of 'real' interests, however, immediately raises the problems of the child audience, and points us towards the traumas that were to come. *Pace* Postgate's injunction, children's producers had little evidence of what children really watched and valued; in classic Reithian fashion, they had a strong conception of what children needed, but did not seek to discover what they might *want*.[29] If they had, they might have paid more attention to the work of the BBC's own Audience Research Department (ARD). In 1949, the BBC had set up its first 'viewing panel' – a means of establishing patterns of taste among television audiences. Analysing the responses of the panel, the ARD found that for each step 'down' the social class scale, there was a sharp increase in a taste for all types of light entertainment and feature films, and a weakening interest in genres such as documentary and arts programmes. Since television ownership was, in the early 1950s, beginning to spread across social classes, it was therefore likely that a majority audience preference would emerge for light entertainment. Moreover, among children, this kind of preference was even stronger. According to Robert Silvey, Head of Research, 'a startling two-thirds of 7–11s claimed to like "cabaret" very much, and the 12–14s stood out as the group with the highest proportion of enthusiasts for cabaret, sports outside broadcasts, newsreels and feature films'.[30] The child audience was not willing to be confined to its little piece of time, and was showing signs that it preferred very different programmes from those produced by the Children's Department: the audience was on its way to being 'lost', and the more its class composition shifted, the more marked its condition would become.

Within the Children's Department, and in the BBC as a whole, this cultural disposition presented a problem. The appointment of Lingstrom rather than Madden had marked the culmination of a sharp dispute within the BBC about the implications of Madden's cultural preferences.[31] Popular culture, particularly in its American forms, was to be opposed: in the BBC, and more generally in elite English culture, American influence was thought to be undermining national traditions and hierarchies.[32] In 1951 Norman Collins, Head of Television Services, warned children's producers against letting 'Children's Hour become simply another vehicle for introducing American dance tunes to English children'.[33] Americanisation was also something that Freda Lingstrom feared. 'Abhorring any hint of commercialism,' she would screen Westerns only 'over her dead body', and despised American animation.[34] Her dislikes extended to the works of Enid

Blyton, the thought of which she would not entertain. 'Real interests and values' were thus only tolerable provided they occurred in an acceptable cultural form: as Lingstrom put it, she had 'very catholic tastes' but drew the line at screening anything 'frightening', 'cruel' or 'vulgar'.

The consequences of this attitude, even though it conformed to the cultural preferences of Lingstrom's superiors, nonetheless alarmed them. 'My Dear Freda,' wrote McGivern in 1954, with the first ITV broadcasts less than a year away, 'I am afraid it was my interest in the television service, not my interest in the programmes, which kept me viewing to the end of transmission on Sunday ... I found this – and I am certain they did too – a very unexcited and unexciting viewing for the majority of children.'[35] Sections of the child audience certainly shared McGivern's opinion: the ARD found that only half of twelve- to fourteen-year olds were enthusiastic about *For the Children*, and its successor programmes were likewise far from universally acclaimed.[36]

During the period of BBC monopoly, although the audience might dissent from Lingstrom's preferences, it could not seriously challenge them. With the arrival of commercial television, there was a rapid change. Once the audience could exercise the power of choice, the viability of the BBC's conceptions of children's television was called into question.

1956–64

Owen Reed, formerly a producer of radio drama in the West of England, took over the Children's Department in 1956. The first ITV companies had begun broadcasting in late 1955. At that time, there were television sets in four and a half million homes – about 30 per cent of British households.[37] By 1960, when ITV broadcasts were able to reach most of the country, the number had increased to ten and a half million. By the late 1950s, ITV was much the more popular channel: BBC research calculated that in the first six months of 1957 ITV programmes enjoyed a 70:30 advantage among viewers who could receive both channels.[38] ITV companies enjoyed, if anything, an even greater lead among child audiences. A 1960 Granada Television survey of children's viewing estimated that ITV's daily audience share ranged from 66 per cent to 85 per cent.[39] This imbalance was all the more significant because it did not occur in the context of a duopoly in which competing broadcasters shared roughly the same ideas of quality, purpose and audience need. Independent (i.e. commercial) television in the late 1950s was sharply at odds with the BBC. It was famous in these years for its break from Reithianism, for what contemporaries alleged was a 'retreat from culture',[40] and what its Director-General described as the creation of 'people's television ... reflecting their likes and dislikes, their tastes and aversions, what they can comprehend and what is beyond them'.[41]

In public, the BBC responded to competition with an alarmed disdain. For Hugh Greene, the existence of ITV struck a blow at the heart of public service broadcasting: it won audiences, but destroyed standards; it 'gave people what they want', but 'was that the full unanswerable argument?' Citing children's television as an example, he described the BBC's commitment to causes which ITV 'by its very nature' could never uphold – a strong educational emphasis, an attention to the needs of the very young, an alertness to minority interests and a willingness to 'encourage children to engage in pursuits other than the watching of television'. ITV, by contrast, gained its success through a debased kind of programming, a main part of which comprised 'wild west and adventure films' containing an unacceptable 'amount of violence' and made in America 'or in England with American money for an American audience'.[42]

Internally, the Corporation (like Greene himself, its future Director-General) was less conservative, both in relation to the excitements of popular drama and to its country of origin. Its immediate response was to enter into competition with ITV on what were – at least in part – commercial television's own terms, buying programmes in the American market and attempting to strengthen its light entertainment output. But it also planned for the longer term a more substantial transformation. Reed reports (but does not precisely date) a meeting in the late 1950s when the purposes and character of this transformation were outlined to BBC staff:

> Gerald Beadle, my old boss when he became managing director of television, he had us all together in the TV Theatre, all the programme staff, and he said, 'We are in a dire situation in which we have got to be able to prove to the next governmental committee that it is the BBC ... that will get the third channel and colour. We have got to prove that we are popular or we shan't survive. We have therefore got to make the good thing popular and the popular thing good, and that is your directive for the foreseeable future.'[43]

In 1956, McGivern had spoken to Reed about winning back the audience without 'sacrificing standards': whatever the implications of his instruction, it was still phrased in conservative terms. Beadle's emphasis was more positive: the BBC had to engage with popular taste and in the process come up with new definitions of 'the good'. But his challenge was just as sharp. The reshaping of public service television was not only driven by a sense of cultural mission, but by competitive necessity: reinvention was a matter of survival. For the Children's Department, which had developed such a strong regulatory approach to its audience, and which had sought even to protect them from the dangers of Enid Blyton, the demand that it should engage with popular taste, and encounter the 'real interests' of children, was an especially difficult task. In terms of competition, it was faring worse than other BBC departments; it remained underresourced; and the background and intellectual dispositions of its members rendered it ill-equipped to recognise the cultural roots of ITV's success. What, then, was Reed to do?

Some decisions had been taken for him. The existence of the 'toddlers' truce' was – as Sendall bluntly puts it – 'costing the ITV companies money'.[44] The ITA lobbied the government to end it. The BBC objected, but in February 1957 both channels began transmitting programmes between six and seven in the evening. The time barrier between children's and adult television had been taken down. Likewise, within children's television, the strong boundaries created by specialisation were eroded by the imperatives of competition. From 1956 until virtually the end of the decade, the scheduling of children's programmes was affected by the

22

BBC's new policy of 'leading with its strongest card', which was usually a programme intended for older children. The Lingstrom policy of starting with the youngest and then moving on to the next age group was temporarily abandoned.[45] At the same time, Reed began screening more American programmes – mainly adventures and Westerns of the kind that Greene had disparaged.[46] (See Figure 2.)

Figure 2:   BBC Programme Schedule, 13 January 1957

4.45–6.00   CHILDREN'S TELEVISION
4.45   Champion the Wonder Horse
5.10   Lenny the Lion
5.20   The Adventures of Peter Simple
         A serial play in six parts from Captain Marryat's novel
5.45   Sunday Special: Come Aboard *The Commodore*

Thus the protectionist climate established by Lingstrom was to some extent modified. Correspondingly, 'action-based' drama became central.

The fundamental problem of popularity required a more considered response, however. Reed spent much of the later 1950s attempting to identify the changing nature of his audience, its tastes and interests, and the ways in which children's television should transform itself to meet them. His starting point was to contest the BBC's time-honoured definition of the boundaries between children and adults. The official line of the Corporation was that 'children's television is directed towards children between the ages of 5–16 ... While their ages vary from 5–16 and even more, it is believed that they are broadly alike in the pattern of their lives.'[47] Reed argued that this definition of childhood was based on a reading of outdated middle-class social habits and attitudes: no one over the age of eleven wanted to be addressed as a child.[48] Rather than try ineffectually to engage an audience which rejected the whole idea of children's television, or to stake their future on the needs of the 'maternal appendages' who comprised the under-fives, producers should recognise that the 'true' child audience now comprised two groups. The first consisted of the 'kindergartens aged 5–8 who like life to be cosy, believe in fairies but have growing horizons and are becoming familiar with the rudimentary entertainment conventions'; the second comprised the 'primaries who like to feel tough, organised and keen, are anti-grown-up, still live in a world of let's pretend but with an increasing appetite for combat adventure and pseudo-man of the world settings'. Reed argued that the BBC had not been 'tough' enough with either section of this audience; it held no appeal for the 'solid, sticky, gang-minded, lolly-sucking and gregarious mob of 5–11s', among whom its failure was 'most conspicuous'.[49]

Reed's department staked its future on its ability to satisfy this core audience. In November 1960, after five years of competition with ITV, it met to review its success.[50] The record of the meeting is a revealing picture of its collective state of mind, and of its continued difficulties in rethinking its established approach. A preparatory paper concisely summarised some of the more measurable effects of competition in the 1955–60 period. The Department had grown in size, from eight producers to twelve, and its weekly schedule had expanded from nearly seven hours to eight and a quarter. It now bought in more American material and produced more light entertainment programmes. Its production values were higher, with the inclusion of outdoor film sequences in many programmes.

Having dropped the formal, on-screen title of 'Children's Television', it was thus able to develop what one producer called a 'more adult approach'. Beyond establishing these basic facts of change, the meeting attempted to situate them in a wider cultural and aesthetic context. The boldest position was adopted by the drama producer Shaun Sutton. The advent of ITV, he argued, had been good for the BBC. It had resulted in more money being spent on children's television; it had accelerated the development towards 'semi-adult programming'; and it had raised levels of technical competence and professionalism. It was true that, despite the BBC's advances, ITV still gained the best audiences, but this was because their schedules were built around a few 'absolute winners' – *Popeye*, *Robin Hood*, *The Mickey Mouse Club* – not because of any overall superiority.

In acknowledging ITV's success and in recognising its basis in popular entertainment, Sutton was saying something that, within the Corporation as a whole, was by now unexceptional. As Burns puts it, 'By 1960, most people in the BBC had been made aware that whatever else it did, it had to deliver programmes that were entertaining' and thus competitive.[51] To some at the meeting these were still scandalous arguments which betrayed the Department's tradition. Reed, however, for the most part accepted them and tried to develop them further, moving towards a definition of what could be called the aesthetic basis of ITV's success. There was a difference, he suggested, between the BBC's pre-ITV programme-making and its later efforts: once it had been 'soft', now it was 'tough'. Others elaborated the metaphor, speaking of the new 'punch' of light entertainment programmes and of the 'stiffening' of programme content. Reed himself linked these rather gendered qualities to a further, novel, aesthetic requirement, that of 'compulsiveness' – an issue he approached pragmatically, rather than with full enthusiasm:

> Since competition has had to be urgently reckoned with, compulsiveness – the art of being compulsive – has become one of the standards of good television: that is to say, whether a programme is good or bad is decided not only on whether it is a good or bad programme for children, but whether it is a useful thing for keeping children with you, which is a different thing.[52]

Praise of compulsiveness was at the same time, of course, a criticism of the BBC's traditional (non-compulsive) output, and a departure from its established criteria of quality. Long before the meeting, Reed had been contemplating a new aesthetic for children's television. In part, his thoughts were technical, and centred on the limited means that the BBC put at the Department's disposal: he felt trapped within 'the static studio situation' and 'spent his life in shouting for film'.[53] ITV's strategy of building its daily programme around a 25-minute adventure film compared favourably with the studio-bound productions that were all he was capable of providing.

But the lack of compulsiveness was not merely technical in origin: limited means combined with established cultural preferences to centre the BBC's output on the somewhat non-compulsive form of the 'classic serial'. Its centrality compounded the Department's problem. As Reed had already pointed out in 1958:

> So far, BBC Children's Television has drawn its strength mainly from the classics . . . But the really compelling factors are speed and space and adventure . . . Children are con-

ditioned by cinema-going into an intoxicating measure of realism. Studio television is stuck at the point where without more film, it must rely on character rather than incident, and this means going back to the leather-bound family favourites.[54]

Reed had come to see that much of the future of children's television lay in the 'romantic adventure film', and that much of the Department's work should be interpreted through the prism of this particular aesthetic. He even saw the magazine programme *Blue Peter*, first screened during Reed's period of leadership, as embodying the principles of action-adventure, incorporating location shooting in far-flung places. According to one account, he spent much of his energy trying to emulate the success of *Robin Hood* – a quest which contributed to his 'undoing'.[55] Certainly, he thought that ITV's success was based on importing into television the aesthetics of Hollywood – a move which suited the new toughness he ascribed to his audience. The 'inescapable' conclusion for the BBC, he maintained, was to 'venture into dollar-earning co-production and . . . the bear-garden of the world telefilm trade'; its failure to do so meant that it tasted the 'bitter fruit' of ITV's success.[56] But in practice, the co-financing of boyish adventures was ruled out. It would have consumed the greater share of available resources, narrowed the BBC's overall output and 'slanted production towards the American market'.[57] Reed's home-grown attempts at an answer to *Robin Hood* – an over-budget *Rob Roy*, a miscast *Hurricane* – were dogged by the incompetence of producers. Reed may have defined a new aesthetic for BBC children's television – or at least borrowed one from the cinema – but in practice he was not able to implement it.

The problems of the Department, however, went further than these particular operational failures. As the transcript of the meeting reveals, Reed and his colleagues continued to be influenced by the aversions and ideals of an earlier period, in ways which made it difficult for them to respond to popular taste. Compulsiveness, even for Reed himself, was a problematic objective as it was all too close to the 'addiction' which Reed and many of his contemporaries saw as the least desirable effect of television.[58] Reed's own preferences were at odds with much of children's television. He spoke longingly of the days of 'relaxed and civilised thinking' before the arrival of competition, and the Reithian administration of 'wise and civilised men to whom one owed one's position and above all one's freedom'.[59] He had a distaste for the most successful choices of ITV's programme buyers, especially in the area of animation. 'I would not touch *Popeye*', he told his colleagues, 'if it was offered to me on a plate for the same reason I would not touch *Huckleberry Hound*, because it is noisy. It harps on a type of violence which', in the aggregate, is far worse than all the duels [in adventure films].' It was 'agony' to watch this sort of thing, he said. His colleagues – despite or because of the fact that the meeting was minuted in full by the BBC's central Secretariat – joined in, remembering with equal fondness the days of 'proper, peaceful entertainment' and regretting the 'thump, thump, thump' of contemporary children's programmes.[60]

This guileless nostalgia was symptomatic of a strategic difficulty. What producers remembered as 'peaceful entertainment' had earlier been described by the market researcher Mark Abrams as 'the atmosphere of a kindly middle-class nursery' – an atmosphere from which young people were escaping in droves.[61] Later in the decade, Abrams characterised the dominant cultural tendencies among young people as 'proletarianisation' and 'Americanisation'.[62] Beadle's slogans about the popular and the good were, among other things, injunctions to engage with these new patterns of culture and taste: anti-American 'rejectionism' of the McGivern type was no longer viable. This was not a dialogue in which children's producers, at the deepest levels of cultural disposition, were well equipped to engage. Their failure to do so had dramatic consequences for the Department.

By 1960 it was clear to those outside the Children's Department that it had failed to win back the lost audience. The pressures on the Department grew to a traumatic point. Their impact was imprinted in the battle-scarred memories of Reed, who, nearly twenty years after the event, recalled with painful clarity the beginnings of a fatal crisis:

> What really altered the position of the Department then, and myself, was the growing influence of the audience figures and the report as it were of casualties day by day from the battlefront. At the weekly programme meeting where the touchstone for everything – for virtue, for success, for validity of programme effort – everything turned more and more on what audience figures were reported back by Robert Silvey and his boys from Audience Research ... What was very difficult to argue against was unfavourable comparisons with the rival programme at the same time, and there appeared on the Wednesday morning conference table in an awful sort of atmosphere of doom what were done as the (competitive) graphs ... And if at any point in time the programme at that moment showed up unfavourably one was judged unfavourably almost automatically with a sort of awful, neurotic, round the table gasp of breath ... and there built up as a result of this unfavourable judgments about the Department and people against which there was really no defence, because no defence on grounds of philosophy, or interest was listened to. It was figures, figures, figures all the way. And because figures tended to be weaker on the children's side, because of our wretched lack of money and our lack of film and maybe our lack of ability for all I know, there was a wave of what I can only describe as paedophobia, a sort of horror of anything labelled with the name of children, swept through the television service in the late 50s and early 60s which was directly the opposite of the Lingstrom tradition ...[63]

What Reed describes so well here was truly an existential crisis. It was not the future of a particular set of programmes which was at stake, nor even just the fate of an entire department. As the boys from audience research measured the ratings of each individual programme, the very principle of a comprehensive children's service was being weighed in the balance, and found wanting. The values and working practices which had developed over more than a decade were called into question; the 'community' of children's producers, and with them the ideas about childhood needs that had sustained public service television, were now under siege – not just from commercial competition, but from the new culture of the BBC. The uncaring 'atmosphere' of which Lingstrom had complained now took on, for people like Reed, a new and suffocating quality. Any attempt to respond to what they thought of as children's needs was likely to be judged in terms only of its success in attracting a wide audience.

This experience of hostility to children's television *from within the BBC* has since become a central part of the collective memory of those involved in public service children's television. The events of the early 1960s gave producers an enduring sense of the precariousness of their work, and of the contrast between the responsibility and intrinsic importance of their vocation and its lowly status in the larger world of television. Developing an awareness of the constant presence of potentially terminal danger, and of the ways in which latent neglect could transform itself into explicit and general opposition, they became alert to the appearance of any new threat to the restored children's service.[64] Underlying the participation of children's producers in later campaigns to defend the service are the experiences so powerfully evoked by Reed. At the same time, though, the passion and pathos with which these events were recalled, in their many retellings, served to obscure the basis of the 'paedophobia' – the psychotic state – which in Reed's account swept the Corporation. It is to a discussion of that basis which we now turn.

It was often acknowledged during this period that the boundaries between children's and adult television were frequently crossed by children themselves. When Hilde Himmelweit and her colleagues, in one of the first major studies of the child audience, had asked children what kinds of programme they liked, three-quarters of the votes went to adult programmes, particularly to crime thrillers. Only among the youngest group they interviewed – eight- to ten-year-olds – did programmes made specifically for children appear among the top five favourites.[65] Himmelweit argued that the advent of choice would inevitably lead to a further decline in the audiences for children's programmes.[66] Reed himself had at least partly accepted the truth of this observation in arguing that the generic title of 'Children's Television', under which the Department's various output was listed in the *Radio Times*, had infantile connotations, was repellent to many children and should be dropped.[67] At the same time, this represented a potential hostage to fortune, as it implied that there was at least some basis for questioning the child/adult distinction on which the separate existence of the Department depended. What translated these arguments from sociological observation or minor questions of signposting were two forces – namely, the Department's competitive failure and the accelerating development of the BBC's engagement with popular taste.

In 1961 Stuart Hood had been appointed Controller of Television. Hood was a Scot, an intellectual, a former partisan, hostile to many aspects of the old BBC, which, he felt, linked establishment politics with an 'uninventive' southern English, middle-class cultural taste.[68] His Assistant Controller was the Welshman Donald Baverstock, who was similarly unappreciative of the BBC's cultural norms, though for less politically-oriented reasons. Together, Hood and Baverstock turned the BBC round, to the point that by 1963 it was winning the majority share of the audience.[69] From his ascendant position, Hood was not particularly interested in children's television, still less committed to its survival.[70] In as much as he did consider it, the Department appeared to embody the less attractive features of the BBC. Like McGivern before him – though for very different reasons – Hood was irritated by the ways in which the Department interpreted 'entertainment'. For him, it epitomised 'the negative side of the Reithian tradition'; like the BBC's Light Entertainment Department, it was peopled by producers whose 'West End' theatrical background led them to an 'instinctive' and uncritical reproduction of middle-class taste and social hierarchies.[71] He had no time for the version of heritage embodied in the classic serial, did not share Reed's conception of drama as a maturational force and told Reed that the days of 'actors dressing up in costume' were numbered.[72]

Recollecting the arguments (in a 1997 interview with the authors), Hood suggests that they took place at a time when 'childhood', a 'nineteenth-century invention', was 'breaking down'. The barriers between childhood and adulthood were eroding, and with this erosion the necessity for a children's service – especially of the kind provided by the BBC – became a matter for debate. This debate took place less on the ground of cultural change than of audience research. By now, the ARD had come to include children in its audience surveys (see Chapter Four), and Hood and Baverstock utilised its findings in a deadly way. Children's demonstrable liking for adult programmes, and the successful exploitation of that liking by ITV, showed, they argued, that audience preferences did not lie where Reed claimed they did. Children's enthusiasm for ITV – particularly marked among working-class groups – was proof that the BBC had failed to address a popular audience.[73] What purpose was there, then, in a service which had so comprehensively lost its audience?

Alongside his critique of existing children's television, Hood had the outlines of an alternative, which he drew less from the specifics of broadcasting for children than from his overall programme for the BBC. Employing audience research into children's preferences, he reinforced the case for one of his strongest motivating principles: 'people should be exposed to various things', and scheduling should avoid attributing particular qualities and interests to specific sections of the audience. There should be a programming mix, which would promote diversity and cultural argument. In the process, he suggested, existing cultural authority would be undermined and the way opened up for a new kind of television in which 'popular' and 'quality' elements would be combined; and so far as children were concerned, this mix would involve eroding the boundary between children's and adults' programmes. These principles were not, of course, peculiar to Hood. They were reflected in other aspects of Hugh Greene's time as Director-General, under whose management was carried through, sometimes against the positions of embedded departmental cultures, a process which Hood describes as a 'revolution from above', the pursuit of the popular by means that were if necessary authoritarian.[74]

It was Hood more than anyone else who deployed these principles against the Children's Department. Reed's fears of paedophobia were realised in the figures of Hood and Baverstock – revolutionaries from above, 'brilliant people' who formed 'the most miserable leadership to work to'. He 'found that in Baverstock I was dealing with a man who never stopped talking and in Hood a man who never talked at all'. They both 'suffered from horror of children to an advanced degree'. With them, he endured 'a year or two of very great misery', 'a most extraordinary atmosphere of fear and tension ... when there were sighs and groans at the children's figures round the table every Wednesday morning'. He recognised 'that in one way or another children's television was heading for trouble'.[75] Reed was right, of course. Hood disliked the cultural attitudes embedded in the children's service: the view was often attributed to him that it was 'too bloody middle class'. Without having a clear idea of what a reformed children's service would look like, Hood determined on a process by which the old service would gradually lose its distinguishing features – the collegial existence of its producers and the comprehensive range of its programmes.

His first cut was the deepest. In 1961, he removed drama – the jewel in Reed's crown – and light entertainment from the control of the Children's Department. Without drama, Reed knew, he was even more unlikely to fight off ITV competition. Left to protest from the sidelines about the 'dangerous' and 'frightening' nature of the new programming strategy, Reed demanded, without success, joint control of drama productions screened during traditional 'children's time'.[76] In particular, he complained about the disturbing nature of scenes in a production of *Oliver Twist*, produced by the Drama Department without reference to the 'very careful, accurate planning' and concern for children's development that Reed saw as the hallmark of the Department. Hood, meanwhile, decided that children's television should lose all broadcast signifiers of its autonomous existence: continuity announcers would no longer refer to 'children's programmes' as such.[77] Reed looked on as a 'sacrosanct minority service' was whittled away, and the 'need for specialist attention, specialist advice, specialist conscience and care' was set aside.[78]

In 1964, the separate existence of the Children's Department came to an end. Hood placed children's television within a new 'Family Programmes Department', and laconically recited the epitaph of the old regime. Its schedules had become 'tired and repetitive'; 'new thinking was required', with an appeal to a 'wide cross-section of children and parents'.[79] Reed had no part in the new arrangements, and became Head of Training. The idea that children's television could develop as a miniature version of public service broadcasting seemed to be at an end. The gap between the commitments of the children's television 'community' and the new cultural orientation of the BBC appeared too great ever to be bridged.

Interlude 1964–7

The closure of the Children's Department did not, however, resolve the problem of the BBC's relation to the child audience (nor, indeed, did the dismissals of producers which followed the closure). The changes were not intended, as it were, to abolish 'children' as a target audience. Their needs were still – at least in a general sense – recognised. But Hood's approach discouraged too close an exploration of these needs, or of the assumed process of their development. Perceiving with clarity the tendency of the child audience to migrate towards adult programmes, and having a strong sense of youth-related cultural change, the approach failed, however, to investigate the new conditions of the childhood which such changes had created. Hood's strategy expected children to satisfy their interest in 'fictional' television by watching programmes produced for adults, or for 'family viewing'. Their 'non-fictional' interests could be catered for by the Family Programmes Department, which would also make programmes for the very young. In this way, the theatrical culture of the old Department could be brought to an end, and children could be addressed in a way that was much more responsive to the social dimensions of childhood and family life. Although programmes for children would still be made, the *segregation* of the child audience – in terms of the institutions which catered for them and the ways in which they were addressed – would disappear.

This was the hope that Doreen Stephens, Head of the new Department, expressed at the start of her brief period of control. She had a 'clear and specific vision' of a department 'operating in the field of children's interests and entertainment, with problems of adolescents, the needs of women with children at home and with children who have grown up ... aspects of health and welfare of special family concern ... household management and consumer research ...' .[80] However visionary, it was also plain from this statement that programmes made specifically for children would not be a priority of the new Department, but would take their place in a long list of commitments. This was an almost inevitable consequence of the new arrangements, but it gave rise, all the same, to a number of problems. There was a gap between the BBC's general acceptance that children had distinct needs in respect of television – needs which social change was redefining – and the institutional provision it was making for those needs to be met. Thus when Stephens, two years after her visionary statement, delivered a public lecture on 'Television for Children', she gave a long account of the BBC's new attitude to children – but a much briefer description of its output. Her treatment of changes in the way television now addressed children was serene to the point of complacency. The past was a period of error, the present was one of enlightenment. In 'middle-class homes of the 1920s and 1930s' children had been brought up 'in cushioned ignorance ... protected as much as possible from harsh realities and surrounded with cosy fairy fantasies and images'. In its radio days the BBC had reflected the attitudes of the period, and these attitudes had been 'carried over into television'.[81] She offered some praise for Freda Lingstrom's programmes: her work on *Watch with Mother* had been a 'breakthrough', but her programmes were all the same – 'soft and sentimental, sometimes self-consciously middle-class and inclined to condescension'. They skirted around proscribed topics – birth, death, ghosts – in a way which amounted to a 'denial of experience' and prevented 'the natural growth and development of the mind'. Their protective, prohibitive attitude belonged to a different age. The present was another country, in which it was recognised that 'the best way to protect children from life and its vicissitudes is knowledge'. Children now were not 'over-protected in the choice and presentation of programmes'; producers, 'working in a competitive situation', now recognised that they could not hold their audience captive: children, fortunately, were free to choose. Television, of course, had the 'duty and responsibility to enrich and enlarge the child's experience', but it could only do this if the viewer was entertained at the same time.[82]

Stephens thus signalled very clearly her understanding that the traditional culture of childhood had changed, and claimed that the BBC had changed with it. Over-protectionism was at an end; children's capacity to choose was accepted and welcomed; television had entered an era in which it could freely and engagingly develop children's knowledge of life. But her lecture failed to refer to the argument that the erosion of child/adult boundaries had lessened the need for dedicated children's programmes. In fact, the general drift of the lecture lay in the other direction: that there really did exist a distinct, historically specific cultural experience called 'childhood', and that broadcasters needed to address it.

Inevitably, therefore, she found herself modifying the severity of Hood's pronouncement and describing the BBC's recent work in terms of its usefulness *to children*, though in truth the achievement she described was not an impressive one. Drama, she explained, had proved too expensive, and there had been fears that in terms of quality it had become a poor relation of adult productions; she hoped, though, that it would be possible to restore it. Other programmes, most of them established under the previous regime, had been improved by the challenge of competition and the helpful work of the ARD: *Play School* (the pre-school programme which she claimed embodied a 'hard-core', non-protectionist approach); *Jackanory* (storytelling); the light entertainment programme *Crackerjack*; *Blue Peter* (a magazine programme aimed at eight- to ten-year-olds); *Tom-Tom* (a science and technology programme for ten- to twelve-year-olds); and *Animal Magic*. These were complemented by a large number of programmes bought in from abroad – not only from the US but also, importantly, from Europe (see Figure 3).[83]

Figure 3:   BBC Programme Schedule, 4 October 1966

1.30–1.45   Watch with Mother
1.45   Closedown
2.05–4.35   Programmes for Schools and Colleges
4.35   Closedown
4.45   Jackanory
5.00   The Stranger: film series from Australia
5.25   Four Days of Gemini IV: documentary about US space programme
5.50   The Magic Roundabout
5.55   News

Hood had left the BBC in 1964, and so exercised no influence on the Family Programmes Department. Stephens stayed on for four years, resigning in 1967 to join London Weekend Television, and eventually to head the ITV Network Children's Programmes Committee. Towards the end of her period feeling grew in the BBC that the Family Programmes experiment, at least as far as children's television was concerned, was in overall terms a failure. The programmes listed by Stephens represented the core of the schedule: ever-popular, they proved to be long-running. But around this core, programming was weak. The resources available for children's programmes within the joint Department were constantly under pressure: in the contest between 'child' and 'adult' demands, there had only been one winner. The decision to pass all responsibility for drama to an 'adult' department had led to some successes – notably *Doctor Who* – but also to the production of programmes that children found 'boring' or 'difficult'.[84]

More important, though, than any of these factors for the future of children's television was the change in the general climate in which the BBC operated. Throughout the 1960s, the BBC's income rose steadily, and its accounts suggest a continuing healthy surplus.[85] This was one sign of a wider security. In 1960, Parliament had set up the Pilkington Committee, instructing it 'to consider the future of the broadcasting services in the United Kingdom'.[86] In its report, published in 1962, the Committee endorsed the BBC as 'the main instrument of broadcasting in the United Kingdom'.[87] It led to government White Papers which awarded the BBC two major prizes: the authorisation to start a second television service (BBC 2) and to introduce colour television. The structure of ITV, meanwhile, was modified, with its central body, the Independent Television Authority (ITA) 'taking a more positive role in regard to programme standards'.[88]

Thus, in addition to its ratings success, the BBC had achieved a higher political and cultural status. ITV appeared to be in a much less favourable position. Restrained, after 1962, from downmarket competition with the BBC, and bruised by the critical judgments of Pilkington about its overall quality, ITV ceased to offer a markedly different alternative to the BBC and itself took on many of the characteristics of a public service broadcaster. It was during this period that the 'regulated duopoly', which formed the basis of television between the 1960s and the 1980s, was born. So far as children's television was concerned, ITV's redefined role led to the emergence of specialist departments in the regional companies, with a remit to provide a comprehensive range of programming in line with the particular characteristics and needs of the child audience.[89] ITV companies began to gather producers who were capable of making successful drama and entertainment series for children, and in doing so increasingly challenged the BBC on its own ground.

1967–80

Such a position of overall security, combined with a perceived under-provision in an area seen as important to public service broadcasting, paved the way for the rebirth of the BBC Children's Department. The head of the new Department was Monica Sims. Initally joining the BBC in 1953 as a radio talks producer, Sims had since moved back and forth between radio and television. From 1964 to 1967 she had edited the radio programme *Woman's Hour*. Briggs suggests that she took up her post convinced that the Family Programmes Department had not been a success: the mix between children's and women's programmes had not worked – 'the cultures were different'.[90]

The new Department faced two problems. The first was to reconstruct it as a functioning unit producing a wide range of programmes, including drama. On her arrival, Sims found that 'there was very little left': 'the drama had gone, the documentary programmes, the magazine programmes …'[91] Nevertheless, with some financial support from sympathetic controllers, she was able, between 1969 and 1972, to achieve an increase in the output, range and acknowledged quality of children's television. In 1969, the Department provided between nine and ten hours a week of television, with a further one and a half or two hours provided by other BBC departments.[92] Sims was still at this point commenting regretfully on the way in which she had to 'make a virtue out of necessity' in 'combing Europe' for drama programmes which could be bought and dubbed by the BBC.[93] But by 1972, she was able to report a substantial change. In the intervening years, partly by stealth and partly by argument, she had re-created the Department's drama capacity and strengthened other aspects of its output. The Department now expected to provide nearly fourteen hours a week of programmes, 'including every kind of output – drama, light entertainment, sport and outside broadcasts, news and current affairs, documentaries, arts, science and general features, magazine programmes, music, films, cartoons, puppets, story-telling and pre-school programmes'.[94] In a modest way, it was a period of expansion, in which the model of children's television as a 'mini-schedule', reflecting the full range of public service broadcasting as a whole, was restored to working order (see Figure 4).

Figure 4:   BBC Programme Schedule, 26 October 1978

1.45 Bagpuss
2.00 You and Me: pre-school series
2.14 For Schools and Colleges
4.20 Yogi Bear
4.25 Jackanory
4.40 Emu's Broadcasting Company
5.05 John Craven's Newsround
5.10 Blue Peter

The second problem was that of reinventing the *culture* of children's television – the ways in which it defined children's needs and attempted through its programmes to respond to them. Reinvention in this case was in some respects a matter of rediscovery, of re-establishing the 'interpretive community' and of applying some of the Department's intellectual resources and traditions to the resolution of contemporary problems. After the interregnum of Hood's reforms, a link was re-established with the thinking of earlier periods. At least in the retrospective eyes of many members of the Department, Sims managed to create a functioning 'community' of producers on a stronger basis than before. Anna Home, a subsequent head of the Department, has recalled the period as a 'golden age of children's television'.[95] From the beleaguered vantage-point of the 1990s, Edward Barnes, another successor to Sims, also looks back fondly on the BBC of twenty years ago:

> It's one of the great things that I always thought was wonderful about the old BBC is that you used to have the right to fail once in a while. As long as you didn't make a habit of it ... And of course one of the marvellous things about working in children's programmes is that (a) I think that children are actually quite tolerant and (b) the bosses aren't watching you ... So you can afford to do things and then assess them on air as it were, to see if they work and what is working for you.[96]

Judy Whitfield, producer of the pre-school programmes *Play School* and *Play Days*, remembers a similar lack of pressure: programme budgets were minuscule, but ratings were never considered an issue.[97] Anna Home likewise recalls a 'freedom to experiment' which made the 1970s 'a very sumptuous time'.[98] Producers felt they had a licence to explore what Kenneth Adam, Director of Television, called in 1964, 'the growing points of society'.[99] Hugh Greene – the BBC's Director-General from 1960 – urged on broadcasters a 'sensitivity to the world around them', a sensitivity which was measured in terms of its alertness to the pace of change in the 'times in which they are communicating'.[100] In the same spirit, Pilkington had valued above all other factors shaping television 'the attitudes, convictions and motivations of those who provide programmes'.[101]

In this environment, those working in children's television, perhaps more slowly and cautiously than those in other departments, began to decipher the signs of their times, and to both reassert and reshape their inherited traditions – a process which began in the late 1960s and did not reach its limits until the middle of the following decade. In doing so, as Sims points out, 'they were no more than a part of everything else'.[102] But in contrast to the period of confrontation between Hood and Reed, the impetus for change in this period did not come from outside the Department. As Anna Home puts it, the movement for change 'wasn't an overall policy – it came absolutely from within the Department'; or, in Sims's words, 'we'd grown up trying to work among ourselves really, with all these things in the world around, trying to make sense of what children really needed.'[103] Thus the Department recognised itself as a cohesive 'community' which was able to work creatively and effectively on the basis of the shared sense it made of the world. Its self-recognition was complemented by praise from outside: the Annan Committee of 1977, for example, saw the Department as the home of some of the best and most creative programme-makers, and connected its success to the 'autonomy' which it enjoyed.[104]

Central to the change was a revaluing of 'childhood', especially of early and middle childhood. Reed's idea of the child was not much more than an eloquent restatement of commonplaces: young children are imaginative and credulous; older children adventurous and gang-minded. In Sims's Department, populated to a significant extent by producers with some background in pre-school education, other representations of childhood came to the fore. Their emergence was not entirely explicable in terms of a change in Department personnel, but was also connected to wider social changes; and of all the 'growing points' of society in the 1960s and 1970s, one of the most central concerned the meaning attached to being a child. The experience of childhood began to be seen – or re-seen – in ways which drew more heavily than before on a broadly romantic 'progressive' tradition within educational philosophy. Earlier generations of producers had celebrated the 'eagerness' of the child viewer. Monica Sims went further, to evoke not just the child's thirst for knowledge but also children's scepticism of adult norms, and the suppression of their questioning instincts by adult society. Children, she wrote, 'have a valuable, questioning awareness of their surroundings ... inborn in every child whatever its cultural or economic inheritance ... and all too soon sacrificed to adult expediency'.[105]

In arguing thus, Sims made use of commonplace ideas to depict an audience considerably more active and critical of adult life than those portrayed by earlier broadcasters. She and her colleagues borrowed from these ideas, too, a conception of learning which dissolved the boundaries between education and entertainment. 'Children learn through play,' wrote Edward Barnes; and Sims, more expansively, wrote of *Play School* that it offered

> no directive to learn but constant encouragement to play – with games, rhymes, stories, songs, movement, sounds, painting and dressing-up. To find out, make, build, watch, enquire, listen and help. To experiment with water, shapes, textures, movement and sounds. To wonder, think and imagine.[106]

Thus the audience was imagined as one engaged in constant creative action, stimulated by the ordinary materials of the home and by television's kindly pedagogy. Despite this conception of it as 'active' and 'questioning', the way of representing the child audience insisted that it was also rooted in a particular way of life, and in a particular mode of experiencing the world in which the new was subordinate to the familiar, and in which development occurred at its own, slow, natural pace.

To this extent, children's television stood against tendencies towards internationalisation and commercialisation, and their technological and aesthetic effects. Nowhere was this brought out more clearly than in the polemics which accompanied Sims's 1971 decision not to buy for the BBC the American pre-school series *Sesame Street*. In Sims's comments the semiotic features of a future period of children's television are, as it were, anticipated and criticised. In the process, some of the deeper preferences of her child-centred account of children's television – as well as the residual anti-Americanism of public service culture – are revealed.

Sesame Street was a project designed to be internationally marketed, and its makers were supported in their export drive by heavy governmental pressure. This perhaps explains the need Sims felt to compile at some length the reasons for her opposition. In her account, a concern to retain a particular televisual pace and rhythm was associated with an idea of healthy child development. The value of children's television was defined in terms of its ability to develop a 'two-way involvement' in which television, by attending to children's 'own life and circumstances', could help them integrate into the national 'pattern of life'. A developmental approach to learning and a project aiming at cultural cohesiveness were thus linked; and in the process child-centredness – of the sort embodied in *Play School* – was inserted into a comprehensive philosophy of national public service broadcasting. In *Sesame Street*, Sims claimed, both pedagogy and cultural effect were very different. Rather than 'giving children the opportunity to conjecture, to solve problems and to be creative', it offered bite-sized pieces of information, segmented and unrelated to each other, presented at a hectic pace, and detached from real-life situations. In doing so it 'destroyed the continuum of experience'. Its fragmented format – a 'system of cartoons with constant interruptions' – not only frustrated the development of children's concentration but also reduced, by means of its constant focus-shifting, the space for children to imitate or elaborate what they watched. The economic reliance of its makers on export orders and repeats meant that it would not be 'immediate, topical and involved in the child's own life and circumstances'; it would disregard the 'pattern of life' in children's own societies. It thus possessed 'an unreality', a 'lack of truth' and failed to 'start from the child's own particular environment and experience'. In consequence, it was 'authoritarian'.[107]

If the remaking of the Department involved an affirmation of the importance of 'child-centred' television for young children, it also entailed a fuller recognition of the cultures of older groups of viewers – and in the process, it needed to address questions of social class and popular taste. Hood had made two main points about children's television: that its audience was in the process of deserting it for adult programmes; and that – in the succinct folkloric version that circulated within the BBC – it was 'too bloody middle class'. The experience of the 1970s proved the first contention wrong, but the second continued to wound. The process of reinventing the culture of children's television required that it be faced. In doing so, producers were again responding to a sign of the times. Issues of culture and class constituted the central set of problems of social policy in the 1960s and 1970s. These were in part problems of inequality and deprivation – including 'cultural deprivation' – and in part problems of what would now be called difference and recognition. In education, for instance, attempts were made not only to reduce class-based differentials in achievement but also to improve the performance of working-class students by engaging more directly with the everyday cultures of learners, an engagement which involved teachers in a more serious effort of cultural interpretation than had previously been the case.[108] The work of the Children's Department was affected by similar concerns. Trainee producers were sent to watch programmes in people's homes, in order to get a sense (particularly) of the reactions of working-class audiences.[109] Sims frequently emphasised that *Play School* had its part to play in the fight against cultural deprivation, and thought that it could compensate for the fact that 'many children do not live in homes where adults hold conversations with them'.[110]

Thus, in a way which again reflected the spirit of the times, the Department moved towards a closer engagement with aspects of popular and everyday culture. Shortly, we shall explore some of the results of this engagement. Its limits, though, should not be forgotten. Reed's utterances, at the meeting of 1960, had revealed a producer culture torn between the 'compulsive' requirements of success and a deep personal allegiance to decidedly non-compulsive forms of television. Something of the same tension shaped the thinking of the post-1967 Department. Whatever its desire to represent previously unscreened aspects of popular experience, it remained attached to a core of values in which middle-class attitudes and universal moral principles had come to be seen as one and the same thing. Monica Sims recalls a meeting in the late 1960s during which Hood's criticism of the class-based values of children's television was repeated:

> Huw Wheldon [Managing Director, Television] was marvellous. He got up and said, 'What are you saying? . . . What is wrong with being middle-class? What is wrong with speaking clearly, grammatically, behaving morally, not throwing things around the studio?' He made a wonderful defence of middle-class values, of which I was able to say, 'Well, you must admit these are working-class values as well'. The BBC was always being tarred with a middle-class image and values . . . I don't think it was true. I think it's true to the extent that all education is middle-class. Has to be. Because to learn and to want to realise your potential is actually a middle-class aspiration . . . I think there was always a realisation that the people with whom the children identified had to accept their responsibility as role models. They would have to behave considerately to each other, they would not be allowed to be very thuggish or eat chocolate or chips . . . There was always this belief in behaving well and considerately to other people, which I don't personally think is a middle-class attitude.[111]

Accompanying the discussion about morality here is of course a strong cultural subtext, which resides not only in the statement about education but also in the dietary symbolism, where the eating of the quintessential people's food is seen as something that children's television must strenuously avoid representing: a concern for children's welfare and a desire to inculcate the norms of a specific kind of culture are merged together.

When Edward Barnes, interviewed in 1982, spoke of belonging, deprivation and integration, he was making similar connections. 'We try in all our programmes', he said, 'to integrate children into our kind of family.' 'It must do more good than harm', he added, 'to children from deprived homes to feel that they have a sense of belonging somewhere rather than nowhere whatsoever.'[112] Likewise, Barnes's defence of what he calls 'paternalism' – a children's television based on the values of a 'loving and caring parent' – has a similar structure, organised around a buried metaphor of rescue. Writing in *The Listener* in 1982, Barnes, who four years previously had succeeded Sims as Head of Department, warned that 'our children must not be the proles of tomorrow'.[113] Children's television could save them from this fate – which otherwise awaited them at the hands of commercial channels – by educating them as viewers. 'One of the prime functions of the Children's Programmes Department', he wrote, 'is to teach children how to watch television before they are conditioned to believe that they are *Crossroads* [ITV soap opera] fodder.'[114] Thus public service television could deliver children from an Orwellian future and draw them away from the wastelands of popular taste, into a different and richer cultural life. In learning to interpret the varied genres offered by the Department, children would develop – emotionally, cognitively and in terms of cultural accomplishment. Rather than being exposed to an indiscriminate mass of adult television, they would follow (as carefully in this respect as the children of Lingstrom's day) the graded path of development pointed out to them by the guiding parental hand of the children's schedule:

> Many children hear their first ever story on *Play School*. When they are five or six, they will have the concentration to follow a half-hour-long story told in dramatic form in *Playhouse*, and between eight and thirteen they will have their minds and emotions stretched by plays and serial stories.

Eventually, as Barnes describes it, this 'training in narrative will bring them to the drama of ideas in [the adult] *Play for Today*'. Likewise, watching the children's programme *Newsround* will lead them to adult news and to *Panorama*. Television thus enables, and embodies, the development of a mature citizenship.[115]

Neither Sims's anecdote nor Barnes's prescription suggests a Department devoted to the overturning of middle-class norms of social behaviour and cultural value. Nevertheless, in limited ways, without departing from an overall cultural protectionism, the Department did expand the cultural range of its programmes so as to address what was represented as working-class experience. Central to this expansion was drama of a new kind – the school-based series *Grange Hill*, first screened in 1978, and the most controversial product of the Children's Department in the 1970s.

As Edward Barnes puts it, *Grange Hill* 'was about working-class children'.[116] Like most ground-breaking programmes, its origins were partly accidental. The Department did not plan to make a controversial programme, but it did have in mind a drama series based in a comprehensive school. The writer commissioned to prepare the scripts, Phil Redmond, broke the conventional mould, and in doing so was able to take the Department, often reluctantly, with him. Redmond wrote in reaction against the 'middle-class type of drama that was getting pushed down kids' throats'. His intention, he asserted, was to 'do something from my own background', in which 'people [were] speaking in working-class accents about working-class issues'.[117] Anna Home, who commissioned the series, comments that it was the first programme to represent what had become in the 1970s the majority form of secondary education – the comprehensive school.[118]

The first series of the programme was received fairly mildly; but the second and third series – which according to Redmond 'were all about student militancy and behind the bike shed and horrendous things like periods and first bras' – were met with hostility.[119] The Department had – arguably for the first time – created a popular programme which effectively separated and sealed off the world of children from the world of adults. In Home's account, adults, who had little experience of the new schooling, 'didn't like the programme': they 'thought it was far too raw'. Members of Parliament were not happy either, and 'teachers didn't like it because they thought it was undermining their authority'.[120] According to Redmond, this 'extreme reaction' led to the programme being put under close surveillance:

> in the end it became one of those things that never happens in television – we were told what we could and couldn't have in it. We'd get in a room and everyone in BBC suits and we'd be told we could do this, but we couldn't do that.[121]

Thus *Grange Hill* shifted the Children's Department, however temporarily, from an area of cultural and moral safety to one of danger. This shift was only partly to do with content and subject matter. It was also a change in mood. For Redmond, 'there's definitely a pre- and a post-*Grange Hill* period in children's television and … in British television [as a whole]'. After *Grange Hill* came a spate of drama series with 'tougher edges', so that 'kids could get a regular dose of misery'.[122] For Sims, too, a 'working-class' subject matter was connected to a greater degree of realism, and a more direct representation of everyday problems; she saw *Grange Hill* as an attempt to be 'more realistic', 'addressing some of the difficulties children face as well as the fun and enjoyment'.[123]

Grange Hill, then, was innovative in two significant respects. First, in tone and content it marked a break with earlier ways of representing children's lives. Second, it had the effect of setting children apart from what were felt by both its creators and its critics to be the norms of conventional adult life. For a limited time, it was able to depict children's experience in a way that extended child-centredness beyond the status of a general principle, and into an area where it involved a more concrete, and in this case class-inflected, engagement with children's cultures.[124]

Drama was not the only area, however, in which this sort of cultural engagement took place. The 1960s, famously, was a decade in which 'youth culture' became both a political issue and a new commercial form. The former aspect was rarely in any direct sense a subject for children's television; but the latter – especially in the 1970s – increasingly was. In the mid-1970s a new format developed – the Saturday-morning magazine programme. This extension of children's television time into a previously unexploited area, and its domination by entertainment values, effectively killed off, almost completely, a once-important form of children's culture, Saturday morning cinema.[125] Its effects on television culture were also considerable. Magazine programmes introduced several elements new to children's television. First, they drew from the DJ culture of Radio 1 and of commercial local radio, a culture which gave the programme presenter a central role and a prominent, idiosyncratic character. In the process, the ways in which programmes related to the child audience came to differ from what had previously been the norm. Magazines made much use of phone-in material and relied heavily on the improvisational skills of their presenters. In doing so, they developed a new and less formal way of addressing their audience and responding to its interests. This mode of address tended to validate children's everyday cultures; the focus was no longer on edifying hobbies or on information thought useful by adults. Adult behaviour, in fact, became an object of mockery; like the more solemn conventions of children's television, it was frequently parodied to the point of slapstick. The final novel element was the programmes' relation to children's musical cultures. Popular music, together with the various representations of sexuality which accompanied it, was an important features of the new magazine programmes.

All these features were more strongly present in ITV programmes than in the BBC equivalent. ATV's *Tiswas*, first screened in 1975, was famously unruly; and ITV's children's time pop programmes of the mid-1970s featured David Bowie and Marc Bolan in all their ambivalent sexual splendour. By contrast, the BBC's alternative, *Multi-Coloured Swap Shop*, was a more cautious affair. Home notes its unrehearsed nature and comments that 'it broke new ground and took many risks'.[126] In retrospect, however, what stands out are the continuities between *Swap Shop* and the BBC's earlier programmes: it contained many items which a previous generation of writers would without difficulty have recognised as 'educational'; and in several of its contributors, it maintained a link with the television of the 1960s. Its engagement with popular culture was more muted and less celebratory than that of ITV's programmes: its pop stars tended to be tamer, its humour less confrontational. As Stuart Hall pointed out, *Swap Shop* was 'carefully and unobtrusively organised around introduction into the respectable part of the teenage scene'.[127] *Swap Shop* was safe where *Grange Hill* was (sometimes) scandalous. But this did not mean that it was unproblematic: looking back in 1997 on the period of *Swap Shop*, Barnes was still troubled by its tendency to cross the boundaries between childhood and adulthood:

> I've often wondered if I wasn't in some way responsible for artificially bringing children into teenage, adult and sexual values before the time they were needed . . . I think that it is the effect of ramming sexual values and of some kinds of values that surround sexuality down people's throats before they've reached puberty. I think it is not a good idea, really, because that is eroding childhood. And I sometimes wonder if I've been a party to that in some way.[128]

In one respect these remarks, which relate to the closing years of our period, lead back to McGivern's concerns about the 'vulgarity' of light entertainment in the 1950s. They highlight the enduring problem of a children's television culture caught between the sense of mission embedded in its occupational culture and the necessity of reaching out in the direction of popular taste – and in the process encountering profound changes in the culture of childhood. But Barnes's discomfort is greater than that of McGivern. McGivern's concerns – explicitly, at least

– had been mainly to do with the contamination of one taste culture by another. Barnes's worries run deeper: in fostering a commercialised sexuality, television may be assisting in the destruction – or the corruption – of childhood itself. His comment suggests that even in the midst of its 'golden age', public service television for children faced the possibility that the child audience of its imagination was slipping away; and that this 'erosion' was at least partly a result of the work of children's television itself. Thus for Barnes, as for Reed, childhood was a condition whose stability was never guaranteed; and just as Sims's comments on *Sesame Street* were filled with a sense of foreboding about the commercial reshaping of children's culture, so Barnes's remarks reflect not just a concern about the future, but a perturbed sense that in some form it had already been born, and that the BBC itself had helped deliver it.

Conclusion

In this chapter, we have tried to show how the BBC Children's Department negotiated the first thirty-five years of its existence. What we have sketched is no neat pattern of development, but rather a persistent field of tension, in which ideas about childhood intersect with cultural, economic and technological change; and in which questions of policy and institutional culture are intertwined with the capacities, professional culture and ideological orientations of individuals. By the end of our period, children's television had become a substantial feature of public service broadcasting – but its fundamental dilemmas remained. As the 1980s advanced towards the era (feared by Barnes) of cable and satellite television, so the status of childhood and the child audience became increasingly problematic. This time, the forces reshaping children's television arose not from the single and ultimately controllable source of ITV, but from a much larger global process involving deregulation and many-sided market competition. In the following chapter, it is these changes in the political economy of children's television – and their impact on public service broadcasting – to which we turn.

Notes

(The abbreviation WAC in these notes refers to the BBC's Written Archives Centre, where the files of the Children's Department (up until the 1970s) are collected. Documents held at the Written Centre are fully referenced here; full details of texts in the public domain are given in the Bibliography.)

1 Reed, unpublished interview with John Lane for the BBC Oral History Project, 1977.
2 Ibid.
3 In researching this chapter, we interviewed or read the work of people who had been production assistants, programme producers and 'managers' with departmental, or Corporation-wide responsibilities. For brevity's sake, we refer to them all here as 'producers'. For the same reason, we mostly use the term 'Children's Department' rather than 'Children's Programmes Department'.
4 Fish (1980).

5 Oswell (1995).

6 Wagg (1992), p. 151.

7 Cecil Madden, TV Programmes Organiser, correspondence, 1947 (WAC File 1 T16/45/1).

8 Richmond Postgate, correspondence with Cecil Madden and others, 28 April 1950 (WAC File 1 T16/45/1).

9 Freda Lingstrom, correspondence with George Barnes (Director of Television) and Cecil McGivern, 17 December 1953 (WAC File 1 T16/45/1).

10 Oswell (1995), pp. 78–9.

11 McGivern's views are summarised in minutes of Children's Department meeting, 4 December 1951 (WAC File 1B T26/5/2).

12 'Sacked', *Sunday Pictorial*, 8 April 1951. See also 'Why change? Ask the televiewers', *News Chronicle*, 9 April 1951.

13 Lingstrom (1953), p. 101.

14 Capon (1952), p. 27.

15 Adams (1950), p. 86.

16 Ibid.

17 Lingstrom, correspondence with Barnes and McGivern, see note 9.

18 Lowe (1988).

19 Walkerdine and Lucey (1989).

20 Hadow (1931), reprinted in MacLure (1986), p. 191.

21 Mary Adams, *Children's Television: Fundamental Issues*, 8 August 1947 (WAC File 1 T16/45/1).

22 Reed, unpublished interview with John Lane, note 1. As we shall indicate below and in Chapter Three, these 'standards' were somewhat abandoned later in the decade, largely in response to the advent of commercial television; although they subsequently re-emerged to form the basis of the developmental 'mini-schedule' which still applies today.

23 Adams (1950), p. 87.

24 Ibid.

25 Lingstrom (1953), p. 99.

26 Reed, unpublished interview with John Lane, note 1.

27 Lingstrom (1953), p. 101.

28 Richmond Postgate, correspondence, 1 April 1950 (WAC T16/45/1).

29 For a fuller discussion of 'needs' and 'wants', see Chapter Five.

30 Silvey (1974), p. 161.

31 Cecil McGivern, note to Cecil Madden, 2 October 1950 (WAC T26/5/1). Among the points at issue was the fact that Madden wished to make instructional programmes about ballroom dancing. 'Have you seriously considered whether this is suitable for normal children?' wrote McGivern. Madden replied, 'I wondered whether children would not like to be taught before Christmas simple dances like the waltz, polka or foxtrot ... Don't you think this is quite suitable for normal children and, in fact, could do a lot of good?'

32 Johnson (1998).

33 Norman Collins to Cecil Madden, 28 October 50 (WAC T16/45/1). Collins later occupied a central position in independent television.

34 Home (1993), p. 29; Edward Barnes, interview with the authors, 1997. Barnes was Head of Children's Programmes from 1978 to 1984. In relation to Westerns, the claim is exaggerated – they were screened, though not in great numbers.

35 Cecil McGivern to Freda Lingstrom, 20 December 1954 (WAC T16/45/11).

36 Mark Abrams, *Child Audiences for Television*, unpublished report, 1955 (WAC VR55/502).

37 Abrams, *Child Audiences*; Briggs (1995), p. 1005.

38 BBC (1957) *Programmes for Children*, 16 September 1957 (WAC T/16/45/2). It is important to recognise, however, that two-channel homes were at this time still in the minority and that, overall, the BBC retained a majority share of the audience (Curran and Seaton (1997), p. 179).

39 Granada Television (1960).

40 Sendall (1982), p. 328.

41 Ibid., p. 317.

42 Hugh Carleton Greene, 'Two Threats to Broadcasting: Political and Commercial Control', speech given in Bad Boll, West Germany, 13 March 1958 (WAC T/16/45/2).

43 Reed, unpublished interview with John Lane, note 1.

44 Sendall (1982), p.245.

45 Reed, unpublished interview with John Lane, note 1. In 1960, Reed argued that this abandonment of the established principles of scheduling was a temporary measure: 'As far as we could gather, we were getting a figure of about 18[%] to their 82. This was a mass desertion of our audience and a situation which could not be allowed to go on. It was a rot setting in at lightning speed. We turned everything upside down to stop the rot. We started with our strongest programme. The priority was to stop the rot. This made nonsense of our normal planned children's entertainment, but ultimately it stabilised the rot and brought about the fairly healthy position we are in now. We have since reverted cautiously to appropriate and considered planning, but we could only do it after we had stopped the rot.' Reed's optimistic diagnosis was not shared by his ARD, nor by his commercial rivals.

46 BBC, report of a meeting on children's television, held on 22 November 1960 (WAC T16/45/3). The most substantial contribution to the meeting was made by Reed.

47 BBC, Study Group on the Nuffield Report (*Television and the Child*), 1959 (WAC T16/45/2).

48 Oliver Reed, memorandum to the Controller of Programmes, Television, 5 July 1957 (WAC T16/45/2).

49 Ibid.

50 BBC, report of a meeting on children's television, note 46. The context of the meeting was the preparation of the BBC's submission to the Pilkington Committee. All departments were asked by BBC management to discuss the balance-sheet of their response to ITV competition. The meetings were attended by a member of the BBC Secretariat, and were fully minuted.

51 Burns (1977), p. 54.

52 BBC, report of a meeting on children's television, note 46.

53 Reed, unpublished interview with John Lane, note 1.

54 Reed, memorandum, 2 June 1958 (WAC T16/45/2).

55 Barnes, interview with the authors.

56 Reed, memoradum, note 54.

57 BBC (1957).

58 As discussed, for example, by Himmelweit, Oppenheim and Vince (1958).

59 BBC, report of a meeting on children's television, note 46; Reed, unpublished interview with John Lane, note 1.

60 BBC, report of a meeting on children's television, note 46.

61 Abrams, *Child Audiences*, note 36.

62 Abrams (1959).

63 Reed, unpublished interview with John Lane, note 1.

64 Home (1993); Barnes, interview with the authors.

65 Himmelweit, Oppenheim and Vince (1958), p. 13.

66 Ibid., p. 15.

67 Reed, memorandium, note 54.

68 Stuart Hood, interview with the authors, 1997.

69 'BBC overtakes ITV in share of viewers', *Daily Telegraph*, 17 January 1963.

70 Reed's memories of Hood were searingly vivid; Hood remembers Reed only slightly.

71 Hood, interview with the authors.

72 Reed, unpublished interview with John Lane, note 1.

73 Hood, interview with the authors.

74 Ibid.

75 Reed, unpublished interview with John Lane, note 1.

76 Oliver Reed, memorandum to the Controller of Programmes, Television, 21 November 1961 (WAC T/16/45/3).

77 Stuart Hood, memorandum, 7 November 1961 (WAC T16/45/3).

78 Reed, memorandum to Controller of Programmes, note 76; unpublished interview with John Lane, note 1.

79 Stuart Hood, memorandum, 9 January 1964 (WAC T31/324).

80 Doreen Stephens, memorandum, 1964 (WAC T31/324).

81 Stephens (1966), p. 7.

82 Ibid., pp. 3–8.

83 Ibid., pp. 12–16.

84 Monica Sims, interview with the authors, 1977.

85 BBC *Annual Reports*, 1967–72.

86 Pilkington Committee (1962), p. 1.

87 Ibid., p. 295.

88 Memorandum by the Postmaster-General to the Cabinet, concerning the 'Second White Paper on Broadcasting and Television', quoted in Briggs (1995), p. 304.

89 Lewis Rudd, interview with the authors, 1998; Judith Mackrell, obituary of Marjorie Sigley, *Guardian*, 10 September 1997.

90 Briggs (1995), p. 347.

91 Sims, interview with the authors.

92 Monica Sims, *BBC Children's Programmes*, internal paper, June 1969 (WAC).

93 Ibid.

94 Monica Sims (1972) 'Children's programmes BBC Television' (draft of an article for *Sound and Vision*, 10 November 1972 (WA T47/113)).

95 Home (1993).

96 Barnes, interview with the authors.

97 Judy Whitfield, interview with the authors, 1998. 'They probably did have overnights (ratings) but nothing filtered down to my level. They may have been going on at a higher level which I wasn't aware of. But we were fairly cushioned from it ... I'm not quite sure when that [ratings] started creeping in. I think it would probably have been about ... the beginning of the 1980s ... We were all very cushioned then. We just got on and made the programmes.'

98 Anna Home, interview with the authors, 1997. Anna Home was Head of BBC Children's Programmes from 1984 to 1997.

99 Tracey and Morrison (1979), p. 45.

100 Hood (1967), pp. 49–50.

101 Pilkington Committee (1962), p. 68.

102 Sims, interview with the authors.

103 Home, interview with the authors; Sims, interview with the authors.

104 Annan Committee (1977), pp. 349–50.

105 Monica Sims, '*Sesame Street*', paper given to the European Broadcasting Union, 14 October 1971 (WAC T47/113).

106 Edward Barnes, information for Vice-Chairman of the BBC's governors, 30 April 1971 (WAC T47/113); Sims, 'Children's programmes', note 94.

107 Sims, '*Sesame Street*', note 105. In some of this, Sims is quoting from the comments of various educationalists about *Sesame Street*.

108 See Halsey (1972).

109 Sims, interview with the authors.

110 Sims, 'Children's programmes', note 94.

111 Sims, interview with the authors.

112 Edward Barnes, interviewed by Stuart Hall for the Open University Television Programme *D102 A Foundation Course in the Social Sciences – Social Integration 1: Children's Television*, 1982.

113 Barnes (1982), TV interview.

114 Ibid.

115 Ibid.

116 Barnes, interview with the authors. A fuller discussion of the origins and evolution of *Grange Hill* will be included in Buckingham (forthcoming a).

117 Phil Redmond, interview with the authors, 1996.

118 Home, interview with the authors.

119 Redmond, interview with the authors.

120 Home, interview with the authors.

121 Redmond, interview with the authors.

122 Ibid.

123 Sims, interview with the authors.

124 Redmond stresses that in his view this achievement was in its strongest form limited to a couple of series. Barnes, from a different perspective, comments that with time it became apparent to critics that *Grange Hill* had 'very, very strong moral values' (Barnes, interview with the authors).

125 Staples (1997), p. 229.

126 Home (1993), p. 131.

127 Hall, *Children's Television*, note 112. A fuller analysis of these programmes will be contained in Buckingham (forthcoming a).

128 Barnes, interview with the authors.

2 Run the Risk
Towards a Political Economy of Children's Television

This chapter brings our analysis of the institutional dimensions of children's tele-vision from the 1980s into the present, and projects some way into the future. The past two decades have seen a steady move away from the principle of public service, towards a more commercial, market-led system. We begin by considering some recent research and debate about the consequences of this development for children's tele-vision. We then offer our own analysis of these technological and economic changes within broadcasting, and their impact on the child audience; and we consider the current state of play among the various sectors of the industry. In the process, we address several key questions that have consistently recurred in public debates about children's television – questions about quality, diversity and cultural identity. As we shall argue, there are several grounds for questioning the view that children's tele-vision in Britain represents a 'Great Tradition' that is now in decline.

Over the past two decades, British broadcasting has been steadily dragged into the commercial marketplace. The comparative equilibrium provided by the regulated duopoly has been progressively eroded, and the principle of broadcasting as a public service has been increasingly threatened. These developments can partly be explained by the end of frequency scarcity and the proliferation of new media technologies; but they have also, of course, been driven by successive govern-ments' ideological commitment to the so-called 'free market'. These developments have had far-reaching, but also potentially ambivalent, consequences for children's television.

As we have shown, children have always been seen as a 'special' audience in debates about broadcasting – an audience whose particular characteristics and needs require specific codes of practice and regulation. Such assumptions have been subject to complex historical changes, yet they continue to inform the work of policy-makers, producers and legislators right through to the present. The pro-vision of a distinct service for children has always been seen as a defining marker of the public service principle, and this continues to be the case, for instance, in the 1990 Broadcasting Act and in documents such as the BBC's *Extending Choice* (1992) and its 'Statement of Promises' (1996).

In this respect, debates about children's television provide an interesting case study for broader questions about the future of broadcasting in Britain, as we move towards an increasingly market-led system. As we suggested in the Introduction, the tone of these debates has largely been pessimistic and conservative. Public discussions of children's television are often infused with nostalgia: it is rare to read press reports of such debates which do not hark back (however ironically) to the 'golden age' of *Muffin the Mule*, *Watch with Mother* or *Play School*. As in many other areas, the invocation of childhood often serves to focus much broader anxieties about loss and decline. The future is seen to promise little more than the destruction of the great achievements of the past. We hope our analysis of the contemporary situation will provide the basis for a more constructive response to change.

The worst-case scenario?

Much of the debate here rests on an implicit comparison with the fate of children's television in the US. While American public broadcasting has been responsible for some of the most significant success stories of children's television – most obviously *Sesame Street* – the provision of children's programmes in the US has been primarily a matter for commercial broadcasters. Just as US critics and lobby groups frequently look to Britain as a model for public service children's television, so British critics look to the US as an object lesson in the ravages of a market-led system.[1]

In fact, commercial broadcasters in the US only gradually 'discovered' children as a potentially valuable target market. As Bill Melody[2] describes, television was initially marketed to parents in the 1950s as an *educational* medium, albeit primarily in order to encourage them to invest in a television set in the first place. As in the UK, this period was marked by a considerable uncertainty about the child audience, and about the extent to which it could be seen as distinct from the family or general audience.

From the late 1950s, however, an increasingly commercial logic came to dominate US television: the medium was essentially conceived as a means of 'selling audiences to advertisers'.[3] Melody and other critics[4] argue that this situation had particularly negative implications for children. Initially, children were regarded primarily as a means of influencing their parents' consumer behaviour – as a source of 'pester power'. They were not widely seen as an economically valuable market in their own right. As a result, there was little incentive to produce material that catered specifically for their needs, or at least to invest significantly in doing so. Indeed, children were predominantly seen as an audience that could be bought cheaply: it was generally assumed that they would watch anything they were offered.

This assumption had several consequences. In terms of scheduling, it meant that programmes for children would only be screened at times when more valuable sections of the audience were unavailable to view. As a result, there were few programmes in the after-school slot (when more valuable 'housewives' could be reached), and children's programmes were primarily confined to the Saturday morning 'kid-vid ghetto'. Smaller subsections of the child audience were even more likely to lose out. Pre-schoolers, for example, could be lumped in with the general child audience, thus making it unnecessary to produce programmes catering specifically for them. While boys were seen to be unwilling to watch programmes aimed at girls, girls would be more likely to do the reverse; and so the industry wisdom became 'if in doubt, use boys'.[5] More broadly, these critics argue, a competitive, market-driven system leaves no room for failure, and therefore for innovation: reliance on the tried and tested is bound to be preferred to creative risk-taking. Taken together, these factors inevitably resulted in the production of cheap, formulaic, 'lowest common denominator' television for children.

According to the critics, these tendencies were accentuated during the 1980s with the deregulation of children's television under Reagan.[6] The limited gains made by lobbyists for children's television during the 1970s were swept aside, as capitalism's inexorable search for new markets focused increasingly on children. Children were no longer perceived simply as a conduit to adult consumers, but as a target for direct marketing in their own right. The advent of the 'thirty-minute commercial' – animation series created by toy manufacturers primarily as a means of advertising new products – was the most controversial aspect of this development.[7] Although there is of course a long history of media-related merchandising for children – dating back at least as far as Disney's Mickey Mouse Clubs in the 1930s[8] – this had always been perceived as a 'secondary' phenomenon. By contrast, the new wave of toy-related cartoons in the 1980s were conceived primarily as marketing devices: key decisions about the narratives and characters were dependent upon the imperatives of the toy companies.[9]

While this phenomenon continues, there has since been a move back towards regulation in the US. The Children's Television Act 1990 required stations to provide 'educational' programming, although the meaning of this term was initially somewhat vague. Some stations argued, for example, that a programme like *The Jetsons* was 'educational' on the grounds that it informed children about life in the future.[10] Under Clinton, however, this legislation has been strengthened: stations are now compelled to provide at least three hours of 'educational children's programmes' per week, although there are as yet no requirements about when this should be scheduled, or the extent to which it should be promoted.[11] There have also been signs that the government wishes to take a more proactive stance, by funding the production of 'quality' children's programming. In general, however, the regulatory body, the Federal Communications Commission, remains comparatively weak, and responsibility for monitoring provision continues to lie with individual citizens and lobby groups.

Despite these recent developments, critics of the US system typically see its poor record in children's television as a logical consequence of commercial domination. The market, they argue, is inherently incompatible with children's interests, with their psychological well-being and with the provision of a broad range of high-quality programming. For such critics, commercial television is little more than an incitement to consumerism, and an exploitation of children's innate vulnerability. Stephen Kline, for example, argues that:

> The marketplace will never inspire children with high ideals or positive images of the personality, provide stories which help them to adjust to life's tribulations or pro-

mote play activities that are most help to their maturation. Business interests trying to maximise profits cannot be expected to worry about cultural values or social objectives beyond the consumerist cultural vector that underwrites commercial media.[12]

This pessimistic view of the consequences of a market-led system represents something of a critical orthodoxy, although it has been subject to challenge. Ellen Seiter,[13] for example, accuses such critics of an implicit snobbery, which is based on unarticulated middle-class (and, to a lesser extent, male) cultural values. Distinctions between 'educational' and 'non-educational' toys, or between 'quality' television and 'trash', are (she argues) little more than a reflection of the 'smug self-satisfaction of educated middle-class people'. Seiter asserts that 'consumerism' is far from confined to the working classes, or indeed to children: the market for middle-class toys, for example, is based on different aesthetic values, but it is just as 'commercial' and 'manipulative' as the mass marketing of companies like Toys 'R' Us. Furthermore, she suggests, this approach neglects the active and diverse ways in which children make sense of the media. In the case of advertising, for example, she argues that the industry has been far readier than many of its critics to acknowledge children's cynicism about commercial messages, and their considerable sophistication as an audience.[14]

These debates obviously reflect much broader questions about the relations between 'culture' and 'commerce', and about the nature of the child audience, which will be the major focus of our analysis in this chapter. At this stage, we would wish merely to caution against the temptation to translate an analysis from the US to the very different social, economic and cultural context of the UK. As the controversies over *Sesame Street* in the early 1970s suggest, fear of 'Americanisation' is a significant strain in British cultural life, at least among some sections of the educated middle classes.[15] 'America' seems to represent a fantasy of a nightmare future – 'we will all be like America in ten years' time' – although it is arguably one which never actually comes to pass. In the 1980s, the fate awaiting adults in the new era of commercial multi-channel television was summed up in the phrase 'wall-to-wall *Dallas*'. In the early 1990s, it was often maintained that children would be bombarded by wall-to-wall American animation. Yet neither scenario has in fact transpired.

As we have indicated, such arguments rest on implicit assumptions about cultural value and identity that are in need of much fuller examination. The notion that children's culture can and should be protected from 'contamination' by commerce reflects a utopian, protectionist notion of childhood that is very questionable. Simply on a factual level, there are several reasons to challenge the assumptions on which these fearful predictions are based, at least as far as they relate to the UK. Ultimately, we would argue that such arguments are based on a form of economic reductionism: that is, a view that a market-dominated system will *inevitably* lead to a neglect of children's social and cultural needs. As we shall attempt to show, the operations of the market in the sphere of culture are both more complex and more ambiguous than such critics tend to suggest.

The 'Great Tradition'?

The most significant recent analysis of the British situation is contained in Jay Blumler's report for the Broadcasting Standards Council (BSC), *The Future of Children's Television in Britain*, published in December 1992. This report was commissioned in the wake of the 1990 Broadcasting Act, amid fears that the changing structure of ITV and the growing commercial pressures on the BBC would lead to a decline in the quantity, diversity and quality of children's television. The report was intended to provide a benchmark against which to monitor future developments; and the BSC subsequently commissioned an 'update' for purposes of comparison, reported in the press story quoted in the Introduction.[16]

Blumler's original report includes a detailed statistical analysis of changes in children's television programming during the 1980s; while the 'update' extends this – using a rather different system of categorisation – into the mid-1990s. We discuss this research and its underlying assumptions more fully in the following chapter, although a brief summary is relevant here. Blumler finds that, while there is a general expansion in the *amount* of programming for children, there is also some contraction in its *range*. Thus, for example, there is an increase in 'animation' and 'entertainment' programming and a decrease in factual and preschool programmes, and in 'storytelling'. As Blumler acknowledges, this does not necessarily imply that *quality* has worsened; although he implicitly assumes that 'quality' is more likely to reside in certain kinds of programming (such as home-produced drama) than in others (such as animation). Nevertheless, Blumler suggests that this does not bode well for the future:

> the trends suggest that competitive preoccupations, intensified cost-consciousness and embroilment in international transactions were already affecting the shape of children's television schedules in the mid- to late 1980s. For the future this raises a troubling question: if so much has changed at a time when the BBC–ITV duopoly was still intact, how much more vulnerable to pressure could children's television be as the new system develops?[17]

These fears are echoed in the second major aspect of Blumler's report, which is his analysis of interviews with leading broadcasters involved in the policy, management and production of children's television. While acknowledging a degree of optimism among some of his respondents, Blumler concludes that none of them 'expected the environment for children's television to be as hospitable in the future as in the past'. Blumler's own predictions are even more gloomy. Unless the work of terrestrial broadcasters can be supported, he argues, the most likely scenario is one of 'creeping erosion'.

Blumler describes British children's television in explicitly Leavisite terms as an internationally envied 'Great Tradition',[18] the cornerstone of public service, an embodiment of 'quality' and of a distinctively British cultural identity. He identifies several characteristics which, he argues, have guaranteed the health and survival of this tradition. These include: the scheduling of children's programmes at times when children are available to view (for example, after school); the commitment to a 'mixed diet' of programming, including drama, information, animation, news, etc.; the targeting of programmes to meet the needs of specific subsections of the audience according to age (for example, pre-schoolers); and the presence of talented and motivated professionals working in the area. These characteristics have, according to Blumler, been guaranteed by the broader structural features of British broadcasting: the commitment to public service; the regulated duopoly; and the strength of regulatory bodies.

Blumler argues that this 'Great Tradition' is now under serious threat as a result of changes in the structure of broadcasting. Along with the many producers and executives he interviews, Blumler fears that the increasing commercialisation of independent television in Britain, and its corrosive effect through competition on the BBC, will lead to an erosion of the commitment to children's broadcasting. The report identifies several specific sources of this threat: the imposition of tighter budgetary constraints; the potential weakening of centralised regulation (following the replacement of the IBA by the ITC); the changing economic structure of broadcasting (for example, the centralisation of the ITV network and the BBC's introduction of Producer Choice); and the growing dependence on international markets. Taken together, these are leading to 'a more pragmatic spirit', in which the principled commitment to public service may come to be seen as merely 'old-fashioned'.

Very much in line with the analyses of US children's television referred to above, Blumler identifies a number of key characteristics that are likely to be threatened as a result of these changes. These include: children's protected place within the afternoon schedules; forms of programming designed for minority subsections of the audience, or which are otherwise believed to be less popular (such as factual programmes); programmes that are less cost-efficient (such as short-run dramas); and 'the innovative spirit' more generally. With the benefit of hindsight, it is notable that Blumler largely neglects the potential implications of cable and satellite television, despite the fact that they might seem to provide further support for his essentially pessimistic predictions. In 1992, of course, only one specialised children's channel was operating (The Children's Channel [TCC]); and the overall penetration of cable and satellite was still very limited. Yet for many contemporary commentators, the potential fragmentation of the audience that may occur in the multi-channel future has become the most significant threat to the 'Great Tradition' of public service broadcasting.

Nonetheless, it is significant to note that the BSC's 1997 update[19] fails to confirm many of Blumler's fears. The most striking finding here is the continuing increase in provision for children, not merely on cable and satellite, but also on terrestrial channels. In terms of the range of programming, the report finds no evidence of a decline in factual or in pre-school programmes or in drama, nor indeed of any 'creeping erosion' of the key late-afternoon slot. While there are fluctuations, the general conclusion here is that terrestrial children's television has 'held the line', although ITV comes in for greater criticism than the BBC. Nevertheless, the report does point to the growing competitive pressure felt by children's broadcasters, and the need to protect domestic production in the new multi-channel environment. Like that of its predecessor, the tone of the second report remains one of foreboding: children's television continues to be seen as an endangered species, and specific forms of regulation are still required in order to guarantee its survival.

Of course, the pessimism of this argument is partly rhetorical: emphasising the potential threat to children's television is necessary if readers are to be persuaded of the need to protect it – and, by extension, public service television more broadly. Nevertheless, the findings of the second report provide some grounds for questioning Blumler's basic assumptions about children's place in a more market-led system: namely, the idea that children are unlikely to prove a very valuable audience for broadcasters, and that they will be seen as easy to please. As we shall argue, these assumptions are difficult to sustain, both in terms of economic forces and in terms of what is known about audience behaviour.

Public voices

The concerns expressed in these reports have been strongly echoed by lobby groups such as BACTV (British Action for Children's Television) and more recently the VLV (Voice of the Listener and Viewer). BACTV was formed in the late 1980s with funding from the British Film Institute, drawing on the inspiration of the US organisation Action for Children's Television (ACT) which had offered an influential challenge to commercial interests throughout the 1970s and 1980s. BACTV was particularly galvanised by the absence of any mention of children's broadcasting in the Green Paper which led to the 1990 Broadcasting Act; and following a concerted lobbying campaign, it was successful in ensuring that a commitment to this area was eventually written in to the Act.[20]

BACTV subsequently foundered and was eventually subsumed within VLV, which came to prominence in the mid-1990s. VLV's membership is diverse, but it is widely perceived as a liberal alternative to the nation's other leading lobby group on broadcasting, the NVALA (National Viewers' and Listeners' Association), founded by Mary Whitehouse. While the NVALA has consistently accused broadcasters of promoting immoral behaviour, and hence of engineering more general moral decline, the VLV could be seen as a defender of the status quo of terrestrial broadcasting as described by Blumler. Indeed, it is perhaps not unduly cynical to suggest that this is why senior broadcasters have been so ready to co-operate with it – although it remains rigorously independent of external funding.

On one level, such groups have been remarkably successful in generating a more informed public debate about the social and cultural functions of broadcasting. The VLV's achievement in capturing the 'middle ground' has helped to marginalise the perspectives of the NVALA and the moral right, which in our view represents a long-overdue development. Claiming to speak on behalf of 'consumers' – and indeed of 'citizens in an informed democracy', as its founder Jocelyn Hay put it – the VLV has placed its main emphasis on the structural and institutional conditions that will guarantee 'positive' public service broadcasting, rather than on complaining about the shortcomings of particular programmes.

Jocelyn Hay's analysis of the current state of children's broadcasting, which she outlined in an interview with us in 1997, is very similar to that of Blumler's report. She fears that the commercialisation of broadcasting and the proliferation of channels will threaten the key public service principles of quality, diversity and universal access, and lead to a growing reliance on US product. While the VLV's primary aim has been to defend the public service principle, it is far from utopian in this respect. Like Blumler, Hay argues that it is the 'mixed economy' provided by the regulated duopoly – rather than simply the BBC – which has guaranteed the range and quality of British children's programmes. Like the BBC's former Head of Children's Television Anna Home, [21] she rejects the notion that advertising in children's programmes should be banned (as it is, for example, in Sweden) on the grounds that this would result in a dramatic reduction in budgets; and she acknowledges that 'controlled exploitation' in the form of merchandising is also a necessary support for programme-making. Nor does she propose a relentless diet of 'educational' or 'improving' programming: there is a recognition that children should be offered a range of programmes, and that they are entitled to relax with 'entertainment' just as adults do. While there is a degree of conservatism here, it is motivated not by an irrational fear of change but by a desire to hold on to what is seen to be of positive value in the present.

At the same time, this position does appear to rest on some rather less even-handed judgments about cultural value; and it is these judgments – which amount to a particular 'taste culture' – that (as we have seen) frequently appear to surface in the press and in other forms of public debate. Thus, despite her insistence on the need for diversity, Jocelyn Hay makes a clear distinction between the 'recycled American junk' which she argues is available on cable and satellite channels and the 'high-quality programming' which is implicitly identified with terrestrial broadcasting:

> we're fighting hard to keep the positive requirements on the public broadcasters. And it's going to be increasingly difficult to keep them on ITV, and Channel Four for that matter ... but in the face of all these growing commercial channels – niche channels – which are probably nothing really but recycled American junk, or cartoons most of it – and children love them. And that's fine. We all enjoy these things now and then. But if you live on a solid diet of that, it's like living on a solid diet of junk food ... And whilst it is taking the audience away from the other channels, then there's huge pressure now on the controllers, both ITV and the BBC and Channel Four, to keep up the size of their audiences, to justify the licence fee or to justify the space to controllers ... it's that kind of high-quality programming that's made with a public service remit that puts the needs of British children above all else; it's just not imported American animation or cartoons with voices and different values and everything else, but is a balance of classic and contemporary drama, magazines, news programmes, *Newsround*, you know, the whole variety of stuff – that's what's important to keep ...
>
> So, if your children want to live on a diet of Mars bars all day, do you let them do that? ... It's exactly the same kind of argument. Children need to be guided. I'm not saying that you come down heavily and they shouldn't have some fun, and they shouldn't have some cartoons and everything else, but it comes back to parents exercising some responsibility for what their children watch, and if they want them to sit down and watch nothing but American cartoons, OK. But it's not going to do the child much good. .... we all need a mixture. And variety and diversity – and *that's* the strength of British television. You've got it now. But once it's gone – it's not going to come back, and that's going to have an impact on our language, on our cultural values, on, if you like, the educational attainment of our children – if you watch nothing but cartoons it doesn't take you very far – and when I say children's cartoons, I mean, *children's* cartoons. There are other – animation, I happened to stumble – BBC 2 has been carrying some bible tales in animation, which is quite a different thing. I mean, and they've done some Shakespearean animation, so it's not necessarily bad. But it's just re-peddling things which have got very often purely commercial values that are made primarily to

sell related merchandise, not even that the programme story is the main driving force behind it ... It's balance – it's very much a question of balance.

Despite the qualifications here, the argument clearly rests on a series of overlapping oppositions, which might be represented schematically as follows:

culture	commerce
public service	an unregulated market
quality	junk
doing children good	exploiting children
what children need	what children want
responsible parents	irresponsible parents
British	American
education	entertainment
terrestrial	cable/satellite
live-action drama	cartoons
fact	fiction

On one level, these oppositions reflect some very traditional distinctions between 'high culture' and 'popular culture' that might be regarded as characteristic of British middle-class taste. Significantly, however, they are justified by appealing to arguments about *childhood*. The fundamental problem here is that children appear to 'love' things that are 'bad' for them; and if these threatening desires are not restrained, the consequences will be potentially disastrous, not only for children themselves but for society as a whole – for 'our' language, 'our' cultural values and the rest. From this perspective, it is not just broadcasting but also *children* (and their parents) who are in need of regulation.

Ultimately, the motivating force of the argument here is a wider concern about the future of public service broadcasting generally. There is a sense in which children's television serves merely as a convenient vehicle for the argument. Certainly, the VLV has made little attempt to address or involve children in its work; and the argument here reflects a considerable distrust, if not hostility, towards the child audience. Indeed, in this respect, it is worth noting that the VLV's origins lie primarily in a campaign to 'save' BBC Radio 4 from attempts to make it more attractive to a younger audience.

On the face of it, however, Hay's position is *not* simply that one side of these oppositions should be favoured above the other, but that there should be 'balance' and 'diversity' – and to this extent, it would seem to be an unexceptionable argument. The question, though, is how this 'diversity' is to be defined. Where is the *point* of balance? And, indeed, what is the balance *between*? In this respect, the broadly liberal emphasis on balance and diversity – which we would certainly support in principle – appears to beg more questions than it answers. It appears only to defer more awkward questions about cultural value, about national identity and about children's 'needs' as an audience – questions which, in a climate of rapid social change, are becoming ever harder to address.

Changing the terms of debate

These contemporary debates about the future of children's television thus raise some very fundamental concerns. While it is not our intention simply to dismiss these concerns, we do feel there are grounds for caution here. Our reservations are theoretical, empirical and pragmatic; and it is worth summarising them briefly before we move on.

Theoretically, the concerns we have identified are based on a set of cultural values, and on assumptions about childhood, that we would wish to question. These values and assumptions have been discussed in the preceding chapters; and they will be considered in further detail in due course. There are three main themes here. First, there is the perennial issue of *quality* – a term that is notoriously vague, and (partly for this reason) one which is frequently invoked in debates about broadcasting. Second, there is the notion of *national identity*, which is explicitly invoked by the fear of invasion by American cartoons. Third, there are assumptions about *childhood* – about the needs and characteristics of the child audience, and about the potential role of television in child development. In questioning some of these ideas, we are not thereby suggesting that the attempt to define 'quality' or 'national identity' or 'children's needs' should simply be abandoned. However, there is a sense in which these concerns often *combine* in discussions of children's television to generate a particular form of cultural conservatism. We would agree with lobbyists such as Jocelyn Hay that it is vital to retain what is of value in the current arrangements; yet this kind of cultural conservatism is, in our view, not only pragmatically unrealistic but also profoundly inadequate as a basis for enabling children to deal with a rapidly changing social and cultural environment.

A second reason for caution here is more empirical. We feel there is considerable room for doubt as to whether the nightmare scenario predicted by such critics will actually come about. On one level, this is because the wholesale marketisation of television in Britain still appears to be an unlikely prospect. Of course, it is possible to argue that public broadcasting has effectively privatised itself, both through the move towards an 'internal market' and through the growing emphasis on generating revenue in areas such as merchandising and international sales. In developments such as digital broadcasting, it is frequently hard to tell the difference between the public and the commercial players. Nevertheless, public broadcasting is still very far from the marginal position it occupies in the US, for example. Furthermore, evidence suggests that audiences don't necessarily want 'wall-to-wall cartoons'. Ratings for 'quality' children's programming (as conventionally defined) remain high; and certain genres which appear to be synonymous with 'quality' have significant commercial potential within the wider global market. While the penetration of cable and satellite is increasing, there now appear to be significant limitations on the extent to which consumers are willing to invest in new technology, particularly given the overall increase in expenditure on entertainment services as a proportion of household income. Even in the US, where such services have been much more widely available for many years, the predicted fragmentation of the audience has actually been quite limited.[22]

Finally, in terms of future policy, we would argue that there is a distinct danger of complacency in seeking simply to defend the status quo of public service broadcasting against the ravages of commercialism. As Ian Connell[23] has argued, it is essential to distinguish here between public *service* and public *sector*. Until very recently, British television took the form of a regulated duopoly, in which public service objectives were imposed upon commercial as well as public broadcasters. As Blumler outlines, children's broadcasting in Britain has benefited greatly from these arrangements. Regulation has ensured that children's programmes have been shown when the audience has been available to view; that subsections of the audience have been specifically catered for; that there has been a strong domestic industry, producing programmes with national or regional content; and (more contentiously, depending upon one's definition) that there have been 'high-quality' programmes in a range of genres, covering education, information and entertainment. Nevertheless, it is important to recognise that this also *depended upon* a limited degree of competition between public and commercial broadcasters. As we have indicated, the success of ITV encouraged the BBC to develop new forms of popular programming; although it is important to emphasise that the BBC's response was not merely imitative, and that the nature of its response also depended upon the character of its own internal organisation. Whether the restructured BBC of the 1990s is now in a position to make an equally creative response to new forms of competition is a matter for speculation.

Ultimately, however, we would question whether it still makes sense – theoretically, empirically or pragmatically – to conceive of this debate in terms of an *opposition* between public service and the market.[24] Broadcasting in Britain has always been a 'mixed economy' – albeit a regulated one, of a particular historical kind. There is no 'pure' form of public service broadcasting, unless we are to look to the early days of radio; nor, even in the US, is there a 'pure' market-led system with which it could be compared. There are certainly some ways in which the mechanism of the market makes it more accountable or responsive to popular needs than public sector broadcasting; although equally there are other ways in which the market cannot – or at least does not – provide. There may well be grounds for conceiving of children as a 'special' audience, who require specific forms of provision if their needs are to be met; and it is vital not to confuse the needs of the citizen with the needs (or perhaps desires) of the consumer. Yet if we are to identify how those needs can be met, we must move beyond the conventional split between 'culture' and 'commerce' that continues to characterise contemporary debates about children's television.

Technological proliferation

Recent developments in British broadcasting have arisen from a complex interaction between technological and economic change. Before we move on to assess the implications for children's television in particular, it is worth outlining a brief sketch each of these areas in turn.

One of the most obvious changes in the contemporary media environment in the past decade has been the proliferation of new technologies of distribution, most notably video, cable, satellite and multimedia. On one level, this has been clearly driven by capitalism's search for new markets.[25] Nevertheless, it has not been an inexorable process, or one with guaranteed results.

One reason why these developments have *had* to be commercially driven is to do with the initial cost of providing infrastructure. In the case of cable television, for example, the UK is in a very different position from the US, where the majority of homes were cabled up decades ago, primarily because of the problems with reception across long distances.[26] In the UK, cable television has been a relative latecomer. Videocassette recorders rapidly achieved a relatively high level of penetration in the late 1980s; and satellite had gained a small but growing corner of the market a few years before cable began to be introduced in most areas.

This sequence of introduction has had significant implications in terms of costs to the consumer. Television has, of course, historically been 'free-to-air' in the UK. The licence fee has steadily risen, although not always in line with inflation; but it has remained at a fixed proportion (and as an effectively compulsory item) of household expenditure. Each of the successive pay-TV options (not to mention more recent innovations such as video on demand) has potentially offered greater choice and flexibility; but it has also represented an increase in the proportion of household expenditure devoted to entertainment services. The key constraint, therefore, is the rate at which consumers are able – or indeed willing – to commit additional expenditure. While some of these options might well be seen as either/or choices (cable or satellite, for example), others clearly provide additional options (digital television or interactive CD-I) – at least in terms of the means of reception, if not initially in the actual content itself. As the rate of technological change accelerates, this issue becomes more acute. How frequently are consumers willing to replace their existing hardware (for example, their video recorders or television sets) with newer, more sophisticated equipment – and, in many cases, to replace the software (such as videotapes) that goes with them?

Part of the answer to such questions depends upon how the technologies are marketed. The product image of the technologies plays a significant role in negotiating household spending decisions. In the past five years, children have come to play an increasingly important role in this respect – just as they did in the 'promotional era' of television in the US.[27] This has been most apparent with home computers, which are increasingly being marketed on the grounds of their educational value for children.[28] Yet it has also been the case in television: along with sport and movies, children have been a major factor in driving cable and satellite subscriptions, as BSkyB's early marketing of *The Simpsons* illustrated. The penetration of video has consistently been higher in households with children than in those without, although the gap has narrowed as availability has increased (it is currently 94 per cent in households with children, 88 per cent in those without). The same is now true of cable and satellite (currently 33 per cent of homes with children, 20 per cent of homes without).[29] Children's video (particularly for preschoolers) is now a substantial element of the sell-through market.[30] Furthermore, at least some of these new technologies have been designed and marketed specifically for children and young people – most obviously, computer games consoles. At least in terms of marketing, children would appear to be in the vanguard of technological change.

As in the US, children have also become a significant target for 'niche marketing'. As we shall indicate below and in Chapter Three, the provision of material for children has dramatically increased in the last decade, not just in the new channels of cable and satellite but also in terrestrial broadcasting. There are currently five UK specialist cable/satellite channels aimed at children and young people, of which three or four are normally included in a basic package. Partly in response to these developments, the terrestrial channels have also significantly increased their output for children: Channel Four resumed programming for children in 1993 (having dropped it in the late 1980s), while the BBC is now repeating its afternoon children's programmes on BBC 2 in the early morning, and Channel Five also has a commitment to this audience.

If only in terms of *quantity*, the short-term effect of these technological developments has been to ensure that children are now extraordinarily well served. The increasing competitiveness in the children's market means that at least some of their tastes and preferences are much more widely reflected than they ever have been in the past. Even here, however, two important qualifications must be made. First, it should be emphasised that these new services are not (and will not in the short term become) available to all: on the contrary, we may be witnessing the beginnings of a growing polarisation between the 'technology rich' and the 'technology poor'. In this context, the material that is provided on terrestrial, free-to-air channels should continue to be a major concern. Second, we should not confuse quantity with *diversity* or *quality*, however difficult it may be to define these things. In purely economic terms, if funding levels remain more or less static, an increase in quantity may well have to be achieved *at the expense of* the budgets devoted to individual programmes. In both respects, there is room for scepticism about the longer-term benefits for children of the technological revolution in broadcasting.

Marketisation

Of course, these developments have not been driven solely by the pace of technological change. On the contrary, both in the US and in the UK, the ideological commitments of right-wing governments have led to far-reaching forms of deregulation. As in many other areas of cultural activity, the guiding assumption has been that the market, and not the state, should provide.

In practice, however, the picture has been rather more complex. For example, the 1990 Broadcasting Act did result in a weakening of centralised regulation in commercial broadcasting, although this has arguably been much less dramatic than was initially feared.[31] Meanwhile, in areas of moral concern, there has been a *tightening* of regulation, through legislation such as the Video Recordings Act 1984 and the Criminal Justice Act 1994, through stricter codes of self-censorship (as in the video games industry) and through the work of new statutory bodies such as the Broadcasting Standards Council (now Commission).[32] Arguably, the balance of regulation has shifted from 'positive' to 'negative': it is now defined primarily as a matter of preventing aspects that are seen as morally bad, rather than laying down and enforcing requirements for quality and diversity. In the area of media regulation, as in many others, Conservative policies reflected a classic split between free-market liberalism and moral authoritarianism – although, if anything, it is the latter that is emerging as the central principle under New Labour.

On the other hand, public service imperatives have increasingly been suffused with commercial logic, albeit in complex and contradictory ways. On one level, the more extreme forms of marketisation have been avoided: unlike many other European countries, the British government has not privatised its main public service television channels, or forced them to accept advertising, nor has the licence fee been significantly cut back. On the other hand, both the BBC and commercial broadcasting have been reorganised along the lines of an 'internal market'. In the case of the BBC, this is illustrated by Producer Choice, the split between Broadcast and Production departments and the legal requirement for outsourcing (25 per cent of programmes must now be produced by 'independents', and the BBC will no longer fund the entire production costs). Like the commercial companies, it has come under increasing pressure to earn more from entrepreneurial activities such as merchandising, co-production and overseas sales. Disgruntled BBC staff (and former staff) regularly complain about the domination of 'accountants'; while others seem to perceive its traditional public service profile as the only remaining constraint on the potential for ruthless commercial exploitation.

Rather than describing this history simply in terms of the creeping marketisation of public service, it might be more appropriate to see it as incorporating four stages. The first, which dates from the advent of commercial broadcasting to the publication of the Pilkington Report in 1962, was in some respects one of direct competition between commercial and public broadcasters – a competition in which the BBC had to struggle just to survive. As we have seen, its eventual response was not merely imitative but also innovative (although in the case of children's television, it had particularly dramatic implications).

By imposing stricter requirements on commercial broadcasters, the Pilkington Report ushered in the regulated duopoly that represented the status quo in British broadcasting until the mid-1980s. While this resulted to some extent from spectrum scarcity, it was primarily a result of the existence of strong social and cultural imperatives for broadcasting.[33] Although there was undeniably strong competition between the public and commercial sectors, the audience was to some degree insulated from the negative consequences of 'pure' market forces. This period was characterised by a high degree of vertical integration between producers and broadcasters; strong centralised regulation; and a high entry cost, along with union closed shops and industry-controlled training.

The third period, beginning in the mid-1980s, might be described as that of entrepreneurial anarchy. This resulted partly from the expansion of the spectrum through the advent of new technologies (noted above), but also from the doctrine of control by market forces. This period was characterised by the break-up of vertical integration (both in the BBC and in ITV); weaker centralised regulation; and the increase in outsourcing, inspired by the example of Channel Four, which resulted initially in the brief flowering of 'workshops' and small, artisanal production companies. This period also witnessed an increasing cross-fertilisation of commercial and public service companies, in which everyone became potentially both a buyer and a seller: the ITV regional companies started selling programmes to the BBC or BSkyB, for example, while the BBC and Nickelodeon began to run each other's programmes (see below). Finally, there were important changes in programme funding: co-production became more common, and merchandising and overseas sales were key considerations.

In the late 1990s we may be seeing the emergence of a fourth phase, one of technological, cultural and economic convergence. According to orthodox Marxist economics, this would arise from the basic tendency of capitalism to monopoly; and parallel developments can be seen, for example, in the early decades of Hollywood.[34] This period is characterised by renewed forms of integration, both vertical and horizontal, based on cross-media ownership; the consolidation of the 'independent' sector into a smaller number of medium-sized companies; and the increasing dominance of multinationals, achieved partly on the basis of risk-taking investments in hardware (as in the irresistible rise of Rupert Murdoch). In this context, however, the leading public service broadcaster emerges as a privileged commercial player, possessing a substantial library of rights and a positive brand image based on history and tradition.

The most obvious consequence of convergence is that it is becoming increasingly impossible to separate television from other media. Particularly in the field of children's culture, the boundaries between TV programmes, movies, computer games, books and videos have become ever more blurred: each text increasingly seems to be a spin-off from another text, or indeed an advertisement for it. Disney is of course the classic example, but even within the protected environment of public sector broadcasting, television has become inextricably connected with merchandising and other media.[35] The BBC's highly successful Saturday-morning show *Live and Kicking*, for example, constructs a self-referential world where the guests are pop stars or actors from soaps, the games and the pop videos are ads for other commodities, and the prizes are various media artefacts; and in the process, it advertises itself and its own magazine to what is effectively a captive audience.[36] Likewise, one Nickelodeon executive described her channel to us as a 'self-contained advertising agency'. Far from merely selling audiences to advertisers, the media are now busily selling audiences to other media – and indeed the boundaries between 'media' and 'advertising' have begun to break down.

Children's production across sectors

Against this broad picture of technological and economic change, how might we assess the specific implications for children's production? We propose to consider these on a sector-by-sector basis, drawing on our interviews and informal discussions with key industry personnel and on our reading of the trade press and other sources.

Cable and satellite
At the time of writing (early 1998), the UK has no fewer than five specialist cable/satellite channels for children and young people. All are wholly or partly US-

owned. They are: Disney (only available as a premium channel in the UK); Nickelodeon (like its sister company MTV, owned by the US media giant Viacom); the Cartoon Network (owned by Turner, which is itself now a Time-Warner company); Fox Kids (part of Murdoch's News International); and Trouble (a spin-off from the now-defunct TCC, and part of Flextech, a British company majority-owned by US giant TCI).

With the exception of Trouble, all these companies possess extensive libraries of rights to past programmes: for example, Turner (and now Warner) owns Hanna-Barbera, the US animation giant, while Saban Entertainment (producers of the notorious *Power Rangers*) have a supply deal with Fox Kids. As we show in more detail in Chapter Three, most (though by no means all) of the programming on these channels is US in origin. Despite its origins as a British company, this is also true of Trouble: like the wholly US-owned Nickelodeon, it attempts to inject a local flavour through its links and continuity material.

Even within this apparently flourishing and diverse sector, there are already signs of a move towards convergence. For example, the projected launch of a Warner children's channel was postponed when the Turner Corporation was bought by Warners in 1996: while there is some competition between Turner and Warner in the US, the company has decided not to compete in overseas markets. Likewise, Sky 1 axed its children's programmes in July 1996 in time for the launch of Fox Kids (both are owned by Murdoch).

The travails of TCC illustrate this most clearly. TCC was founded in the mid-1980s, and was originally a wholly British-owned company. Until 1993, it was the only cable/satellite channel catering specifically for children. The advent of competition effectively destroyed it. The company was almost sold to Fox/Saban Entertainment in 1995, and it subsequently struggled to reposition itself in the market. In 1997, it spun off Trouble, a new channel aimed at the pre-teen/teen market, leaving TCC to focus on the younger age group. However, competitive forces proved too strong and the channel was finally wound up early in 1998.

As these attempts to reposition the channel imply, age is seen as one way of segmenting the market in the cable/satellite sector. Disney, of course, would define itself as a 'family channel', rather than a 'children's channel'; yet, like the Cartoon Network, it is mainly targeted at younger viewers (aged three to nine). By contrast, Nickelodeon and Fox Kids are aiming more at older children. It will be interesting to see whether the audience is segmented further as a means of resolving competitive pressures: late in 1997, for example, Disney was rumoured to be contemplating a relaunch, with a new emphasis on UK-produced material, including pre-school programmes. As we shall indicate in Chapter Four, audience research plays a much more significant role in the cable/satellite sector than in terrestrial television: as five channels compete over what is at most 30 per cent of the target audience, questions of 'branding' or channel image are obviously vital.

Aside from Disney, Nickelodeon is the major international success story in this sector. There are now 'local' Nickelodeons in Germany, Scandinavia, Australia and in several Latin American countries; and while the company is sensitive to accusations of cultural imperialism, it is clearly attempting to rival Disney in its status as a global brand – not least through its use of merchandising. As we shall indicate in Chapter Five, Nickelodeon's rhetoric of 'kid empowerment' seems to derive from a different world from the child-centred discourse of UK terrestrial broadcasters. The notion of the channel as a 'kid-only zone', consistently reinforced in its publicity and on-screen continuity, has been described by one terrestrial executive as a kind of religion. Nevertheless, Nickelodeon UK prides itself on its close – or, in its own terms, 'interactive' – relationship with its audience: according to its own figures,[37] 250,000 attempted calls are made to the station each week (see Chapter Five). Unlike the notoriously paranoid Disney, representatives of Nickelodeon UK have participated energetically in public debates about children's television, despite the hostility they sometimes encounter from terrestrial broadcasters. Within the industry, much of this success is attributed to the leadership (in the UK) of Managing Director Janie Grace, who has a background in both public and commercial broadcasting.

In fact, however, ratings for these channels have been far from impressive. Nickelodeon's figures, for example, have fluctuated slightly, and have recently shown a decline; although their typical audience share of around 1.5 to 2 percent in cable/satellite homes is fairly minuscule in any case. The major success story in this sector is the Cartoon Network, which enjoyed a reach of 7.5 million viewers in late 1997, although these figures may well include significant numbers of adults. These channels are also particularly popular with metropolitan and ethnic-minority viewers; and they appear to pose a greater threat to ITV than to the BBC. Nevertheless, as we shall indicate in Chapter Four, there is considerable doubt about the reliability of ratings, particularly in relation to cable and satellite.

The BBC

At present, the BBC is the undisputed market leader in UK children's television. Following a significant turn round in the last few years, it is currently winning the ratings battle. Most of the current top-rated children's shows are BBC productions, many of them (such as *Blue Peter*, *Newsround* and *Grange Hill*) of very long standing; it enjoys supremacy in the key Saturday-morning slot with *Live and Kicking*; and it has recently scored notable ratings and critical successes with original dramas such as *The Demon Headmaster* and *The Queen's Nose*. In 1995, it increased its investment in the area to an annual £60 million (as compared, for example, to Nickelodeon's budget of £2 million for new UK production), although this has since dropped back to £55 million.[38]

Despite this relative buoyancy, BBC children's television is in the midst of substantial change. The implications of the restructuring of the Corporation – particularly the split between Broadcast and Production departments – remain to be seen; although the retirement of Anna Home and the departure of several 'old guard' children's producers have to some extent undermined the continuity of 'dedicated professionals' Blumler saw as characteristic of British children's television. Concern has been expressed, for example, that the new Head of Children's Production, Lorraine Heggessy, does not have a history of working in children's programmes, and may be wanting to move towards a more inclusive form of 'family entertainment' – although such fears have been firmly dismissed. Meanwhile, there have been press rumours that in-house production in this field would be closed down in favour of a schedule wholly commissioned from independents;[39] while there is also talk of a possible merger between the Children's and Schools departments, a move which both have always strenuously resisted. Nevertheless, the BBC has made several high-profile public commitments to children's broadcasting in recent years, notably in its 1996 Governors' Seminar, which may at least represent an attempt to compensate for its relative neglect of this area in previous policy documents.

At the same time, the BBC has increasingly recognised children's television as a key area for commercial exploitation, through merchandising, video and overseas rights. To some extent, of course, this has always been the case. It is not only US cartoons that can be described as thirty-minute commercials: on the contrary, some of the most apparently innocuous creations of children's television, both in the commercial and the public sector, have been extremely lucrative – from Muffin the Mule and Sooty through to Postman Pat and Thomas the Tank Engine. BBC Worldwide (formerly BBC Enterprises) now energetically promotes and licenses a whole range of children's TV tie-ins, from the extensive range of Noddy merchandise through to magazines such as the market-leading *Live and Kicking* and *Playdays*; while the massive success of the new pre-school series *Teletubbies* has generated substantial new opportunities for spin-off toys, magazines, books, records and videos.[40]

Likewise, the UK is second only to the US in international sales of children's programmes; and (like Nickelodeon or Disney) the BBC is a universally recognised brand name. It has an enormous library of rights, of which some (notably big-budget costume dramas such as *The Chronicles of Narnia* or *The Phoenix and the Carpet*) are highly marketable overseas; although the logic of scheduling means that such shorter-run dramas are now becoming less attractive than those which run in blocks of thirteen weeks. Here again, *Teletubbies* is an exemplary case: it is generating considerable international sales, although it has been strongly criticised in some countries.[41] At the same time, the BBC has relied increasingly on co-production deals with foreign producers, of which the best known is probably the successful animated series *Animals of Farthing Wood*, the result of a pan-European collaboration between public television channels. Meanwhile, in the home market, the boundaries between the BBC and the cable/satellite sector have become increasingly blurred: two of the shows screened during the BBC's *Live and Kicking*, for example, are Nickelodeon productions (*Rugrats* and *Keenan and Kel*); while Nickelodeon has bought parts of the BBC's pre-school sequence for screening in the UK.

As we have noted, the BBC has always possessed a symbolic importance as the upholder of a national 'Great Tradition' in children's broadcasting; and this role generates a degree of sensitivity to parental and public criticism which is much less necessary in the cable/satellite sector, for example. In some ways, the key issue for the BBC in this more competitive, commercial environment is that of its *distinctiveness*. What can the BBC claim to be doing that other channels cannot? And how can it justify this to parents and other members of the adult public, since it is they who pay the licence fee? Two contrary indications of the BBC's strategy are evident in recent publicity materials. A full-page advertisement (1996) run in the upmarket broadsheets – and hence aimed at parents – stakes a claim for Children's BBC on the grounds of its *educational* merits. Children's programmes, it argues, are effectively 'delivering' the National Curriculum. By contrast, a trailer for the perennial *Blue Peter* run on Children's BBC in the same year featured its ever-more youthful presenters jiving enthusiastically to a recent chart hit, in a manner that would have had Lord Reith spinning in his catacomb.[42] How the distinctive-ness of the service is defined clearly depends upon the target audience; and the balance between 'education' and 'entertainment' is crucial in this respect. The BBC's particular problem in relation to children's television is that it has to please children and adults at the same time – even though the latter rarely watch the actual programmes.

ITV and Channel Four

At the time of writing (early 1998), children's broadcasting on ITV appears equally fraught by contradictions and tensions, albeit of a different kind. ITV is trapped between what some clearly perceive as the devil of public service require-ments (as imposed by the ITC) and the deep blue sea of unfettered commercial-ism. Critics of the ITV system see it as constrained by its regional structure and its shrinking budgets. Following the centralisation of the network in the early 1990s, fully funded productions have become a rarity; and (as in the BBC) regional ITV companies are increasingly looking to co-production deals with overseas broad-casters and other regional companies, and to sales of video rights. Meanwhile, there is a surprising uncertainty about whether children are a valuable audience in commercial terms: many of the advertisements in Children's ITV slots, for example, are aimed at adults (particularly mothers) rather than the children themselves. Children's ITV has been particularly condemned for its failure to mar-ket itself and to establish its unique selling points.

As its immediate rival, Children's BBC enjoys significant advantages over ITV, not only in its stronger brand image but also in its ability to schedule in the 5.10–5.35 slot and in its range of successful long-running shows (which signifi-cantly include factual programmes). There are several areas in which the BBC is winning hands down in the ratings, notably on Saturday mornings. ITV is also hampered by a widespread perception that 'quality' is the preserve of the BBC,[43] despite the fact that it produces programmes which are very much within con-ventional definitions of quality, such as factual programmes (*Art Attack*), drama (*The Treasure Seekers*) and literary adaptations (*The Famous Five*). Meanwhile, in terms of its audience profile, ITV potentially has most to lose from the growth of cable and satellite. It has been rumoured that some senior figures in ITV would abandon children's television altogether if they were permitted to do so; although recent personnel changes may lead to a more proactive approach to children's pro-gramming.

It is too early to say much about Channel Five, beyond noting that a commit-ment to children's programmes was included in its bid for the licence, and is hence subject to regulation by the ITC. [44] In this area, as in many others, it is facing an uphill struggle to establish its distinctiveness and hence its market share. Interestingly, at least some of its early successes have been with what is sometimes termed 'kidult' programming, albeit of a particularly kitsch variety, such as *Xena: Warrior Princess* and *Hercules*.

Channel Four, on the other hand, has an interesting history in terms of the status of children as an audience. Despite its statutory requirement to reach minority audiences, children were not initially seen as a high priority. Its children's department was abolished in 1988, only to be revived in 1993 under a new Commissioning Editor, Lucinda Whiteley. (The historical parallels with the BBC in the 1960s are relevant here.)

In some ways, the dilemmas of Channel Four reflect those of children's departments in terrestrial television more broadly, and may serve as a pointer to the future. With its wholly commissioned schedules, Channel Four is unique in British television, although other channels may well be heading in this direction; and while its remit is also unique, it reflects a symptomatic combination of public service and commercial commitments. Externally, the children's department at Channel Four must strive to establish a brand identity in competition with other channels; while internally, it has to compete with other departments for scarce resources. The Children's Commissioning Editor has to establish popularity with the audience and credibility with colleagues; and in children's television, these two requirements are not only not synonymous but are also often quite contradictory.

Perhaps the inevitable consequence here – and it is one which may be endemic to children's television – is the gap between rhetoric and reality. Thus, Channel Four representatives will actively promote programmes which they feel are innovative, albeit within the public service tradition, such as the award-winning children's access show *Wise Up* and the collection of programmes made by and about children transmitted under the scheduling title *Look Who's Talking* in October 1994. As with Nickelodeon, it is argued that the channel is 'giving kids a voice'. On one level, these programmes do offer a model for meeting public service objectives within a commercial framework, although *Wise Up* is not exactly a ratings winner, and *Look Who's Talking* was considered by some other children's broadcasters to be 'not children's television' (a judgment which raises interesting issues in itself, of course). However, as our analysis in Chapter Three will show, the bulk of Channel Four's children's schedule is in fact made up of bought-in cartoons and sitcoms; and it is not unduly cynical to point out that this is likely to generate substantial new revenue from toy advertising.

Another consequence of this situation is the tendency to blur the boundary between children and other audiences, particularly 'youth', which has long been a Channel Four speciality. Lucinda Whiteley's most expensive commission, for example, was the teen soap *Hollyoaks*. Channel Four's new Commissioning Editor for children's programmes, appointed early in 1998, is the former children's presenter Andi Peters; and while his background in children's television may be significant, his published statements thus far seem to reflect a wish to combine youth and children's programming. As in the case of the BBC, children's programming is enjoying a new-found status here; but the distinctions between children's and other forms of programming may become increasingly uncertain. Despite the broader tendency towards niche marketing, there remain clear economic gains in merging children with more valuable sectors of the audience.

The consequences of commercialisation

Inevitably, much of the information presented here will be out of date by the time this book is published – not least because of the accelerating pace of change within the industry itself. Yet our analysis has value as a case study, if not as a topical report: it clearly shows the way in which commercial and public service imperatives have become inextricably entwined. The past decade has seen an undeniable shift towards the commercialisation of British children's television. Yet for the foreseeable future, we will still be living in a mixed economy, in which the boundaries between 'culture' and 'commerce' are being crossed in sometimes unexpected ways. The current context presents a complex mixture of commercial opportunity and insecurity, in which the child audience has come to be seen as significantly more valuable, albeit primarily as a consumer market. Yet children do not necessarily stand only to lose from this new situation, as criticisms of the US system would seem to suggest.

Of course, advocates of commercialisation typically present such changes as a matter of increasing consumer choice. On one level, marketisation and increasing competition clearly do give increased status to the audience. As we have indicated, the advent of commercial television led to a broadly positive democratisation of public service broadcasting: the BBC could no longer afford to ignore the audience in the sublime confidence that it alone knew what was best. Similarly, in the current context, one could point to the way in which increasing competition has led to a much greater emphasis on research, particularly in the commercial sector, although we should also be sceptical about the notion that research necessarily guarantees accountability to the audience (see Chapter Four). At least in principle, however, contemporary broadcasters can no longer afford simply to give children what they think children ought to have, or indeed what they believe they can get away with.

Nevertheless, there are distinct limits to 'consumer sovereignty' in television, not the least of which is that the viewer is positioned as a consumer in the first place. Commercial interests are only concerned with children's needs or motivations to the extent that these will make them either watch or not watch – or indeed buy or not buy. This kind of logic does not necessarily *prevent* the possibility that children's needs will in fact be met – or indeed that the public will be served. Contrary to Stephen Kline, we would assert that the market *can* provide quality and diversity; it *can* foster children's social, cultural and intellectual development; it might even be said to 'empower' them in certain ways. It is simply that *these are not its primary aims*. Whether it achieves these aims will depend partly on the ways in which it is regulated; but it will also depend on a complex balance of cultural and economic forces. In the following sections of this chapter, then, we consider the ambiguous implications of the developments we have outlined for the provision and organisation of children's television.

Quantity

On one level, the market clearly *has* provided for children. There is now a great deal more television available for children, at least in terms of viewing hours, not just on cable and satellite but also on terrestrial channels. As the BSC reports indicate, and as our analysis in Chapter Three confirms, this increase began to gather pace in the 1980s and accelerated rapidly through the 1990s.

However, very little of this increase has been achieved through the provision of new programming – particularly home-produced programming. Despite (or perhaps because of) the massive investment in new hardware, and in view of its small audience share, funding for new production in the cable and satellite sector remains extremely limited. Meanwhile, channel controllers on terrestrial television have more hours to fill, without any proportional increase in their budgets. In practice, therefore, much of this expansion of provision has been achieved through the increased scheduling of repeats: for example, the BBC now repeats most of its afternoon children's programmes on BBC 2 during the following day's breakfast-time slot – largely in response to the phenomenal success with children of Channel Four's *Big Breakfast*. Most of the rest of the increase can be accounted for by the purchasing of inexpensive imported programming, mainly from the US. Meanwhile, the schedules of the new cable/satellite channels are largely reliant on bought-in programming which also runs on terrestrial channels, and on substantial amounts of repeats (see Chapter Three).

If children do now appear to have become a valuable, sought-after audience, then, the assumption that they can be bought cheaply still remains. Indeed, children's value in the television market is to a large degree based on the cheapness with which a service can be put together out of existing copyrighted material. As we have noted, most of the new cable providers have significant advantages in this respect, since they own substantial libraries of rights; although at present the BBC is of course in a similar position. None of the new cable/satellite providers is investing in home-produced programming for children anything like the funding they are pumping in to sport: it would be fair to guess that the annual expenditure on original programming at Nickelodeon UK is less than BSkyB would pay for one premier league football match.

Ultimately, this lack of new product will present significant constraints on future development. Cable channels, particularly Nickelodeon, have undoubtedly introduced new styles of programming to UK viewers, particularly in areas such as animation and comedy; but in filling a daily service, this material is endlessly repeated and soon loses its freshness. At least some US material is (correctly) judged to be inappropriate for British viewers; yet the lack of investment in home-produced programming may make it harder to sustain the presence of new and original material, which will be necessary over the longer term. Meanwhile, other genres which are regarded as less attractive to international audiences – such as factual programming and realist drama – are much less likely to be found on such channels.

The other potential consequence here is the fragmentation of the audience – and hence, perhaps, the demise of the 'common culture' which the shared experience of broadcasting has historically represented. There is increased competition, not only between the growing number of channels but also between television and other forms of screen-based entertainment. Furthermore, viewers have limited amounts of time in which they are available to view. Children's actual viewing hours have not increased in line with provision: indeed, they have actually decreased by almost two hours a week since 1992. As a result, the audience for any single programme is likely to decline as the audience fragments: no one children's programme has been seen by more than 30 per cent of them since 1992.[45] In cable/satellite homes, children's viewing of terrestrial television is declining quite fast (in 1996 it was around 50 per cent of their total viewing), although the decline has been less dramatic in marked-out children's slots, for example in the afternoons.

Nevertheless, there are reasons to be cautious here. Given the high penetration of video ownership in this country and the overall increase in expenditure on entertainment services, consumers are likely to be sceptical about whether these new technologies are really offering them anything new. While audiences for terrestrial children's television are falling, two-thirds of children in Britain still live in terrestrial-only homes – a figure that has declined fairly slowly since 1995. Even in the US, the four main networks still enjoy a 60 per cent audience share; and the predicted fragmentation of the mass audience appears to have reached a limit.[46]

At least in cable and satellite homes, however, we might expect to see significant changes in children's viewing behaviour. As we shall indicate, many producers and industry researchers no longer seem to conceptualise children as a 'captive audience', but as incorrigible 'zappers'. Indeed, some research suggests that a majority of US children under the age of sixteen have never seen a complete television programme.[47] In practice, inheritance remains a key factor in scheduling: audiences still tend to stay with the same channel from one programme to the next. However, there are increasing questions about how children (and, of course, viewers in general) will find their way around in the new multi-channel environment. British responses to US television – from Raymond Williams onwards[48] – have often been characterised by a sense of bewilderment in this respect; although it is likely that children will come to see certain channels or scheduling slots as 'home', and hence to avoid less familiar material.

Ultimately, while the expansion in provision for children does represent a benefit in itself, there are significant reasons for questioning the view that 'the market will provide'. First, as we have implied, the children's market may already have reached saturation point: too many providers are chasing a fixed (or, in fact, declining) audience. The demise of TCC effectively proves this; and it may be that in the medium term, other channels will go to the wall. The longer-term prospects for commercial expansion are also far from rosy, even with the promise of digital television. The production of substantial amounts of new programming is unlikely to be commercially viable, unless costs are dramatically reduced – although we may see the emergence of new low-budget television genres. Furthermore, given the range of other options in screen entertainment and the limits on household expenditure, only a minority of families are likely to subscribe to premium digital channels. Children in digital homes will have many more opportunities to watch the same programmes, and they may watch them in different ways; but the logic of the market clearly sets limits to what it can provide.

Second, it should be emphasised that the market provides for some but not for all. As in the case of children's television in the US, the privatisation of communications may well be leading to a polarisation between the 'technology rich' and the 'technology poor', in which those with access to cable and other pay-TV options are significantly better served than those without.[49] This is, of course, already a controversial issue here in relation to the coverage of sporting events. In this context, the principle of universal access – which is one of the central tenets of public service – is bound to become a key policy issue.

Quality

Of course, quantity should not be confused with quality. Yet here too, the picture is complex. As we have indicated, analyses of children's television in the US have suggested that quality is an inevitable casualty of commercialism, both because children are not seen as a valuable audience, and because of the assumption that they will watch whatever they are given. In the UK, such debates are often implicitly premised on what are assumed to be shared values – for example, that imported programming is necessarily lacking in quality, or that certain genres are incapable of achieving it. As numerous critics have maintained, such arguments typically reflect the tastes of particular class groups[50] – and in this case, perhaps one might also add *age* groups. Many laments for the decline of quality in children's television seem to be founded on a preference for historical costume dramas based on 'classic' novels, and on a nostalgia for childhood favourites from the 1950s and 1960s such as *Watch with Mother*, *Jackanory* and *Blue Peter* (as it used to be). As we have indicated, such arguments often appear to rest on a protectionist construction of childhood and an assumption that 'quality' children's television should function as a corrective to children's own instinctive tastes – that it should ultimately be leading them on to 'better things' than just watching television.

Such arguments are also often based on an extraordinary degree of ignorance about the material itself. For example, the fear of 'wall-to-wall American cartoons' is one which belies their diversity. To be sure, the dominance of animation is partly a consequence of the globalisation of the children's television market: animation is easier to dub into other languages, it is generally less culturally specific than live action and has a longer shelf life. There is also a mythology within the industry that animation will always 'work'. Nevertheless, it is meaningless to talk about 'quality' in this area without making distinctions, for example, between different genres of animation or between animations which are targeted at different age groups. Arguably, the most innovative and creatively imaginative children's programmes of the last ten years have been animated; and many of these have been produced by commercial channels, most notably Nickelodeon. Series like *Ren and Stimpy* and *Rocko's Modern Life* have effectively redefined the possibilities of cel animation, and attracted a considerable 'cult' audience among young adults in the process. *The Simpsons* and *Daria* have demonstrated that cartoons can be a vehicle for social commentary; while *Rugrats*, *Doug* and *Hey Arnold!* have shown that it is possible for them to tackle children's real-life concerns in entertaining and incisive ways.

Similar assertions could be made about comedy dramas for children. Of course, one could name several cheaply produced schedule-fillers that simply recycle tired comic stereotypes and situations, although the BBC is no less guilty in this respect than commercial providers. Nevertheless, channels like Nickelodeon have introduced forms of social comedy that do relate specifically – and sometimes incisively – to young people's everyday concerns with relationships and family life (for example, *Sister Sister*, *Moesha* and *The Secret World of Alex Mack*); as well as comedies that are more formally innovative, at least by the standards of children's television (*The Adventures of Pete and Pete*, *Sabrina the Teenage Witch* and *All That*). However, comedy is an area in which we might expect to find significant differences between adults' and children's tastes: irony, subtlety and verbal wit – which might be taken as markers of 'quality' in comedy for adult audiences – are unlikely to have much appeal to the majority of younger children. Here, perhaps, it is 'bad quality' television that might be more in need of protection from the criticisms of would-be regulators.

Perhaps even more reassuring for advocates of public service broadcasting is the evidence about what children are actually choosing to watch; although the messages are mixed here too. The fact that the majority of children's viewing is given over to adult programmes is well established, although this fact is still frequently met with expressions of horror in certain quarters. Currently, the list of top twenty programmes watched by children includes only one children's show (in 1985 there were eight); although children's programmes still account for ten of the top fifty. However, the 'top tens' for children's shows are consistently occupied by home-grown dramas such as *Grange Hill* and *Byker Grove* and factual programmes such as *Art Attack* and *Blue Peter*. The notion that, given the choice, children will only watch US cartoons seems to reflect an implicit distrust of the child audience that is far from justified. On the other hand, one can point to the growing significance in the ratings of 'kidult' programming – such as *Neighbours*, *Gladiators* or *Baywatch* – that still has mass 'family' appeal; although this, too, is far from being a new development.

The debate about quality also has a significant economic dimension. In the global television market, what is conventionally defined as 'quality' drama is an extremely marketable commodity; and as such, it is often well placed to attract finance from co-production or video sales. This is just as true of children's programmes: 'classic' literary adaptations such as the BBC's *The Chronicles of Narnia* or HTV's *The Famous Five* are cases in point. On the other hand, some less expensive genres – game shows, access or factual programmes – are much less likely to attract international interest. As we shall argue below, this may have broader implications in terms of representation.

Ultimately, then, 'quality' does not necessarily equate with a lack of mass popularity, or with material which cannot be marketed. Furthermore, if we define quality in broad terms, it is clear that commercial broadcasters can provide it – and indeed that they *have to* provide it if they are to retain their audiences. And yet throughout these debates, 'quality' itself is often very narrowly defined. Despite the discursive centrality of the term in debates about children's television, and its inscription within legislation (for example, in the remit of the ITC), there is considerable uncertainty and confusion about how one might actually *measure* quality. If the notion of quality is to have any purchase in future attempts to regulate children's broadcasting in the new commercial environment, it is surely essential that it should be more precisely and rigorously defined.

Diversity

Despite the apparent neutrality of the term, similar problems arise in attempting to assess diversity. Here again, analyses of children's television in the US would suggest that the move towards a more commercial system will lead to a steady narrowing of diversity in children's programming, although empirical research suggests that this tendency is not actually very marked.[51] Thus, one might expect a decline in genres with higher production costs (such as live-action drama), or those which are perceived to be less attractive to audiences (such as factual programmes). Our analysis (reported in full in Chapter Three) does indicate patterns of generic change, although again these are not straightforward. Some genres decline or disappear (live action-adventure, Westerns), while others emerge (access and consumer programmes); and there is a blurring of genres (and particularly of 'education' and 'entertainment') which is characteristic of contemporary popular culture more generally.

In the context we have outlined, it is perhaps not surprising that factual programmes or live-action drama (particularly contemporary 'social realist' drama) have declined *relative to other categories* – not least because these barely feature in the kinds of material that are bought in, particularly on cable/satellite stations. Nickelodeon, for example, has brought in a broad range of animation and situation comedy; yet it is singularly lacking in factual programming and in non-comedy drama – precisely the areas in which the terrestrial channels are currently so successful.

Yet a decline in proportion is not the same as a decline in overall amount – nor indeed does it necessarily imply a decline in popularity. Indeed, as we have noted, it is precisely these kinds of programmes which are consistently the most popular children's shows. Furthermore, measures of audience *share* should not be confused with those of audience *reach*: public broadcasting may continue to enjoy legitimacy on the grounds that it offers specialist provision which cannot be obtained elsewhere, even if its audiences are comparatively small.[52]

Diversity is not only a matter of genre, however: it might also be defined in terms of the target audience. Critics of the US system have argued that marketisation means that certain segments of the audience are less well catered for than others, on the grounds that they are perceived to be less valuable to advertisers. As we shall indicate in Chapter Four, gender and age, rather than social class, are the main operational categories among industry researchers; and there is a sense, particularly in the cable/satellite sector, that broadcasters are jockeying for position among the demographics. Thus, as we have noted, TCC spawned Trouble as a means of repositioning itself towards a teenage market, while Channel Four may also be looking to this age group – one which is, of course, of significant interest to advertisers. On the other hand, pre-school programming is also of value to advertisers, because it is felt that mothers are more likely to watch it, which would suggest that the value of the demographics is not solely a matter of the primary target audience. It is also thought that some audiences are more easily targeted or satisfied than others. For example, some of the broadcasters we interviewed suggested that boys were generally easier to reach than girls; but they also argued that girls will watch what boys watch, but not vice versa. The empirical basis for this kind of industry wisdom is somewhat questionable, although this does not prevent it from exercising a powerful influence on programming decisions. Yet in the more unstable, competitive situation that currently prevails, the basis on which the audience is segmented – and the 'value' that is attached to each segment – have become harder to define and predict.

Cultural identity and globalisation

The globalisation of culture, which has been such a dominant theme in recent academic debates, is of course partly driven by an economic logic. For domestic broadcasters, it is simply cheaper to buy in programming from overseas than to produce it themselves. US media dominate world markets because they are inexpensive: traditionally, the size of the home market has been such that production costs can be amortised on the basis of home receipts, thereby enabling material to be offered very inexpensively overseas – although in fact US producers (particularly in the field of animation) are now themselves increasingly looking to co-financing deals. Like the UK and Australia – which are strong second-division players in children's television – the US can also trade on the fact that English is becoming the global *lingua franca*. For this reason, it is hardly surprising that the *proportion* of home-produced programming is falling in relation to overall provision; and even if the *amount* has not significantly fallen, this fact alone is bound to result in a fall in its ratings, as the audience is spread more thinly.

Traditionally, critics on the left have interpreted the dominance of US media as a form of cultural imperialism; and such arguments are often most emotive when tied to notions of childhood innocence.[53] This concern was forcefully expressed – albeit in rather more liberal terms – at the two World Summits on Children's Television, held in 1995 and 1998;[54] while the Charter for Children's Television, discussed more fully in Chapter Five, draws on the UN Convention on the Rights of the Child in arguing for children's right to have their cultures and experiences represented. In countries such as Australia, this concern has led to (or at least been used to justify) protectionist policies – such as quotas – designed to support the domestic production industry.

On the other hand, it could be argued that – like youth culture – children's culture is not narrowly tied to its physical location. As has been suggested in relation to the advent of ITV in the 1950s, there are ways in which US media speak to popular sentiments that 'official' British culture is unable to reach. Studies of the international reception of US television suggest that it is interpreted in very diverse ways, and often in a manner which supports the values of the various home cultures that receive it. A preference for such material does not necessarily represent a supine capitulation to 'American values' – and in some cases, it can provide material for a powerful critique of such values.[55] Meanwhile, in terms of ratings, domestically produced children's programmes remain more popular with children than those from the US, a pattern that is repeated in many countries around the world.

Ultimately, then, the call to represent children's national cultures and experiences raises more questions than it answers. To what extent are children's experiences specific to local or national cultures? *Whose* 'national' cultures will be represented here? Does a strong domestic industry necessarily result in children's experiences being represented? And to what extent do measures such as quotas result in a strong domestic industry in the first place?

The economic position is also somewhat complex, at least in the case of the UK. Britain is, of course, not only on the receiving end in this respect: it is also a major exporter of children's programmes. As we have noted, UK companies (not least the BBC) are increasingly reliant on sales in international markets and co-production deals. In this context, 'quality' sells – at least if it is traditionally defined. As in television in general, the most easily exportable material is that which comes closest to the British national stereotype: literary adaptations about middle-class white children having exciting adventures, preferably in rural and historic settings (for example, *The Phoenix and the Carpet* and *The Chronicles of Narnia*), all do extremely well in overseas markets. And of course, these children's versions of Merchant-Ivory reflect a certain construction of 'British' national identity which may well be quite close to the hearts of those who see children's television as under threat from the encroachment of 'American trash'. It is no coincidence in this respect that the BBC has revived its Sunday late-afternoon 'family' slot in which these kinds of programmes were first transmitted.[56]

What are less easily marketable, however, are more socially realist dramas which reflect the contemporary experiences of children from other social classes or ethnic groups, such as *Grange Hill* or *Byker Grove*; and even contemporary literary adaptations such as *The Demon Headmaster* and *The Queen's Nose* do less well overseas. In this respect, the globalisation of children's media culture may be leading to a narrowing (even a stereotyping) of particular national identities – a kind of cultural tourism. Interestingly, however, US representations of minority groups – as in sitcoms such as *Moesha* and *Fresh Prince of Bel Air* or the younger children's cartoon *Waynehead* – do appear to be more internationally marketable, and are in fact very popular with young black British audiences; although these series could not really be categorised as 'social realism' either.

Structural guarantees

Finally, what of the organisation of the industry itself? As we have noted, Jay Blumler's original report for the BSC identified several structural conditions which, in his view, guaranteed the commitment to children's broadcasting.[57] The years since Blumler's report have seen a further move away from the stability of the regulated duopoly and the settled assumptions about the child audience it helped to sustain. The steady commercialisation of the BBC in particular could be seen as a fundamental dismantling of the structural arrangements on which the 'Great Tradition' of children's television was built. And yet the consequences of this situation are also ambivalent.

In terms of the industry, there are two unresolved issues that have particular implications for children's television. The first is that of training. According to Blumler, the success of children's broadcasting was guaranteed partly by the continuity of personnel working in the sector. Contrary to popular cynicism, children's television has not functioned solely as a stepping-stone for people on their way up, or a resting ground for those who have been put out to grass – although it is possible to think of examples of both. In fact, its history has been marked by people who have carved out long-term careers in the field, and hence by a sustained professional culture – what we have termed an 'interpretive community' – which bridges the divide between public and commercial broadcasting. Significantly, several senior positions in the cable/satellite sector are now held by such people, who often have a background in the BBC.

However, the commitment to outsourcing has been accompanied by the breakup or decline of traditional routes of access and training. On the one hand, this has begun to open up the industry to hitherto under-represented groups, not least young people themselves: the age profile in cable television, for example, is much younger than in its terrestrial equivalent. On the other hand, the sense of an occupational tradition has begun to disappear, as television becomes much more of a 'revolving door' industry: many of the people we interviewed for this research are no longer in the same jobs, for example. Furthermore, there are now several areas of skill shortage, which have been accentuated by the advent of new technologies.[58] Such changes are likely to have a significant long-term impact on children's television in particular.

Second, the future for regulation also appears uncertain. As we have indicated, it is important to distinguish here between the 'negative' forms of regulation concerned primarily with moral issues and the more 'positive' forms that address questions of quality and diversity – although of course in practice these often overlap. As we indicated in the Introduction, contemporary anxieties about changes in childhood have come to focus particularly on the impact of the media. Calls for stricter regulation of media violence appear to be increasing just at the point when the whole enterprise is becoming even more impossible – not least for technological reasons. More positive forms of regulation, however, are likely to command less and less political will. As the range of providers proliferates, the job of regulation is becoming ever more demanding: the ITC, for example, does have a brief to regulate the new cable/satellite providers, although much of its work is now conducted 'after the fact'. The potential consolidation of the various agencies into a single media regulator, proposed by one of the think-tanks currently influencing government policy,[59] might introduce a welcome degree of coherence, but it would not reduce the enormity of the task.

Conclusion: towards new policies

The broader implications of our analysis for children's television policy will be discussed in more detail in Chapter Six. This brief conclusion will serve merely as a trailer. In the previous chapter, we pointed to some significant problems with the legacy of public service broadcasting – or, more accurately, with public *sector* broadcasting, in its statist, bureaucratic form. In the case of children, the public service ethos has been more strongly sustained than in most other areas of broadcasting; although there has always been an uneasy balance between the need to 'give children what they want' and the attempt to protect them against their baser instincts. Yet while more overt forms of paternalism have been steadily abandoned, the history of public broadcasting in Britain has been characterised by a lack of accountability to the public it is claiming to serve.

This is not to challenge the fundamental principles of public service – the notion of broadcasting as a guarantor of the public sphere and of citizenship, and the key tenets of quality, diversity and universal access. Nor is it to deny the significant achievements of public broadcasting in relation to children – its success both in particular areas of programming and in terms of the overall service (for example, in maintaining provision at times when children are available to view). These are principles and achievements which should be sustained and preserved. As we have indicated, the obligation for universal service – both in broadcasting and in relation to new communications technologies – is likely to become an increasingly urgent policy issue; and here we will need positive and imaginative initiatives that seek to overcome growing inequalities in provision.

However, we would argue that in some instances, the market can and does provide for children – and indeed that it serves them in ways that public broadcasting has sometimes failed to do. This has been true historically, and it will continue to apply in the more commercially driven multi-channel future. The BBC's success in children's broadcasting has *depended upon* the existence of commercial competition – for example, in its introduction of new programmes in the 1960s – and indeed upon commercial exploitation – as in the case of *Teletubbies*. It has often been commercial programmes, both from the UK and the US, that have pushed at the boundaries between childhood and youth culture, and thereby forced the pace of innovation. Furthermore, several ITV companies and Channel Four have offered successful examples of public service within a commercial framework, of which programmes such as *Art Attack* and *Wise Up* are a couple of the better-known examples. Nevertheless, it is crucial to emphasise that this environment has been a *regulated* one, albeit of a particular kind. As we have indicated, government reports such as Pilkington and Annan established a kind of regulatory ambience – a set of expectations about the social and cultural functions of broadcasting – rather than relying on a more mechanistic approach, for example in the form of quotas.

More controversially, however, we would argue that the new cable/satellite providers are also serving children, in ways that the regulated duopoly has not always managed to do. Thus, for all the criticisms one might make of it, Nickelodeon *is* offering children distinctive new forms of television which address their concerns and reflect their experiences. It is successful not only because it gives them what they want but also because it meets needs that are not being met elsewhere. This – rather than some misguided addiction to 'junk food' – is why they are choosing to watch it. Of course, Nickelodeon does not meet all their needs, and it does not in itself provide the diversity of programming which can currently be found on terrestrial channels. But the fact that children spend most of their viewing time watching adult programmes would suggest that children's television in general is also failing to meet some of their needs. Obviously, these new services are only available to a minority who can afford to pay; and (at least in the UK) it is likely that this will continue to be the case at least over the medium term. But the notion that the market is somehow *inherently* incapable of delivering quality and diversity, or of meeting children's needs – that it has a uniformly negative influence on the provision of cultural goods – is one which must be challenged.

The advent of a new Labour administration may to some extent have allayed the fears of the defenders of public service broadcasting. The threat of privatisation of the BBC and Channel Four would seem to have receded; although there is also considerable scepticism surrounding the government's apparently cosy relationship with Rupert Murdoch. Nevertheless, the stability of the regulated duopoly is unlikely to return: public sector broadcasting will have to stake out its territory in a much more commercially competitive environment. However one may read the history, the context in which future broadcasting policy will be devised is one that cannot be seen simply in terms of an *opposition between* public service and the market.

Nevertheless, these are early days. What we have witnessed in broadcasting over the past two decades has been an encounter between a set of traditions and institutions founded in the mid-century and a new set of forces which have developed since 1980. Because this encounter is still in its early stages, it may be that we overestimate the resilience of public service traditions. Ten or twenty years down the line, those traditions may well appear much weaker; and the BBC's current strength as a player in the global market – which is of course based on its history as a public corporation – may prove impossible to sustain. Nevertheless, our response is not simply to leap to the defence of those traditions. To be sure, we need to find ways of furthering public service objectives within a market-led, global system. But we also need to consider how we might *reform* and *redefine* public sector broadcasting in order to make it more accountable to the diverse publics it claims to serve.

Ultimately, we do not feel that a defence of the status quo of terrestrial broadcasting is either realistic or sufficient in the current context. In the case of children's television, such arguments often reflect a form of cultural conservatism, and a rather paternalistic construction of childhood. By contrast, we would place a central emphasis on children's *rights*, rather than simply on their *entitlements*. In other words, we would argue that children should be seen as social actors in their own right, rather than as passive recipients of a culture generated by adults on their behalf. This means devising mechanisms for access, democratic accountability and control, through which children are enabled to articulate their *own* needs and concerns as an audience, and to create their own media culture.

Notes

1 On the US side, this view is frequently voiced by representatives of lobby groups such as Action for Children's Television or the Center for Media Education. See also Palmer

(1988). The British position is particularly apparent in Jay Blumler's work (Blumler, 1992; Blumler and Biltereyst, 1998).

2 Melody (1973).

3 This phrase derives from the work of the Canadian critic Dallas Smythe (e.g. 1981).

4 For example, Kline (1993); Kunkel (1993).

5 This famous quotation is taken from Cy Schneider (1987).

6 See Kunkel and Watkins (1987).

7 Englehardt (1986).

8 See de Cordova (1994).

9 Kline (1993).

10 See Kunkel (1993).

11 Intriguingly, these requirements have been criticised by some 'free speech' advocates as a violation of the First Amendment, on the grounds that they represent a form of 'enforced speech'.

12 Kline (1993), p. 350.

13 Seiter (1993).

14 For further discussion, see Buckingham (1995a).

15 See Hebdige (1988); Webster (1991).

16 Blumler (1991); Davies and Corbett (1997).

17 Blumler (1992), p. 5.

18 This was the term used by the literary critic F. R. Leavis (1948) in his attempt to define a limited 'canon' of great English authors.

19 Davies and Corbett (1997).

20 It is worth noting that the statistical analysis included in Blumler's report was undertaken by Chris Mottershead, then Secretary of BACTV; and that Blumler places a key emphasis on the power of organised 'public opinion', represented by groups like BACTV, to counter threats to children's television.

21 See Home (1995).

22 For a discussion, see Neuman (1991).

23 Connell (1983).

24 The 'classic' statement of this position is Nicholas Garnham's (1983).

25 See Garnham (1990), Chapter One.

26 Hollins (1984).

27 As discussed above: see Melody (1973).

28 For a provocative analysis of such marketing discourse, see Nixon (1998).

29 Figures here are taken from the British Video Association (BVA) Annual Report 1996 and from the ITC's annual research review, *The Public's View* (1997), respectively.

30 This is discussed in more detail in Chapter Four. Pre-school videos (including Disney) feature prominently in the BVA's charts of top ten video sales (as opposed to rentals, where they appear much more rarely).

31 Goodwin (1992), for example, is very sanguine about the role of the ITC.

32 For a discussion of recent tendencies in this field, see Buckingham and Sefton-Green (1997).

33 See Garnham (1990); Curran and Seaton (1997).

34 On 'monopoly capitalism', see Mandel (1974). On Hollywood, see Balio (1976).

35 Marsha Kinder (1991), Chapter 4, describes this as a 'supersystem' of 'transmedia intertextuality'.

36 See Wagg (1992). *Live and Kicking* used to feature the game-show segment 'Run the Risk', which provided the title for this chapter.

37 From an interview with research executive Shari Donnenfeld, December 1996.

38 Such figures are approximate, and cannot necessarily be taken as an indication of the amount invested in actual programming, given that the methods for calculating overheads, staffing costs, etc. are constantly changing. Of course, production costs also need to be seen in relation to (actual and projected) income, for example from merchandising and overseas sales.

39 For example, Maggie Brown, 'The square window', *Guardian*, 5 June 1996.

40 Quite how much of the income generated here finds its way back into children's production is an interesting question. Not all of it is returned to the BBC: character rights, for example, are often owned independently, at least in some markets. In the case of *Teletubbies*, the BBC retains rights in the UK and overseas, with the exception of US rights, which are retained by the production company, Ragdoll. How the money that comes into the BBC is divided is harder to identify.

41 This was particularly apparent in the debate conducted at the Second World Summit on Television for Children held in London in March 1998. Among the most scathing critics were Ada Haug of the Norwegian public service channel NHK and Patricia Edgar of the Australian Children's Television Foundation. For more on the *Teletubbies* controversy, see Buckingham (1998).

42 It should be noted that newspaper publicity at least is not the responsibility of the Children's Department.

43 See Brunsdon (1990).

44 Significantly, however, a commitment to children's programmes was not actually *required* by the ITC.

45 As reported by William Phillips in *Broadcast*, 12 April 1996, p. 22.

46 See Neuman (1991) for a critique of such arguments about audience fragmentation.

47 This intriguing but somewhat dubious statistic is quoted in Tuman (1992), p. 69.

48 Is it sacrilegious to suggest that Williams's (1974) notion of US television as 'flow' might have been based on a somewhat superficial encounter with TV in US hotel rooms?

49 See Murdock and Golding (1989); Wartella et al. (1990).

50 See, for example, Brunsdon (1990); Corner, Harvey and Lury (1995).

51 See Turow (1981) – although this analysis predates the wholesale deregulation under Reagan.

52 See Goodhardt, Ehrenberg and Collins (1975).

53 See Dorfman and Mattelart (1975).

54 A report of the first summit was published by the Australian Children's Television Foundation (1995).

55 See Liebes and Katz (1990); Tomlinson (1991).

56 These programmes were not produced by the Children's Department.

57 Blumler (1992): see pp. 49–50 above.

58 See Varlaam et al. (1990); Collins and Murroni (1996).

59 This idea is floated in the IPPR (Institute for Public Policy Research) publication by Collins and Murroni (1996). There were strong rumours that this was about to become Labour policy immediately before the 1997 election, although these were subsequently denied. Nevertheless, such a development would conform to government policy on regulation in other public services.

3 Vision On
Mapping the Changes in Children's Programming

In the two previous chapters, we have identified a series of historical changes in the institutional contexts of children's television. Our primary focus thus far has been on changes in policy, and on the political economy of television production. As we have argued, these changes have significant implications for the status of children as an audience, and for the ways in which that audience is defined and constructed. While there have been several changes in these respects, this history does not easily fit into a narrative of 'rise and fall'. Thus, we have challenged the idea – which currently dominates much public debate about children's television – that we are now witnessing the decline of a 'Great Tradition'. On the contrary, we regard this history as a kind of continuing debate – and at times an overt competition – between contrasting definitions of the child audience, and ultimately of 'childhood' itself. As we shall indicate in more detail in Chapter Five, these competing (and overlapping) definitions of the child audience continue to circulate within the industry, and in public debate more broadly.

One of the most obvious questions to be raised here concerns the consequences of these developments in terms of programming. How have the programmes specifically provided for children changed over the past forty years? In this chapter, therefore, we present some results from a wide-ranging statistical 'audit' of the children's television schedules since 1956. On one level, this is an exercise in straightforward description; yet it also raises fundamental questions about how we define and categorise television programmes, and hence how we might identify evidence of change. Here again, we question the notion that children's television should be seen as a 'Great Tradition', and that this tradition is necessarily in decline; although we also seek to identify some rather more complex – and in some ways more far-reaching – developments, with significant implications for future policy.

The gradual shift away from the security of the regulated duopoly has generated considerable alarm – and no small degree of pessimism – among those concerned with the cultural role of broadcasting. As we have seen, children's television has been a particular focus of anxiety here, not least because the very mention of children automatically seems to invoke much broader fears of cultural change. Research and debate in this field appear to relate a straightforward story of decline. Many commentators apparently agree that children's television is 'dumbing down', as home-grown, quality programmes steadily lose out to cheap, imported animation. Prognostications for the future of children's television are consistently gloomy: few critics believe that it will be possible to sustain diverse, high-quality programmes appropriate to children's needs in the increasingly commercial, multi-channel environment that is now emerging.

One persistent problem with such narratives of cultural decline is that of evidence. It is always tempting to agree with the assertion that things aren't as good as they used to be; but we need to be clear about what we are comparing. Judging the present or the future solely in terms of their inability to live up to the great achievements of the past can blind us to other changes that may be taking place; and it can lead to a form of conservatism which leaves us incapable of responding positively to the challenges of the future.

In attempting to identify evidence of historical changes in children's programming, we conducted a detailed quantitative audit of television output across five decades. Using published schedules, we analysed the provision of children's programmes during three sample weeks in the months of January, April and October, in the years 1956, 1966, 1976, 1986 and 1996.[1] We examined this material in terms of several key variables: overall time in minutes; channel and time screened; repeats as opposed to first showings; country of origin; fiction as opposed to non-fiction; format of presentation (e.g. live action, animation, human presenters); content (in the case of non-fiction) or genre (in the case of fiction); and original source (e.g. literary or other media adaptation).

Our analysis is in some ways an extension of – and a response to – Jay Blumler's 1992 report for the BSC, and to the subsequent 'update' published in 1997.[2] These reports undertook similar audits, designed to provide 'benchmarks' against which future changes in programming could be identified – although, as we shall see, the categories used in the two reports are somewhat different. Our analysis extends over a longer time period (the earliest date covered by the BSC reports is 1981), although in most other respects our approach has been similar; and there are few areas in which we would dispute their findings, at least in respect of the period they address.[3]

At the same time, we do want to challenge some of the assumptions on which this kind of analysis (including our own) is based. As we have implied, the BSC's interventions in the debate about children's television have been part of a wider project, whose fundamental concern is to preserve the status quo of terrestrial public service broadcasting; and these motivations inevitably lead to a certain way of accounting for historical change. As well as presenting some of our own findings, therefore, we also want to point to the need for some rather different ways of understanding and responding to change.

Defining terms: questions of method

The first problem we faced in this research was in identifying our object of analysis. How do we define what *counts* as a 'children's programme'? As we have noted, research has consistently shown that children do not only watch programmes made specifically for them. Indeed, the most popular programmes with children have *always* been those intended for a general audience.[4] This is not to say that children's preferences are necessarily identical with adults'; and as we shall indicate in Chapter Four, some interesting questions are raised by considering the programmes that are most *popular* with these different audiences. Nevertheless, for the purposes of our audit, we needed a narrower definition. We chose to adopt the terms used in the BSC reports: a children's programme is any programme produced or commissioned by a children's department and/or one placed in scheduling periods set aside for children, or on a dedicated children's channel. This would seem a sufficiently practical definition; although it too raises several methodological difficulties.

In fact, the boundaries between children's television and television in general are not consistent over the decades. This inconsistency is particularly marked when examining specific programmes. The same episodes of *Batman* or *Thunderbirds*, for instance, have been screened at different times of the day and on different channels over the past thirty years. Broadly speaking, such programmes have evolved from family entertainment (in the 1960s), through children's television (the 1970s) to 'cult' or 'kitsch TV' (the 1980s and 1990s) – a development which in itself raises interesting questions about the changing relationships between 'child' and 'adult' audiences. A similar problem occurs with programmes that appear on more than one channel. For instance, there is now a growing number of programmes aimed at teenage or 'tween' audiences. On the whole, these programmes have not been made or commissioned by children's broadcasters, or shown in the traditional children's slots – although there are recent exceptions, such as Channel Four's soap *Hollyoaks*. For these reasons, we omitted programmes such as *Neighbours*, *Heartbreak High* and *Sister Sister*, which are extremely popular with children, but do not feature in defined children's slots on terrestrial channels. However, we had to include these kinds of programmes when they featured on the dedicated children's channels such as TCC and Nickelodeon. Significantly, it is these kinds of 'tween' dramas that often attract adult controversy about their focus on sex and relationships: they are held by some to be an indication of how adolescence is encroaching ever further into childhood.

Additional problems arise in attempting to categorise programmes, particularly in terms of genre. Jay Blumler's initial BSC study acknowledges some of these problems,[5] although the categories it uses are occasionally quite problematic. Some of the distinctions between programmes implicitly rely on judgments about cultural value. For example, some illustrated narrative programmes are categorised as 'animation', while others are regarded as 'storytelling'. It would appear that British animation programmes aimed at the under-fives – such as *Postman Pat* – fall into the latter category, while 'animation' is implicitly confined to imported programmes aimed at older children. However unintentionally, this runs the risk of downgrading animation as something synonymous with cheap US imports. In our analysis, we therefore attempted to distinguish between form and content (however crudely defined). Thus, animation and live action (and so on) were coded separately as programme *formats*, rather than as genres, and in terms of subject matter.

In place of Blumler's eleven genre categories, the more recent BSC study uses five, which are taken from the BARB (Broadcasters' Audience Research Bureau) classification. While this might appear to guarantee a degree of objectivity, or at least consistency, it does make it problematic to then compare the findings of the two reports, as the second report does.[6] Even here, some categorisations are based on form (such as animation), some on target audience (pre-school) and some on even vaguer notions (entertainment).

Ultimately, there are no easy solutions here. Generic classification is an inherently unstable, slippery process. Indeed, research with children suggests that they may not categorise programmes in the same way as adults, and that how they do so varies significantly depending upon the context.[7] Furthermore, genres themselves are obviously subject to historical change: the boundaries between 'storytelling' and 'animation', or between 'entertainment' and 'factual programmes', shift over time. Judging the present using the categories of the past – or vice versa – is thus bound to be problematic. These difficulties are not merely methodological. Imposing *any* single set of categories inevitably entails assumptions and judgments: it is not simply a matter of neutral description.

Reading the schedules

A further complication arises when we consider the 'syntagmatic' dimension – that is, how these different elements (programmes) are combined in the schedule. Measures of the amount of programming in any single category are obviously significant; but we also need to take account of where these programmes are located in the schedules. Thus, there may indeed have been an overall increase in the amount of animation or imported programmes; but these new programmes may not have been scheduled at times when children are most likely to be available to view, or on channels which children are currently most likely to be watching.

In this respect, we would share the assumption, which is implicit in the BSC reports, that 'peak viewing time' for children on the terrestrial channels remains crucially significant, not least in terms of regulatory policy. Children are entitled to have programmes specifically designed for them; but these programmes also have to be scheduled at times when they are most likely to be available to view. Traditionally, this has been the 'after school' slot; although (as we shall indicate in Chapter Six) there may be grounds for questioning whether this will – and indeed should – continue to be the case in future.

Our primary sources of data for this research were the published schedules found in listing magazines.[8] These schedules are of course *representations* of the actual experience of viewing; although in some respects, the changes in how children's schedules have been presented are as suggestive of cultural shifts in perceptions of the child audience as the programmes themselves. Before outlining some findings from our statistical analysis, therefore, we want to provide a more descriptive account of the schedules in each of our sample years across the five decades, and raise some broader questions about how children's experience of television viewing is represented by them.

Separate worlds: the 1950s

Children's television first appeared on BBC 1 in 1946, and an hourly service late on Sunday afternoons began in 1948. Output gradually expanded during the next few years, but it was not until after the creation of a Children's Department in 1950 that a regular daily service was established (it began in 1951). The *Radio Times* was the primary means of presenting information about the schedules, and appeared to be aimed both at children and their parents (see Figure 1). During the early 1950s, radio was still the dominant service within the BBC, and daily television listings came after those for radio.

As Paddy Scannell has argued, the schedule serves as a way of 're-temporising' or organising time: it marks out specific time zones during the day by providing

Figure 1

material which is seen to be 'appropriate to who in particular is available to watch or listen at what time and in what circumstances'.[9] In the case of children, this involves distinguishing them both from the 'youth' audience and from the general 'family' audience; and as we shall see, these distinctions are made in different ways, and are more or less significant, in different historical periods.

Thus, in these early days, children's programmes were 'ring-fenced' within the service, and programmes for pre-schoolers were scheduled separately from those for older children. These were clearly marked out by the use of the collective titles *Watch with Mother* (for under-fives) and *For the Children* or subsequently *Children's Television* (for older children), titles which were also prominent in the published schedule.[10] *Watch with Mother* featured a different fifteen-minute programme on each day of the week, such as *Andy Pandy* (Tuesdays), *The Flowerpot Men* (Wednesdays) and *The Woodentops* (Fridays). This strand was shown at 3.45 p.m., alongside programmes aimed at women in the home, thus allying the pre-school audience very clearly with the 'housewife'.[11] Following an hour of adults' programmes, the main sequence of children's television was shown between 5 p.m. and 6 p.m., clearly reflecting an assumption about when older children would be likely to arrive home from school – although in fact this sequence also ran at this time at the weekends. This was followed by the 'toddlers' truce', between 6 p.m. and 7 p.m., during which broadcasting was suspended. This was intended, on one level, to provide an opportunity for parents to get their children to bed; yet, as we have noted, it also served a more symbolic function of marking a clear boundary between the world of children and the world of adults.

The BBC also used the *Radio Times* and television announcers to indicate the *suitability* of programmes for the child audience, defined primarily in terms of age. For instance, the description of the *Friday Western* specified that it was a programme 'for older children'. By the time we reach 1956, however, the 'developmental schedule' introduced by Freda Lingstrom (see Chapter One) had been partly abandoned: the late-afternoon sequence usually began with programmes aimed at younger children, but after this point it was less obviously structured in terms of age. Scheduling was more thematic, with different days tending to focus on different kinds of programmes. For instance, Wednesday 11 January 1956 featured a drama, *Bobby in France*, followed by a variety/game programme, *Playbox*, whereas the following day appeared to be more 'educative', and included *Children's Newsreel*, followed by *Steps into Ballet* and *Something to Read*. Programmes shown on Fridays and Saturdays tended to be entertainment-based, such as *All Your Own*, which was followed by an adventure drama, *Children of the New Forest*.

By contrast ITV's children's programmes in 1956 were less well established: partly due to the regional structure, there was no separate children's department and no period of time set aside and labelled as 'children's'. Nevertheless, the channel was increasingly successful at reaching the child audience, and was beginning to take the lead in the ratings. A number of formulaic aspects of the service were no doubt 'borrowed' from the BBC. For instance, ITV had an equivalent of *Watch with Mother*, called *Small Time*, shown daily at 4.05 p.m. and including *Oliver Pollip the Octopus* (with Rolf Harris), *Toybox* and *Johnny and Florry*. On the whole, programmes had a more 'populist' flavour: for instance, ITV's *Junior Television*, shown on Saturdays and Sundays between 4 and 6 p.m., tended to start with programmes for younger children, such as *The Adventures of Noddy*, followed by a magazine programme, such as *I-Spy*, and imported adventure dramas, most famously *Robin Hood* and *Roy Rogers*. However, during the week children's programmes were transmitted on some days but not on others; and some programmes appearing in the children's afternoon slot, such as *Hopalong Cassidy*, seem to be aimed at a general family audience, rather than specifically at children. The commercial service, then, was already beginning to threaten the established 'nursery school' atmosphere of children's television by calling into question the boundaries between adults and children.

The 1960s: the emergence of the 'mini-schedule'

The BBC's response to competition and the institutional changes that ensued in the early 1960s inevitably impacted on the organisation of the children's schedule. The most important developments here were the three-year merging of the Children's Department into a Family Department and the advent of an 'alternative' second channel, BBC 2. During the afternoon, children's programmes now lasted for over an hour, typically beginning at 4.45 and ending at 5.55 p.m. Significantly, children's programmes were no longer listed in a ring-fenced format, but simply given their individual title, description and exact time. The 'toddlers' truce' had ended in 1957, largely as a result of pressure from the new commercial companies; and children's programmes were now followed by early evening news magazine shows (such as *Tonight*) and programmes aimed at the more elusive teenage audience (such as *Six-Five Special*).[12] In both respects, the distinctions between children and 'youth' or adult audiences had become blurred; although the gradual introduction in the early 1960s of the 9 p.m. watershed clearly marked the boundary of what was considered acceptable for children, as it continues to do today.[13]

As we have indicated, the dissolution of the BBC Children's Department was partly an attempt to claw back the audience that it had lost to ITV; and the new afternoon schedule was accordingly more 'populist', featuring more material imported from the US. By 1966, repeats were beginning to become an important part of the children's schedule, not least as a result of the extension of broadcasting hours. Programmes for pre-schoolers, for example, included a mixture of old favourites, such as *Andy Pandy*, as well as a number of new additions, such as *Camberwick Green* and *Pogle's Wood*. As well as offering recycled favourites, the new channel, BBC 2, was the site for the new, broadly educative magazine programme *Play School*, screened daily at 11 a.m.

As we have noted, the Pilkington Report on broadcasting, published in 1962, criticised ITV for its reliance on entertainment genres such as Westerns, particularly for the younger audience. According to Bernard Sendall,[14] it was not until the end of the 1950s that ITV began to take a 'serious but also informative grip on children's television'. By the mid-1960s attempts had been made to include a greater variety of material; and both BBC and ITV developed what is sometimes referred to as the children's 'mini-schedule' – a mixed menu of programmes, organised developmentally in terms of the increasing age of the target audience.[15] This approach remains standard practice on these channels today. For example, the ITV schedule began at 4.45 with a programme for younger children, such as the magazine *Playtime* or animation such as *The Adventures of Twizzle*. These were usually followed by a non-fiction programme (for instance, the natural history magazine programme, *Zoo Time*), quizzes (such as *Junior Criss Cross Quiz*) and entertainment magazines (such as *Disney Wonderland*). The final programme in the schedule tended to be fiction, aimed at a slightly older audience (and no doubt also appealing to adults, who might be arriving home from work or tuning in early for the programmes that followed): these included American Westerns and British dramas, such as *Orlando* and *The New Forest Rustlers*, and a whole series of 'mid-Atlantic' puppet dramas produced by Gerry Anderson, such as *Supercar* and *Fireball XL5*.

The final significant change, for both BBC and ITV, was the demise of specific programmes for children during the late afternoon weekend slots. The BBC still maintained the Sunday teatime dramas, often adaptations of literary classics such as *David Copperfield*, although these were no longer the responsibility of the Children's Department. Saturday late-afternoon and early evening programmes were blended into a 'family' slot, which included programmes such as the pop music show *Juke Box Jury*, the sci-fi serial *Doctor Who* and the police series *Dixon of Dock Green*, all of which were extremely popular with children. While the emergence of the mini-schedule reflected a more systematic attempt to address what were seen as children's distinctive needs, in other respects adults and children were increasingly being combined into a 'family' audience.

Consolidation: the 1970s

The 1970s was a period of consolidation and relative stability for children's television in general. The developmentally organised mini-schedule was extended by a further thirty-five minutes on BBC 1, and now began at 4.25 p.m., significantly earlier than in the 1960s. It also gained in diversity (see Figure 2). At the BBC, several of the key series launched during the late 1950s and 1960s, such as the storytelling programme *Jackanory*, the factual magazine *Blue Peter* and the variety show *Crackerjack*, had become standard fixtures; and these were joined in the mid-1970s by *John Craven's Newsround* and subsequently *Grange Hill*. All these programmes contributed to a degree of predictability, which enabled them to become part of domestic family routines; and this in turn helped to guarantee good – or at least stable – ratings. The ITV schedule was more variable in terms of time, although it was generally much shorter than the BBC's (around an hour, as against the BBC's 105 minutes). ITV still screened a higher proportion of US imports, and remained somewhat more 'populist', particularly later in the afternoon, when it could hope to attract adult viewers. On the other hand, ITV was less successful in establishing credible, long-running series, and in some cases still appeared to be following the BBC's lead, notably with *Magpie*, a slightly more 'trendy' version of *Blue Peter*. Nevertheless, such programmes were rarely scheduled competitively, in the sense that similar programmes would not appear oppo-

Figure 2

site each other: as with schools programmes, there was a tacit agreement that the two channels would complement each other's strengths. As we shall indicate in the following chapter, it is only comparatively recently that the 'art of scheduling' in children's television has come to be ruled by the imperatives of competition that govern prime-time television.

Pre-school television was also especially strong at the BBC. *Play School* was now shown twice a day: during the mornings on BBC 2, and in the afternoon on BBC 1, at the beginning of afternoon children's television – which may have reflected the increasing numbers of young children now attending nursery schools. The *Watch with Mother* title had now been dropped, and pre-school programmes appeared under their individual titles, mainly at lunchtimes. While this could be interpreted as a response to feminism, it perhaps also reflected a willingness to address young children as individuals in their own right rather than merely as appendages to mother.[16]

Meanwhile, children's programming was also reaching into hitherto untouched areas of the schedule. Programmes began to be screened on weekday mornings during school holidays. These were mainly repeats and imported animation, but there were exceptions, notably the BBC's *Why Don't You (Turn Off Your TV and Do Something More Interesting Instead)*, the symptomatically titled children's hobby magazine show. Meanwhile, Saturday-morning programmes also began to appear during the mid-1970s, although initially these were also mainly repeats and imports. However, the anarchic ITV series *Tiswas* (which was launched on the regional channel ATV in 1975 and went national the following year) was quickly countered in October 1976 by the BBC's somewhat milder new entertainment magazine show, *Multi-Coloured Swap Shop*. These programmes were partly scheduling devices in themselves: they attempted to combine cartoons, occasional dramas and music videos with live material into a seamless programme that would discourage channel-hopping. They also helped to establish Saturday mornings as a key viewing time for children – a development which had occurred decades earlier in the US, largely because older viewers were seen to be less available to view at this time. They also contributed to the demise of traditional Saturday-morning cinema screenings, which had previously restricted children's availability to view.[17]

Continuity and change: the 1980s

The changes that began to sweep through television in the 1980s had a somewhat belated impact on the children's schedule. Towards the end of the decade, the afternoon mini-schedule was extended further on both channels: it now began significantly earlier, suggesting that the two terrestrial channels were now competing to 'catch' child viewers as soon as they arrived home from school – although ITV was still behind the BBC in terms of quantity, with 75 minutes as opposed to 125. Nevertheless, the range of programmes provided here was essentially the same as in the 1970s – even if (as we shall indicate) the balance had begun to shift.

In a sense, the most significant changes affecting the child audience occurred outside the designated children's schedules; although they also began to have an impact on the schedules themselves. The advent of 24-hour television created new slots and the need to repackage and recycle existing material. Breakfast television, for example, opened up a new arena for competition; and after initial promises about its public service commitments, the ITV franchise-holder TV-AM began to succeed in the ratings with a more informal, entertainment-driven style, featuring characters like Roland Rat who were partly designed to appeal to the child audience. Meanwhile, the advent of 'youth' programmes on BBC 2 and Channel Four, like *The Tube* and *Network 7*, led to new forms of address and a more wholehearted embrace of popular culture; while Channel Four initially brought in minority voices and more challenging subject matter. On one level, the boundary between the child audience and the youth audience became increasingly blurred. This was certainly reflected in scheduling. Towards the end of the decade, for example, both BBC and ITV began to schedule youth-oriented programmes which were seen to have 'child appeal' immediately after the children's slot: the BBC's bought-in Australian soap *Neighbours*, originally scheduled at lunchtime, was given an afternoon repeat at 5.35, and ITV countered with another Australian soap, *Home and Away*, which in some regions was shown at 5.10, in direct competition with BBC children's programmes. Both became massively popular with the child audience, although they also provoked concern among some adults because of their focus on the ever-changing romantic relationships among the characters. Similar developments were to occur with a wave of youth-oriented situation comedies, largely imported from the US, such as *Fresh Prince of Bel Air* and *Saved by the Bell*, which were initially screened in the early evenings on BBC 2 and Channel Four during the early 1990s.

By contrast, within children's television itself, the 1980s also saw the creation of separate billings on both the major channels, which in some respects reinforced these boundaries. ITV created 'Children's ITV' in 1983, with presenters such as Bernie Winters and Tommy Boyd; while the BBC responded with 'Children's BBC' in 1986, presented from the 'Broom Cupboard' by Philip Schofield and others.[18] However, these designated children's spaces were very different from the ring-fenced Children's Hour of the 1950s. While they were clearly targeting and addressing children as a distinctive audience, they also took great pains to avoid the paternalistic 'nursery school' style of the 1950s, which had caused such concern for Owen Reed. If anything, children's television presenters began to address the audience as if they were grown-up children themselves.[19] At the same time, 'CITV' and 'CBBC' (as they came to be known – thus significantly avoiding the dread word 'children') also represented a powerful form of 'branding', which became a significant new imperative in the increasingly competitive environment of the late 1980s and 1990s. In this context, the role of continuity sequences became much more significant: the presenters were increasingly acknowledged as the 'stars' of children's TV, and the sequences themselves were extended to include guest interviews, trailers and other forms of publicity for the programmes that surrounded them.

Competition and deregulation: the 1990s

As we have indicated, the wider technological and institutional changes affecting television began to catch up with children's television in the 1990s. The first dedicated non-terrestrial children's channel – the British-owned TCC – had appeared in 1986. This was joined in 1993 by the Cartoon Network and Nickelodeon; and subsequently by Disney and Fox Kids. While these channels still reach relatively small audiences and rely chiefly on imported and repeated material, their impact on children's television has been significant, not only in the introduction of new programmes (particularly animation and situation comedy) but also in new styles and forms of address. As the schedule (Figure 3) amply illustrates, the amount of material available to children in cable/satellite homes at all times of the day is

CARTOON NETWORK

5.00am Omer **5.30** The Fruitties **6.00** Blinky Bill **6.30** Tabaluga **7.00** Johnny Bravo **7.15** Beetlejuice **7.30** Animaniacs **7.45** Dexter's Laboratory **8.00** Cow and Chicken **8.15** Sylvester and Tweety **8.30** Tom and Jerry Kids **9.00** Cave Kids **9.30** Blinky Bill **10.00** The Magic Roundabout **10.15** Thomas the Tank Engine **10.30** The Fruitties **11.00** Tabaluga **11.30** Scooby Doo **12.00** Tom and Jerry **12.15pm** Bugs and Daffy **12.30** Road Runner **12.45** Sylvester and Tweety **1.00** Popeye **1.30** Droopy **2.00** Yogi **2.30** Top Cat **3.00** The Addams Family **3.30** Beetlejuice **4.00** Scooby Doo **4.30** Dexter **5.00** Cow and Chicken **5.30** Animaniacs **6.00** Tom and Jerry **6.30** The Flintstones **7.00** Batman **7.30** Mask **8.00** Scooby Doo **8.30–9.00pm** Dynomutt Dog Wonder

DISNEY

6.00am Bear in the Big Blue House **6.30** Classic Toons **6.40** Gummi Bears **7.00** Aladdin – the Series **7.25** Classic Toons **7.35** 101 Dalmatians **7.55** Goof Troop **8.20** Classic Toons **8.30** Timon and Pumbaa **8.45** The New Adventures of Winnie the Pooh **9.00** The Adventures of Spot **9.05** The Animal Shelf **9.15** Pocket Dragons **9.30** Bear in the Big Blue House **9.55** The Toothbrush Family **10.00** Alphabet Castle **10.10** Tots TV **10.25** Let's Wiggle! **10.30** The Big Garage **10.50** PB and Jelly Otter **11.00** Sesame Street **12.00** The Adventures of Spot – cartoon fun **12.05pm** The Animal Shelf **12.15** Pocket Dragons **12.30** Bear in the Big Blue House **12.55** The Toothbrush Family **1.00** Alphabet Castle **1.15** Tots TV **1.30** Let's Wiggle! **1.35** The Big Garage **1.50** PB and Jelly Otter **2.00** The New Adventures of Winnie the Pooh **2.30** Quack Pack **3.00** The Little Mermaid **3.30** Timon and Pumbaa **3.45** Aladdin – the Series **4.15** 101 Dalmatians **4.45** Art Attack **5.00** Smart Guy **5.30** Recess **5.45** Pepper Ann **6.00** The Wonder Years **6.30** Boy Meets World **7.00** Brotherly Love **7.30** Student Bodies **8.00** FILM: Slam Dunk Ernest – see Movie Planner **9.30–10.00pm** Home Improvement – comedy

NICKELODEON

6.00am Fraggle Rock **6.30** Muppet Babies **7.00** Hey Arnold! **7.30** Rugrats **8.00** Doug **8.30** The Animals of Farthing Wood **9.00** Children's BBC on Nickelodeon **10.00** Wimzie's House **10.30** Babar **11.00** The Magic School Bus **11.30** PB Bear; Towser; Magic Mountain; Clangers **12.00** Rugrats **12.30pm** Blues Clues **1.00** Bananas in Pyjamas **1.30** Little Bear Stories **2.00** Rocky and the Dodos; Mr Benn; Mr Men **2.30** Children's BBC on Nickelodeon **3.30** Angry Beavers **4.00** Catdog **4.30** Rugrats **5.00** Sister Sister **5.30** Kenan and Kel **6.00** Sabrina, the Teenage Witch **6.30–7.00pm** Alien Strange

---

2.15 Home and Away

Attempts are made to talk Tiegan and Aaron out of going on the road with the band. Meanwhile Marilyn receives an extremely threatening phone call.
Repeated at 5.10pm Subtitled 131303

2.45 Dale's Supermarket Sweep

Shopping game show, with Dale Winton.
Subtitled 130674

3.15 News Subtitled
Regional News and Weather 1029113

3.25 CITV

Children's entertainment, presented by Danielle Nicholls and Stephen Mulhern.

3.25 Wizadora Wizadora tries out her new "disappear quick spell". Repeat ..8626194

3.35 The Slow Norris Puppetry, animation and live action tales with the amiable giant and his friends. Allie shows her Russian doll to the Slow Norris. 6102484

3.45 The Animal Shelf Model animation about five toy animals that live in a young boy's bedroom. 6182620

4.00 Rupert Cartoon adventures with the lovable bear and friends. Repeat ..6392129

4.25 The Rottentrolls Fantasy comedy series about a boy who becomes king of the Rottentrolls.
Commander Harris Loses It. Commander Harris takes Princess Kate, Yockenthwaite and Penyghent on an all-night yomp in the forest – and falls into a hallucinatory trance. With Holly Grainger as Princess Kate, and narration by Martin Clunes.
Written by Tim Firth Subtitled 8332484

4.40 Mad for It Weekly live entertainment show, featuring guests, dating games, outside broadcasts, talent contests and competitions. Today's guests include chart band Another Level performing their latest single, *Guess I Was a Fool.* Presented by Mike McClean and Yiolanda Ttokkallos. 6534858
WRITE TO: *Mad for It,* PO Box 555, Nottingham, NG7 2TT
TELEPHONE: Call free on 0800 389 3879
COMPETITION LINE: Call 0894 222555 (calls cost a maximum of 25p, children must ask permission from the person who pays the phone bill)

5.10 Home and Away

Shown at 2.15pm Subtitled 7170113
Followed by **The Missing File**

5.40–6.00pm Early Evening News

Weather Subtitled 569674

1.40 Neighbours

It's opening night at "Little Tommy Tuckers". Sarah is put in an embarrassing situation.
Repeated at 5.35pm Subtitled 20898378

2.05 Breakers

Terri is forced to confess to Steve about the lies she and Eve have told. ..75003199

2.25 Quincy

Aftermath. In the wake of an air disaster, Quincy's investigations lead him to suspect sabotage. Repeat 8999216

3.15 The Weather Show

Topical weather stories.
Subtitled 1107945

3.25 Children's BBC

3.25 King Greenfingers
Shown at 8.35am on BBC2 Repeat 8713674
3.30 Playdays The Roundabout Stop. Today adventures with trains.
Repeat 9178668
3.50 Chucklevision More comedy with the Chuckle Brothers. Chaos ensues when Barry and Paul train to be butlers. With Doyne Byrd and Jennifer Rose.
Written by Nick McIvor Repeat 9158804
4.10 Get Your Own Back Game show in which children and adults compete. With Dave Benson Phillips. Subtitled 5091552
4.35 Microsoap Second in a seven-part comedy drama about a brother and sister whose parents have separated. Joe and Emily meet Roger's kids – the children from hell – and wonder if Mum having a boyfriend is such a good idea. Then Attila the Hun arrives with 20,000 horsemen.
Joe PAUL TERRY, Emily REBECCA HUNTER, Attila the Hun and others RICHARD DIXON, David RYAN CARTWRIGHT, Felicity LUCY EVANS, Robbie ALBEY BROOKES, Colin JEFF RAWLE, Jane SUZANNE BURDEN, Roger IVAN KAYE, Jennifer LOU GISH
Written by Mark Haddon
Repeated next Sunday on BBC2 Subtitled 4173620
5.00 Newsround Subtitled 7165262
5.10 Blue Peter Stuart Miles and Konnie Huq present another film from the *Blue Peter* summer expedition to Mexico. They visit Copper Canyon, wider than California's Grand Canyon, go mule trekking and brave a precarious balancing rock.
Repeated tomorrow at 7.45am on BBC2
Subtitled 7028736

5.35–6.00pm Neighbours

Shown at 1.40pm Subtitled 580552

3–9 OCTOBER 1998 *RadioTimes*

Figure 3

---

extensive and potentially quite bewildering when compared with the stable, ring-fenced provision of the 1950s. In terms of scheduling, these channels depend upon 'stripping' – that is, running the same programmes at the same time each day – in order to introduce a degree of stability and predictability.

Both ITV and BBC continue to provide the developmental mini-schedule in the afternoons, although both now begin at around 3.30 p.m. On the other hand, Children's ITV has lost the 5.10–5.35 slot, which is now scheduled by regional companies and generally contains 'adult' programmes which rival those screened on Channel Four. The BBC thus enjoys an uncontested position in this slot, and screens many of its most successful 'flagship' programmes for older children at this time, allowing an effective lead-in to the still successful *Neighbours* at 5.35. As this implies, the complementary scheduling that characterised children's television in the 1970s and 1980s has largely given way to head-to-head competition. The BBC schedule in particular has become increasingly anchored around what are seen as fail-safe, long-running shows such as *Blue Peter*, *Grange Hill* and *Record Breakers*. As in other areas of popular television (most obviously soap opera), there has been a growing tendency to capitalise on such successes in preference to developing new product. *Blue Peter*, for example, is now scheduled (or effectively 'stripped') thrice-weekly, while the Saturday-morning show *Live and Kicking* has extended into Friday afternoons; and there is a growing tendency to provide extended runs (i.e. more than six episodes) or subsequent series of proven, popular dramas such as *The Demon Headmaster*.

At the same time, terrestrial children's programmes have continued to spread into new slots in the schedule. Perhaps in response to the success of Channel Four's anarchic breakfast magazine show *The Big Breakfast*, which gained a substantial young audience at the height of its success, the BBC now repeats much of its afternoon sequence the following morning on BBC 2 – and the repeats frequently gain higher ratings than the original showings. Meanwhile, the commercial breakfast channel GMTV has also included shows aimed at younger children, such as *Disney's Wake Up in the Wild Room* and the controversial *Mighty Morphin' Power Rangers*. Both BBC and ITV have also substantially expanded their weekend schedules. ITV's Saturday-morning slot is competitively scheduled against the BBC's, matching cartoon for cartoon. There has been some expansion beyond this slot, with more 'youth'-oriented pop programmes like *The Noise*. The BBC has also now begun to schedule children's programmes on BBC 2 on Sunday mornings, to rival those on Channel Four, which began to develop its profile with the appointment of a new children's Commissioning Editor in 1993. Both slots are dominated by bought-in programmes (mainly sitcoms and animation), supplemented on BBC 2 with 'retro' repeats of series like *Grange Hill* (which clearly also appeal to the twenty-something audience who can remember them first time round). However, both channels also schedule innovative original programmes in this slot, such as the BBC's *Short Change*, a children's consumer advice programme, and Channel Four's access show *Wise Up* – programmes that might not normally have been given airtime during weekday afternoons.

Accounting for change

Changes in the scheduling of children's programmes obviously reflect broader changes in television as a whole. The most significant development since the 1950s has been the steady expansion of broadcasting hours. There has been an enormous increase in the *amount* of children's television, partly as a result of the increasing number of channels, but also because of the move towards 24-hour scheduling. In cable and satellite homes, it is now possible to watch children's programmes at almost any time children are likely to be awake; yet even in terrestrial-only households, the availability of children's television has dramatically increased. As we shall indicate, this has significant implications in terms of what 'watching television' actually *means*, and will mean in the future – implications that are partly apparent simply from comparing the appearance of the printed schedules themselves.

As we have implied, these changes also reflect broader social changes, particularly in the relative positions of adults and children. The boundaries between 'children's programmes', 'youth programmes', 'family programmes' and 'adult programmes' that are institutionalised in the schedules have shifted over time. Like the boundaries between adults and children themselves, they have been blurred in some respects and strongly reasserted in others, often for quite different reasons (see Introduction). The 1950s, for example, saw a struggle between the desire to contain the child audience within its designated slots and the move to incorporate it into the 'family' audience; while the 1980s witnessed both a merging of the child audience with the 'youth' audience and the simultaneous reappearance of designated (and strongly 'branded') children's slots. Yet the extent to which children are now defined as a distinctive or 'special' audience is not so much because of their protected status but because of their perceived value as a *market*. Crudely, commerce has increasingly replaced morality as the guiding principle in defining the child audience – although (as we have indicated) the consequences of this in terms of how adequately children are 'served' by television are not necessarily negative.

These broader questions will be addressed in more detail in due course. Our central aim in what follows is to trace the consequences of these changes in terms of the programmes themselves. On one level, the economic logic here would seem to be obvious. With so many new slots to fill in the schedule, and without proportional increases in budgets, broadcasters have inevitably come to rely on inexpensive solutions: imported programmes, easily recyclable genres and forms (such as animation and situation comedy) and more and more repeats. Yet to what extent does this tell the whole story?

In reporting just some of the results of our audit, we attempt to identify changes, not merely in the *amount* of different types of programming but also in their *proportions* in the overall output, and their *locations* in the schedules. In the following tables, figures in minutes represent the total number of minutes in our three sample weeks;[20] although some figures are expressed in terms of the numbers of discrete *programmes* when this measure is more relevant. Most tables refer to terrestrial television only, given that the data about cable and satellite channels are only relevant to 1996 (although when cable and satellite figures are factored in we have made this clear).

Quantity

Since the 1950s, champions of a dedicated children's service have feared that a combination of economic, political and institutional factors could result in the disappearance of children's television or, more realistically, a decline in the amount that is offered. Children's television has not only been subjected to competition between channels but also to internal pressures and constraints from more powerful departments serving other audiences – most obviously illustrated by the annual conflict over moving children's programmes during major sporting

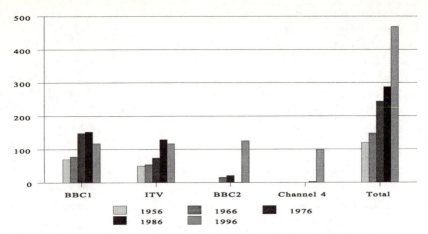

Table 1: Number of children's programmes on terrestrial television 1956–96

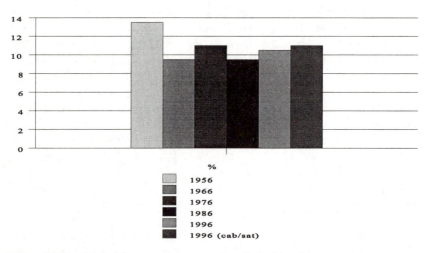

Table 2: Children's television as a percentage of total television time 1956–96

events such as Wimbledon. The first aim of our investigation, therefore, was to assess the amount of children's television provided in our sample years. More subtly, we were interested in how the amount varies between channels over time and at particular times of the year, such as school holidays; and particularly in how designated children's slots shift and develop over time.

The most noticeable trend is that the amount of children's television on terrestrial channels steadily increases with each decade until the huge leap between 1986 and 1996 (Table 1). Each year in our sample records an overall increase in both the number of children's programmes and the amount of minutes they take up in the three sample weeks. This increase becomes even more dramatic if we factor in cable and satellite, rising from 2,433 minutes of children's programmes in the three sample weeks in 1956 to 65,520 minutes in 1996.

To some extent, however, these global figures are somewhat misleading. Given that television output overall has increased substantially during this period, a

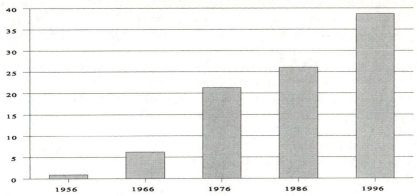

Table 3: Proportion of repeats on terrestrial children's television 1956–96

more telling figure is the *proportion* of children's television compared to total television output (Table 2). The picture here is quite different. While there have been fluctuations in the proportion of children's television over time, there is no clear pattern of increase or decline: the overall figure is relatively stable. Of course, the amount and proportion of material varies throughout the year, as well as between the decades. Of our sample weeks, April was deliberately chosen, as it coincided with the Easter school holidays. From 1976 onwards, the proportion of children's programmes rose during the April months, due to an increase in output during the Easter holidays.

These overall figures, whether in terms of volume or proportion, also disguise the amount of repeated programming that is shown. Particularly outside the traditional afternoon slot, the huge rise in the amount of available children's television is substantially made up of repeats. As Table 3 indicates, the proportion of repeats on terrestrial television has risen substantially. On cable and satellite channels, repeats are not specifically identified in the schedules, not least because programmes are so frequently repeated.

Scheduling

While there has been an overall increase in the amount of children's programming, we also need to identify where in the schedule this has occurred. For example, in our sample months in 1956 there is no special scheduling of children's programmes to coincide with their presumed availability to view during the school holidays; and there is only a limited recognition of this in 1966. The absence of children's programmes during the school holidays in early decades may be indicative of assumptions about the character and expectations of the child audience – namely, that they should not be 'wasting time' in the holidays watching television.[21] But it may also be explained by the lack of sufficient repeatable or bought-in material; and it needs to be seen alongside the overall absence of early morning/daytime television provision for *adults* during the 1950s and 1960s.

In fact, new time slots have rarely been created with the sole intention of providing for a child audience – BBC 2's scheduling of *Play School* being a rare exception. More commonly, children's programmes have been attached to existing schedules. For instance, *Watch with Mother* was initially broadcast alongside afternoon programmes aimed at women in the home, partly because broadcasters were not prepared to open the transmitters up solely for the pre-school audience. Likewise, children's programmes only began to appear in the early mornings on weekdays following the advent of breakfast television for adults in the mid-1980s.

Weekday afternoons

In practice, the afternoon slot is the linchpin of the children's television service on terrestrial channels. As we have argued, the provision of programming for children *at times when they are available to view* – and perhaps at the expense of programming for more commercially 'desirable' viewers – is a key indicator of broadcasters' commitment to the child audience. Table 4 indicates that there has been a steady increase in the overall *number* of children's programmes being shown on terrestrial television during the afternoon slot. On the other hand, it also reveals a gradual decrease in the overall *proportion* of children's programmes being shown in this slot, from roughly three-quarters of children's programmes in 1956 to just under half in 1996. This shows that in 1996 children's programmes are more widely dispersed throughout the schedule, but also that the afternoon slot itself has not been significantly eroded.

Year	% of children's programmes shown between 12 p.m. and 6 p.m.	number of children's programmes between 12 p.m. and 6 p.m.
1956	76	91
1966	75	111
1976	73	178
1986	68	194
1996	47	215

Table 4: Children's programmes on terrestrial television between midday and 6 p.m.* (percentage of total children's output and number of programmes) 1956–96

Breaking the figures down by channel, it becomes clear that, while BBC 2 and Channel Four have expanded their children's television output, ITV and BBC 1 have always been the main providers at the time when children are most likely to be watching. Furthermore, the increase in the amount of provision in 1996 is largely due to Channel Four and BBC 2 scheduling children's programmes during the afternoon: Channel Four was showing *Sesame Street* daily, as well as additional programmes during the school holidays, and BBC 2 also added a small number of pre-school programmes in the early afternoon. For both BBC 2 and Channel Four, the proportion of children's programmes screened during the 12–6 p.m. period represents a much lower percentage of their children's output: 17 per cent for BBC 2 and 27 per cent for Channel Four compared to 75 per cent for BBC 1 and 67 per cent for ITV.

*includes pre-school lunchtime and mid-afternoon programmes

In addition to measuring the number of minutes, it is important to consider the *length* of individual programmes and the *number* of discrete programmes being shown, as possible indicators of changes in the diversity of children's programmes. For instance, although Channel Four output during the 12–6 p.m. slot in 1996 comes close to matching ITV's in terms of time (roughly nineteen hours to ITV's twenty-two), the number of programmes it shows is around one-third of ITV's (twenty-seven to ITV's seventy-eight), suggesting that there is less diversity here. Although there have been differences between BBC 1 and ITV, the late-afternoon slot has traditionally consisted of a range of shorter-length programmes, designed to reach different subsections of the audience, defined primarily in terms of age. This was particularly the case during the 1970s and 1980s. BBC 1 reached a peak in 1976, with 117 separate programmes between 12 and 6 p.m. (including lunchtime pre-school programmes and afternoon repeats of *Play School*); while ITV peaked in 1986, showing 86. By the mid-1990s both BBC 1 and ITV begin to show a decrease in the number of programmes in these slots, although not in the overall time, which might suggest a decline in diversity. Shorter programmes like *Jackanory* and some British-made cartoons have disappeared, which could indicate that programme length is becoming standardised, as in the US (it is worth noting that cable and satellite schedules consist almost entirely of half-hour segments).

Weekends

By contrast, the weekend slot has changed considerably over the decades. As we have noted, there was no Saturday-morning children's television in the 1950s and 1960s: Saturday transmissions began around midday with sports programming, although there were children's programmes in the late afternoon. During the 1970s, both BBC and ITV began to show programmes on Saturday morning, mainly in the form of repeats or imported programmes. The success of ITV's *Tiswas* and the BBC's *Multi-Coloured Swap Shop* and its successors encouraged the breakfast TV companies TV-AM and then GMTV to schedule animation and magazine-style programmes at an earlier hour, aimed at younger children. As Table 5 demonstrates, the amount of Saturday-morning programming has increased for all channels: it rose from one-fifth of overall children's output in 1976 to more than one-third in 1996. This makes for an interesting comparison with the US, where the 'kid-vid ghetto' of Saturday morning has historically been the main window for children's programming; but given the continuing strength of the weekday afternoon slot, it would be misleading to see this as evidence of Americanisation.

Similarly, there were no children's programmes scheduled on Sunday mornings until the 1970s. Programmes began to appear occasionally during that decade, usually repeated programmes for pre-schoolers such as *Chigley*. Further into the 1980s, ITV began to schedule magazine programmes aimed at a younger child audience, such as *WAC Special*; and this has continued into the 1990s with, for example, *Disney Club*. Sunday programmes on ITV and BBC 1 remained limited because of the commitment to religious and current affairs broadcasting during the morning slots. In 1994, Channel Four and BBC 2, who previously had shown no weekend programmes for children, began to fill Sunday-morning schedules

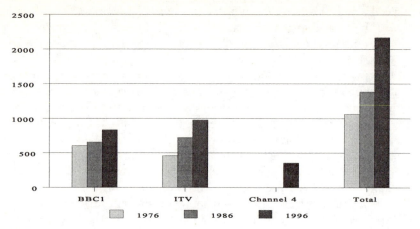

Table 5: Amount (minutes) of Saturday-morning children's programmes by channel 1976–96

with children's programmes. This partly accounts for the considerable increases in the amount of programmes being shown on these channels, representing nearly a quarter of BBC 2's and Channel Four's overall output for children. These increases are largely accounted for by imported animation and sitcoms, such as *Street Sharks* or *Sister Sister* (Channel Four), and repeated weekday schedules or vintage 'classics', such as *Grange Hill* (BBC 2) – although, as we have noted, not all the programmes that appear in these slots are necessarily reruns or imports. As Table 6 demonstrates, the growth of Sunday-morning television has been even more dramatic than the growth of Saturday-morning programming – increasing from just over 1 per cent of overall children's television output in 1976 to over 14 per cent by 1996.

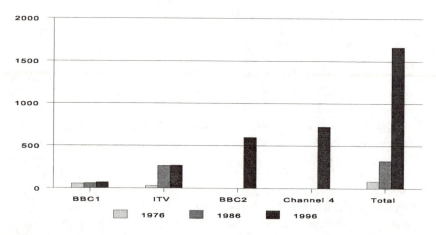

Table 6: Amount (minutes) of Sunday-morning children's programmes by channel 1976–96

Weekday mornings

As we have noted, another key area of expansion in children's programming has been in weekday mornings, particularly during school holidays. No programmes were shown during the mornings in 1956. In 1966, a small number of programmes appear during the morning slot, such as *Watch with Mother* and *Play School*, aimed at the pre-school audience: these account for 14 per cent of the total children's output, although there were no additional programmes aimed at children during school holidays. By the time we reach 1996, programmes scheduled during weekday mornings had increased to 17 per cent of total output, although these were almost wholly concentrated in school holidays. Between 1986 and 1996, these programmes were also steadily moved across from the major channels to the minority channels.

Similarly, children's programmes shown at breakfast time (i.e. prior to 9 a.m.) did not feature in the schedules until 1986, where they accounted for less than 3 per cent of total children's output. These programmes largely consisted of cartoons shown on ITV during the school holidays. By 1996 the figure had risen to 10 per cent of output. Again, this was largely accounted for by school holidays, but also by the BBC's practice of repeating parts of the previous afternoon's programmes on BBC 2 during weekday breakfast time.

Consequences of expansion

As we have implied, therefore, arguments about the expansion of children's television and the perceived decline in quality or diversity have to take into account the expansion of television generally. Most of the expansion has occurred by moving into new slots in the early mornings or at weekends. These new children's slots have emerged on the back of a general increase in television hours, and the discovery that there are significant numbers of children available to view at times when other, more valuable audiences are not. Yet in many respects, the programming here is similar to adult programming in the daytime schedules: because of limited budgets, it is bound to be inexpensive, which in practice means that much of it is imported or repeated. The *proportion* of this kind of programming has thus inevitably increased in relation to the overall provision for children; although there is little indication of a decline in the *numbers* of new original programmes being screened.

As such, we would argue that these developments cannot be seen as a deliberate attempt to marginalise the child audience by attempting to direct it into obscure time slots, or fobbing it off with poor-quality programming. At least in terms of quantity, there has been a continuing commitment to 'children's prime time' in the late afternoons; although the BBC's record here is better than that of ITV. Nevertheless, the dispersal of children's programmes (and the advertising revenue that accompanies them) may put pressure on the maintenance of the dedicated children's afternoon schedule; and it is this slot that has always been seen as crucial to the provision of a children's television service. As daytime television becomes more competitive, the temptation is to target the stay-at-home audience with inexpensive 'lifestyle programming'. Whether children will continue to be served by terrestrial channels at times when they are mainly available to view will depend upon how *valuable* they are perceived to be, both

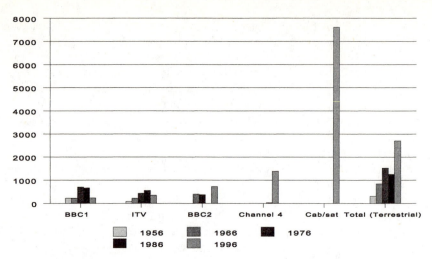

8000				
7000				
6000				
5000				
4000				
3000				
2000				
1000				
0				

BBC1   ITV   BBC2   Channel 4   Cab/sat   Total (Terrestrial)

1956   1966   1976
1986   1996

Table 7: Amount (minutes) of pre-school programmes by channel 1956–96

commercially (in terms of advertising and merchandising) and symbolically (in terms of their privileged status within the public service remit).

Pre-school programmes

This issue is most acute in relation to particular subsections of the audience, most obviously pre-school children. Pre-school programming is by definition only going to appeal to a small audience; and the viewers that it serves are unable to defend their programmes (in contrast to more powerful audiences such as Radio 4 listeners). In terms of the proportion of pre-school output, the 1970s and 1980s appear to be the 'golden age' for pre-school programmes on the two main terrestrial channels (see Table 7). BBC 1 and ITV had the highest number of minutes during these decades, and pre-school programmes made up a larger proportion of their overall output (around one-fifth). By 1996, these figures had declined considerably, largely in response to the greater competition for daytime adult audiences: ITV, for example, has dropped its lunchtime slot, and no longer shows pre-school programmes in the mornings or during the school holidays.

In fact, however, the scheduling of such programmes has largely shifted to the minority channels. As Table 7 shows, the overall output of pre-school programmes on terrestrial channels has actually risen significantly in the past decade, making up nearly a quarter of all children's programmes. Arguably, ITV's decline is compensated for by Channel Four's output, which accounts for 42 per cent of its total children's programming. On the other hand, a sizeable chunk of this is comprised of imports of *Sesame Street*, which is shown daily.[22] Similarly, a high proportion of BBC 2's increased pre-school output is made up of repeated material – although again, this high level of repeats has always been characteristic of pre-school television.[23] More recently, the BBC has made a major new investment in the form of *Teletubbies*, perhaps the first British programme directed at the younger end of this age group (albeit one which enjoys a substantial cross-over 'cult' audience among much older viewers); while, as our table shows, cable and satellite channels have also begun to schedule substantial numbers of pre-school programmes. In addition, over the past ten years, pre-schoolers have become one of the most significant target markets for sell-through video; although this is, by definition, not free-to-air, many of the most popular tapes with this age group are compilations of programmes that have already been aired on terrestrial television.

Ultimately, the notion that increased competition would impact most nega-tively on more specialised subsections of the audience has proven to be distinctly questionable, at least in this case. Interestingly, the industry ratings system (as operated by BARB) only begins with four-year-olds; and despite the fact that it is this system that is used for establishing advertising rates, this does not appear to have resulted in an overwhelming neglect of this age group. Of course, it is this age group that is still most likely to be 'watching with mother' (or, more rarely, father) – and this may account for some of its continuing commercial and symbolic value for broadcasters. Yet despite their status as a minority audience, pre-schoolers have clearly been 'discovered' in recent years as a very significant market in their own right.

Imported programming

Of course, debates about the future of children's television have not only focused on questions of quantity and scheduling. Indeed, in many respects, it is the issue of 'quality' that has been the central concern here. As we have noted, 'quality' is often inadequately defined; yet in the case of children's television, several key issues consistently recur in the debate. The first of these is to do with the danger of 'Americanisation'.

On one level, this concern is nothing new.[24] As we have noted, debates about children's television in the 1950s were just as preoccupied with the encroachment of US programmes as those taking place in the 1990s. During the 1950s, ITV relied on imports such as *Roy Rogers* and *Hopalong Cassidy* to win over audiences from the BBC; and it also produced the successful *Robin Hood*, which was partly co-financed by, and aimed at, the US market. The BBC Children's Department was initially resistant to US imports, and looked to European productions; but by the late 1950s it was increasingly using US programmes to compete with ITV. As this suggests, there is often an implicit distinction here between 'good' imports – Czechoslovakian folk tales, perhaps – and 'bad' imports – principally in the form of US cartoons. Nevertheless, as Table 8 demonstrates, the majority of imported children's programmes on British screens have always derived from the US.

In fact, the amount and proportion of imports fluctuate over time. For example, as a percentage of children's television output, imports steadily rise up to 1976, but then decline steeply in 1986. However, by 1996, imported US material has risen again sharply and accounts for just over 40 per cent of the overall out-put of terrestrial children's television (Table 9). It should also be noted that these figures are likely to be underestimates, as they do not account for the significant proportion of US material that is inserted into British magazine programmes,

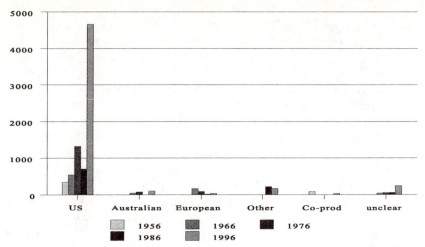

	1956		1966		1976
	1986		1996		

Table 8: Amount (minutes) of imported programming by country of origin 1956–96

such as *Disney Club* or *Live and Kicking* (which at the time of writing incorporates two successful Nickelodeon productions, the cartoon *Rugrats* and the sitcom *Keenan and Kel*).[25]

In addition, the proportion of imported programming varies significantly between channels. It is hardly surprising to discover that the proportion of imported material on the new cable and satellite channels is staggeringly high, since these stations are mostly US-owned (see Table 10). For example, on the Cartoon Network, only ten discrete programme slots out of a total of 253 were non-US productions; and all of these are accounted for by only one programme, *Thomas the Tank Engine*. The only exception to this is TCC, which was the only dedicated children's channel not owned by a big US media giant with access to a library of rights: its schedules had a significantly higher percentage of British and Australian programmes.

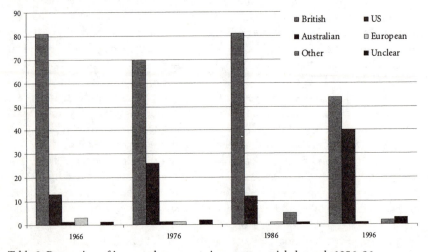

Table 9: Proportion of imported programming on terrestrial channels 1956–96

100

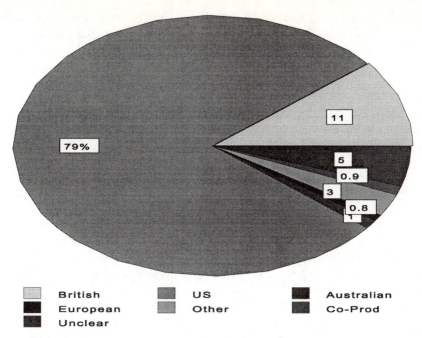

British		US		Australian	
European		Other		Co-Prod	
Unclear					

Table 10: Proportion of imported programming on cable and satellite channels 1996

The large overall increase in the amount of imported programming that takes place on terrestrial television between 1986 and 1996 is also less dramatic when broken down channel by channel, particularly when comparing the weekday afternoon slot. For instance, BBC 1's output fluctuates over the decades, but British-made programmes continue to dominate this part of the schedule. It is notable that British-made programmes register their lowest percentage during the 1960s, but still make up over two-thirds of the children's output. Although European programmes are somewhat higher during the 1960s, they still represent a nominal proportion of programmes. While US imports have steadily risen, they continue to make up only around one-fifth of all programme output in this slot. In addition, programmes shown at these times rarely exceed twenty-five minutes in length, so it is unlikely that US programmes are 'hidden', as in the case of the cartoons that are incorporated within Saturday-morning magazine programmes.

Thus, although there has been a rise in US imports, the afternoon slots continue to be dominated by British programmes. In fact, the rise in US imports is explained largely by Channel Four's entry into the children's market, particularly during the school holidays, and to a lesser extent by the expansion of programmes outside the 'core' hours – such as early Saturday and Sunday mornings. For instance, out of the ninety-nine programmes shown on Channel Four during our sample weeks, seventy-five of them (almost two-thirds) were imported. Similarly, although Channel Four has no comparable late-afternoon slot, its afternoon output of children's programmes is composed of 80 per cent US material – largely accounted for by *Sesame Street*. On the other hand, it is interesting to note that international co-productions still represent only a tiny proportion of children's output: As far as we could tell, ITV and BBC 1 clocked up just one each over the three sample weeks in 1996.

Diversity

Thus far, we have identified a huge increase in the amount of children's television, and a growing reliance on imported programmes, at least in some areas of the schedule. The next obvious question would seem to be: what kinds of programmes are they? Has the expansion been limited to particular types of programming at the expense of more demanding – or simply more costly – material? As we have noted, diversity is a key tenet of public service; and the commitment to a 'mixed menu' of children's programmes is often seen as a central aspect of the 'Great Tradition'. In the case of children's television, the economic logic would appear to dictate a move away from factual programmes and shorter drama series towards animation – in other words, towards programmes which are both cheap to buy in and (if home-produced) easier to market overseas.

There are significant methodological difficulties in attempting to assess diversity in broadcasting. The BSC reports approach this primarily in terms of genre, although in fact they use different systems of categorisation. As we have argued, it is necessary to differentiate here between *genre, format* and *content,* however crude such categories may be. Animation, for example, is not a genre but a format (or a mode of representation); and it is important to distinguish between, say, action-adventure animation (*Spiderman*) and more socially realist animation (*Hey Arnold!*). Likewise, in the case of non-fiction programming, it is vital to make distinctions in terms of format – for example, between magazine programmes, documentaries and quiz shows – and in terms of content. In this section, we present a selection of our findings on these issues.

Fiction and non-fiction

First, can we detect any shifts in the proportion of fiction and non-fiction programmes over the years? We divided programmes into three broad categories: fiction (including drama, animation and storytelling); non-fiction (including informational magazine programmes, news and documentaries); and 'entertainment magazines' (covering programmes that include both fiction and non-fiction elements – primarily Saturday-morning shows such as the BBC's *Multi-Coloured Swap Shop* and its successors). On occasions, such a division may appear arbitrary: for instance, the difference between *Blue Peter* (non-fiction magazine) and *Live and Kicking* (entertainment magazine) may be as much to do with the mode of address and the visual style of the programme as its content. Indeed, the differences here may be reducing with time, reflecting a more general blurring of the boundaries between 'education' and 'entertainment'.[26]

As Table 11 shows, fiction has always dominated the schedules on every channel. While entertainment magazines have become a more significant category, the proportion of non-fiction has not in fact significantly declined. In contrast, as Table 12 shows, cable and satellite schedules are overwhelmingly fiction-based.

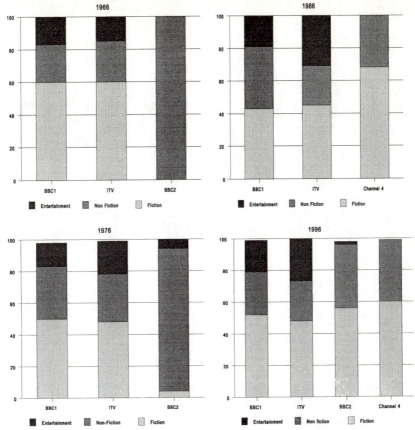

Table 11: Programme type by channel (proportion of overall children's programmes) on terrestrial television 1966–96

Format

Within these larger categories of programme type, we were also interested in the presentational formats of children's programmes. Particular forms of address inevitably embody assumptions about the audience that change over time. For example, the direct-to-camera storytelling of *Jackanory*, which began on BBC 1 in 1967, was felt at that time to be particularly appropriate for the cognitive and emotional abilities of the child audience.[27] When the programme was finally scrapped in 1996, it was argued that this storytelling mode was out of keeping with the much more visual style of television fiction in the 1990s. Of course, there are forms of address that are seen as particularly appropriate for children, as compared with adults – puppets, for instance – although the balance between these forms shifts across time. (Here again, a statistical analysis gives us only a limited insight into such changes, and would need to be supplemented by a more qualitative approach.)

For the purposes of this analysis, our categories of format were: animation, live-action drama (e.g. *The Famous Five, Grange Hill*), documentary (e.g. *The Lowdown*), direct human presentation (e.g. *Blue Peter, How?*) and puppets (e.g.

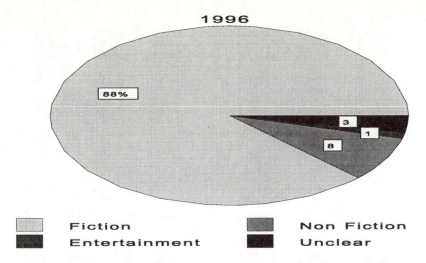

1996

88%

3
1
8

| Fiction | Non Fiction |
| Entertainment | Unclear |

Table 12: Programme type (proportion of overall output) on children's cable/satellite channels 1996

Pinky and Perky). We also included two mixed categories: humans and puppets (e.g. *Rainbow*) and humans and animation (e.g. *Rolf Harris's Cartoon Time*). As Table 13 shows, the proportions of these different formats are quite uneven over time. Nevertheless, there is a steady increase in animation: the figure for 1996 is almost double that for twenty years previously. This overall pattern is replicated in the crucial afternoon mini-schedule on ITV and BBC 1, with animation making up 37 per cent of BBC 1's afternoon schedule in 1996, up from 26 per cent in 1976. On ITV the rise is even sharper, with animation jumping to 37 per cent from only 20 per cent in 1986. However, these rises seem to be at the expense of direct human presentation programmes, rather than of drama, which actually increases

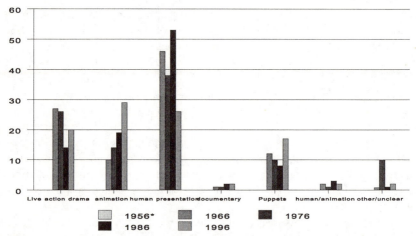

| | 1956* | 1966 | 1976 |
| 1986 | 1996 | |

Table 13: Proportion of children's output on terrestrial television by presentation format 1956–96

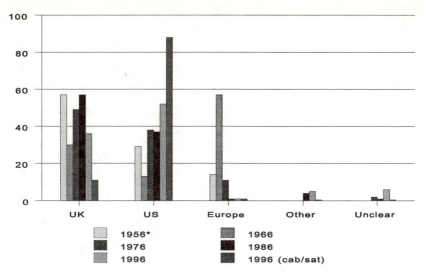

Table 14: Proportion of animated programmes by country of origin 1956–96

on both channels between 1986 and 1996. This would support the earlier finding about the overall dominance of fiction programmes.

Animation

As we have noted, animation is in many ways a demonised format that is implicitly associated with 'Americanisation' and the decline of the public service tradition. During the 1950s and 1960s, animation made up a much smaller proportion of children's output; and while some of this was bought in (for example, Hanna-Barbera cartoons), it also consisted of home-produced pre-school programmes such as *Captain Pugwash* or *Chigley*. It is likely that the comparatively low figure at this point was as much to do with the lack of available material, and its relatively unsophisticated nature, as any resistance to animation *per se*. From 1976 onwards, the number of animation programmes imported from the US begins to rise, to such an extent that by 1996 they represent over half of all animated output (see Table 14). This rise is clearly at the expense of British and European animation; and it is particularly explained by the decline in pre-school output (which accounts for a significant proportion of British animation). Nevertheless, at least in terms of the number of programmes, British animation continues to make up over one-third of animated output on terrestrial television. By contrast, cable and satellite channels (the last column in Table 14) are dominated by US cartoons. This is unsurprising, given that most of these channels are US-owned and have a large library of animation on which to draw. On the other hand, one could argue that this volume of output enables cable and satellite channels to provide animation programmes for a wider range of audiences in terms of age and taste; whereas British animation has historically tended to concentrate on the very young.

As we have indicated, 'animation' is a relatively crude category, which encompasses a range of differences in technique, subject matter, length and style:

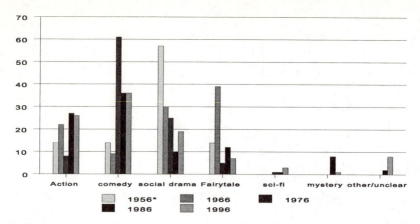

	1956*		1966		1976		
	1986		1996				

Table 15: Content of animation as proportion of all animation programmes (terrestrial only) 1956–96

Postman Pat is obviously very different from *Biker Mice from Mars* or *Rugrats*, although all three are animated. For this reason, we chose to analyse programme format and 'content' separately. Inevitably, the categories we used proved to be quite crude and somewhat arbitrary: many animated programmes could well be categorised as 'crime' and/or 'mystery' and/or 'comedy' (*Scooby Doo*, for example). Nevertheless, this analysis enabled us to focus on the diversity *within* contemporary animation, rather than implicitly defining it as an homogeneous category (see Table 15). Our key finding is that the overall increase in the amount of animation has been matched by an increase in the *range of content* that animation attempts to portray.

Despite the moral panics about violence and animation, and the accusation that they are essentially a 'boys' genre', action-adventure cartoons have always made up a minority of overall output, reaching around a quarter during the 1980s and 1990s. In fact, from the 1970s onwards, comedy appears to be the dominant focus of cartoons, accounting for over one-third of output. What we have called 'social drama' cartoons have actually increased between the 1980s and 1990s, perhaps signifying a levelling off of action-adventure and comedy: cartoons dealing with realistic situations and characters of the kind usually associated with live-action drama account for some of the most successful animated series of the 1990s, such as *Rugrats, Doug* and *Hey Arnold!* (and one can point to the emergence of similar forms of animation for general or adult audiences, with programmes like *The Simpsons, King of the Hill* and *Dr Katz*).

Drama

If animation has often been demonised in debates about children's television, live-action drama clearly occupies a key place in the 'Great Tradition'. As we have noted, the significance of drama rests on assumptions both about representation and the role of storytelling: it is seen as an important way of reflecting children's everyday lives and concerns, and as a means of developing their imagination. Again, there would appear to be an inexorable economic logic here: the cost of live-action drama is high in comparison to other programmes, and in the current climate of intense competition there is concern that drama production is being squeezed – particularly less economical forms such as one-off dramas or short-run series with no obvious international appeal.

As Table 16 shows, the narrative of inevitable decline is an oversimplification. The overall amount of children's drama on terrestrial channels has in fact increased, particularly between the 1980s and 1990s. However, as a proportion of overall output, drama has somewhat declined, although it shows a nominal increase in 1996; and while the amount of drama has increased very significantly during the 1990s, over two-thirds of the programmes are now repeats. In other words, the amount of 'new' drama programmes between the 1980s and 1990s has remained at more or less the same level (595 minutes as compared with 570 minutes of non-repeated material), despite the arrival of Channel Four.

Like animation, 'drama' is a misleadingly inclusive category. One key distinction here is in terms of the *source* of drama. As we have noted, the 'classic' literary adaptation has been seen as a staple of the 'Great Tradition' in children's television: such programmes have been advocated both as a way of introducing children to the literary heritage and (more instrumentally) as a means of encouraging them to read books.[28] Such adaptations are almost invariably 'costume dramas', and consist of short-run, self-contained series; and as such, they can prove more expensive than contemporary drama such as long-running series like *Grange Hill* which permit significant economies of scale. Here again, economic logic might appear to dictate that this category of programme would be squeezed from the schedule.

In our analysis, we therefore coded fictional programmes in terms of their source – original, literary, myth/legend and other media (such as films or comics). Here again, such distinctions can be misleading. For instance, while some literary adaptations are taken from 'classic' children's literature – such as *The Secret Garden* or *The Prince and the Pauper* – others derive from contemporary fiction, as in the case of *The Demon Headmaster*. Likewise, original drama can cover anything from one-off plays, such as those included in ITV's *Dramarama*, to long-running serials like *Grange Hill* or series such as *Flipper*. Similarly, dramas based on myths and legends or adapted from other media sources, such as films and comics, are often very loosely based on the original characters, as in the case of *Robin Hood*.

As Table 17 shows, there has been a steady rise in 'original' material, which consistently dominates drama programmes. During the 1950s, BBC children's drama relied heavily on literary adaptations from a range of sources, including novels such as *Jane Eyre* and *The Silver Sword*. Conversely, ITV dramas at the time were often long-running action-adventure formats, loosely based on popular heroes, such as *Roy Rogers*. Interestingly, however, literary adaptations were at their highest during the 1960s – a period often associated (at least in 'adult' television) with the shift away from the 'classics' towards original social realism typified by programmes such as *Z Cars* and *The Wednesday Play*. Despite a decrease in literary adaptations over the last decade, the lowest point actually occurred in the 1970s.

This emphasis on the value of literary adaptations is often accompanied by an unease about the origin of contemporary children's drama. As we have indicated,

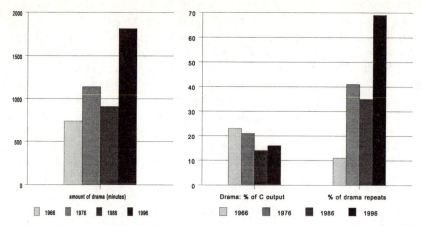

Table 16: Children's drama on terrestrial channels by amount (minutes), proportion of children's output and proportion of repeats 1966–96

the impact of US material has been a subject of concern since the advent of ITV in the 1950s; and imported drama in particular has become associated with a deregulated, commercial system. However, as Table 18 shows, the ratio of UK to US drama in the 1950s is very similar to that in the 1990s. During the 1960s, the amount of both UK and US drama decreases, but it still makes up three-quarters of the total. The decline in UK material at this point is unsurprising, given that responsibility for drama was taken away from the Children's Department; although the deficit was made up largely from sources other than the US.

While there is a higher number of US than UK programmes in 1976 and 1996, this is the result of more imported US drama being shown during April – the

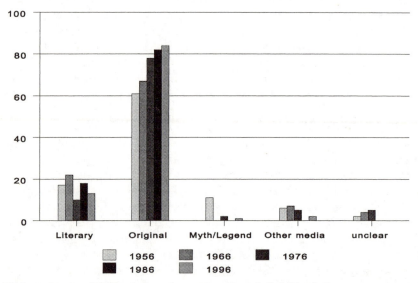

Table 17: Source of children's drama as a proportion of all children's drama programmes (terrestrial only) 1956–96

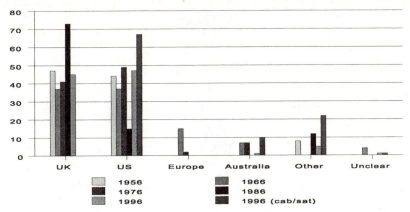

	1956		1966
	1976		1986
	1996		1996 (cab/sat)

Table 18: Country of origin of drama as a proportion of children's drama programmes 1956–96

school holidays. For example, in 1996, Channel Four's drama output shoots up from an average of five specific children's drama programmes in January and October to twenty-two in April – twenty-one of which are US imports. Without the addition of Channel Four holiday programmes, drama output would consist of a much higher proportion of British programmes (around 60 per cent UK to 29 per cent US). Again, this would indicate that the increase in imports has occurred largely outside of 'prime-time' children's television.

More strikingly, the cable and satellite children's channels show no British-made drama whatsoever, although TCC occasionally did so in the past. Non-terrestrial channels are dominated by US material, with some additional Canadian and Australian dramas. This absence of British-made drama is partly a matter of cost: to date, these channels commission only a small percentage of their own programmes from domestic producers.

Non-fiction

Finally, let us consider non-fictional programmes, another key area of children's television that has recently been viewed as under threat. Here again, we divided non-fictional programmes by presentational format (as described above), 'genre' and content. In terms of genre, our categories included: quiz/game shows, such as *Run the Risk* and *Screen Test*; news programmes, such as *Children's Newsreel* and *Newsround*; documentaries, such as *Treasure Houses* and *The Lowdown*; and magazine programmes, such as *Animal Magic, The Book Tower* and *Blue Peter* (this category excluded entertainment magazine programmes).

As Table 19 indicates, there has been very little change in the balance between these categories across the decades.[29] The 1950s tended to be a more experimental period in terms of presentation, typified by a number of 'one-off' or short-term projects, often in the form of film material shown by BBC 1; while the 1960s were notable for their lack of variety, since no specific news or documentary programmes were transmitted at this time. From the 1970s onwards, as the schedules became more predictable, these categories became more routine and stable. The most significant feature here, however, is the dominance of the magazine format

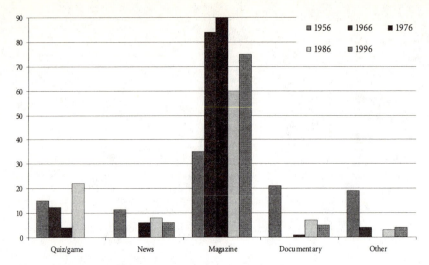

Table 19: Non-fiction format as a proportion of overall children's non-fiction output (terrestrial only) 1956–96

as a means of presenting non-fiction material. The magazine format is clearly used as a way of covering several informational or educational topics, and hence including viewers with the widest possible range of interests. At the same time, it also offers a way of striking the balance between education and entertainment. Magazines tend to be informal and chatty; and they are able to jump between topics, thus perhaps reflecting dominant assumptions both about children's limited attention span and their restless appetite for information.

We also examined non-fiction programmes in terms of their content. As with fiction, the findings here are less robust, as programme content is open to considerable interpretation. In addition, the schedules of the three sample weeks may be less than representative, given that non-fiction programmes tend to be

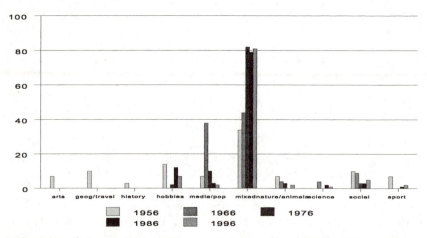

Table 20: Non-fiction content on BBC 1 as a proportion of overall non-fiction output 1956–96

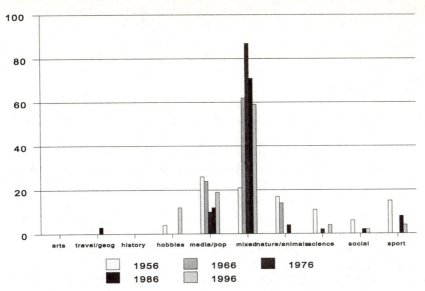

Table 21: Non-fiction content on ITV as a proportion of overall non-fiction output 1956–96

transmitted in shorter runs. However, Tables 20 and 21 do indicate some general changes throughout the decades on BBC 1 and ITV. In the case of the BBC, 1956 exhibits the widest range of material, and this is fairly evenly distributed through-out most of the categories. As we have explained above, this reflects the Children's Department policy, which was more inclined towards discrete 'one-offs' or short series, such as *Steps in Ballet*. However, by the mid-1950s, the Department had also established an increasing number of longer-running magazine series such as *Whirlygig* and *All Your Own*, so that mixed material accounted for around one-third of non-fiction output. By the 1960s, the range has shrunk. Entertainment-based variety magazines, such as *Crackerjack* and *Pinky and Perky*, were more predominant – and were more likely to feature other media, such as pop music. In addition, there were more magazine programmes, most notably *Blue Peter*, that included subjects that might otherwise have been covered by discrete pro-grammes. The balance of non-fiction programmes since the 1970s appears relatively stable. The proportion of programmes with media-based subject mat-ter declines, but is no doubt swallowed up by the huge growth of mixed non-fiction magazine programmes (these figures also include the range of Saturday-morning entertainment magazines, such as *Live and Kicking*, and *Number 73*).

ITV's output is more erratic. As with BBC 1, output in the 1950s covers a wider range than the 1960s and 1970s, where non-fiction output is limited to only three categories. ITV has tended to include other media much more in its children's output, particularly pop music.

Despite these differences, some categories remain fairly consistent across the decades, assuming a kind of timeless status as 'children's issues'. As in the 1950s, being interested in animals, hobbies and pop music is still assumed to be an inherent characteristic of childhood in the 1990s – thus reflecting a distinct set of assumptions about children's relationship with the social and natural world.[30]

Keeping accounts

The word 'audit' suggests some kind of keeping of account. Indeed, the original purpose of the 1992 BSC report was to provide a 'benchmark' for children's programming on mainstream terrestrial television, so that any shift or decline in output could be highlighted and (theoretically) rectified. While such benchmarks are undoubtedly necessary, the flaw in this kind of endeavour is that the moment when auditing begins inevitably becomes the point against which all future changes are measured. By contrast, the wider historical perspective we have adopted here illustrates the impossibility of positing some kind of timeless 'ideal'. As we have indicated, the whole process of auditing and comparing provision across time is highly problematic. Yet the findings of our research suggest that the pattern of change across the decades has been very uneven: it has not simply been a case of growth followed by relative decline.

The most striking finding here – which is supported by the BSC reports – is that there has been a huge increase in the *amount* of children's programming over the decades. This stands in stark contrast to the claims of campaigners who have argued that children's television is at risk of disappearing as we move towards a multi-channel, more commercial system. However, the gradual deregulation of television has transparently not led to the disappearance of dedicated children's programming, either in Britain or the US – with which it is often (in our view sometimes quite misleadingly) compared.

Of course, this development needs to be seen as a function of the steady increase in broadcasting hours, and the overall move from scarcity to abundance, both on terrestrial channels and (of course) on cable and satellite. There is more children's television on terrestrial channels now than there has ever been; although the *proportion* of children's television has in fact not increased significantly relative to television as a whole. Furthermore, most of this increase has occurred in the margins of the schedules, on new channels and at new times when children were not previously catered for.

Economic logic would seem to dictate that this increase in programming will lead to a decline in its diversity and quality. Overall budgets for children's programmes have not grown in line with the increasing number of hours that must now be filled; and hence it is inevitable that broadcasters will rely on inexpensive programmes (such as US imports) and repeats. From this perspective, one would also predict that less popular areas of children's programming (in terms of ratings) – such as factual or pre-school programmes – would be increasingly threatened.

However, our analysis suggests that some important qualifications should be made here. The *proportion* of imported programmes and of repeats has indeed risen significantly; but much of the increase has taken place in these new or marginal slots in the schedule. Some forms of programming are certainly in limited supply. More in-depth, specialist factual material (in the form of documentaries, for example) is conspicuously absent from the schedules – although, to be fair, it always has been. Likewise, there is a striking lack of material from non-English-speaking countries, despite the fact that many are now producing innovative and challenging films and television programmes for children[31] – although, as we have shown, such material has never been exactly abundant on British screens. Nevertheless, we have found little evidence of any dramatic *erosion* of provision in any of these apparently 'threatened' areas across the decades we have studied, or specifically in more recent years. There is little evidence that the balance of programming in the crucial 'prime-time' late-afternoon slot – which coincides with children's peak availability to view – has shifted significantly. The proportion of animation in these slots has increased, certainly, but so has the overall amount of children's drama; while the proportion of non-fiction has remained fairly constant.[32]

In attempting to identify changes in the diversity and quality of children's programmes, however, we have also tried to look beyond the broad (and somewhat crude) categories which are typically employed. Obviously, this can be no substitute for the detailed qualitative analysis that is undoubtedly necessary; and this will be a later outcome of our research.[33] Yet even by adding in crude statistical measures of content and presentational format, we have shown that the pattern of change is more complex. 'Animation' or 'drama' cannot meaningfully be seen as singular categories, let alone as inherently possessing or lacking in 'quality'.

It is here that the limitations of 'benchmarking' become particularly apparent: the assumption that programme categories can be defined and fixed at a particular point in history, and that any subsequent change can be measured relative to them, is effectively to ignore much of the nature of that change itself. In this way, the narrative of inevitable decline seems to be written into the process of auditing changes in television programming. As our analysis has begun to suggest, there have undoubtedly been changes, not just in the balance between programme categories but also in the categories themselves. The four decades we have considered have seen significant shifts in dominant modes of storytelling, in the characteristic formats and modes of address of children's television and in the relationship between (and indeed the definition of) 'education' and 'entertainment'. To judge these changes solely in terms of past categories, as though such categories were merely timeless, is to misread the significance of what is taking place.

Furthermore, these changes cannot be seen in isolation from broader developments, both in dominant conceptions of childhood and in the material realities of children's lives. 'Children' are not a constant in this equation, any more than 'television' is. As we have suggested, changes in the scheduling of children's programmes – as well as being defined by changes in broadcasting more generally – reflect shifts in the ways in which the child audience is imagined and defined. On one level, this is simply about the organisation of children's time: the introduction of programmes for children in the school holidays or on weekday mornings, for instance, was symptomatic of new ways of thinking about children's availability to view. Yet it also reflects broader shifts in the ways in which children are addressed. The growth of 'edu-tainment' formats – most obviously magazine programmes, on both sides of this (perhaps illusory) divide – marked a conscious attempt to address children more informally and to move away from a didactic, paternalistic approach. More recently, the increasing importance of animation in the schedules has resulted in cartoons that seek to represent and engage with children's everyday concerns about family or school, rather than simply providing superhero adventures or slapstick comedy. While specialist non-fiction programmes are clearly in decline, this may in part reflect a broadening of ideas about how to approach 'educative' programming: so, rather than imparting information about health or careers advice in a documentary, it will be assimilated into an entertainment magazine programme or appear in fictional form in a children's soap like *Byker Grove*. Likewise, the expansion of children's scheduling has, in some cases, resulted in new types of programming such as consumer programmes or access shows. All these developments represent responses to perceived changes in 'childhood' itself, and in the boundaries between child and adult audiences; but they clearly cannot be seen simply as an abandonment or dilution of some 'Great Tradition'.

In attempting to resist the pull of this compelling narrative of cultural decline, it has not been our intention simply to suggest that all is well. With growing competition from cable and satellite providers, it is vital that the public service responsibilities of terrestrial channels should be supported and protected, particularly in respect of domestic production and the late-afternoon 'prime-time' slot. Nevertheless, television itself is changing so dramatically that these kinds of criteria may prove simply irrelevant. As the number of channels expands, a similar amount of product is being spread ever more thinly across an ever-broadening schedule. All these television hours have to be filled with something – and in the case of children's cable and satellite channels, their ten hours a day are filled by endlessly repeating the core schedule, so that seventy hours of programming are effectively made up of only twenty or thirty actual programmes. In a multi-channel environment, the whole concept of a repeat becomes almost meaningless: the economics dictate that nothing can only be shown once. In the process, the audience is beginning to fragment: while broadcast hours are increasing, children's overall viewing of television is in decline, which can only mean smaller audiences for any single broadcast. Although programmes transmitted during 'prime time' on the terrestrial channels continue to gain the highest ratings for children's television, these very programmes are repeated at different times of the day and on different channels, to the point where the idea of 'prime time' may also have become somewhat notional. Meanwhile, the globalisation of the media industries and the rise of cross-national media brands mean that the geographical origin of a programme may be increasingly impossible to identify, or at least for ordinary viewers to recognise. In the longer term, perhaps, many of the working concepts that have informed our analysis here – and the studies that have preceded it – will be regarded as virtually redundant.

Comparing the schedules for 1956 with those for 1996 suggests that there has been a dramatic shift in what 'watching television' is seen to mean, and in how the child audience in particular is defined and addressed. The secure, ring-fenced space marked out in 1956 has given way to the seemingly open, borderless

114

landscape of 1996. The garden, we might say, has been replaced by open country-side. On the face of it, it is hard to imagine how children will be able to find or identify 'their' space amid the bewildering proliferation of options now becoming available with digital television. Nevertheless, it is crucial to distinguish between distribution and reception. Television may have changed significantly, but it is more debatable whether most children's everyday routines have structurally altered since the 1950s: they are still legally obligated to attend school, and they are still primarily dependent on parents or other adults. They may be going to bed a little later,[34] and some of them may have access to a much wider range of technological options,[35] but whether they now watch television in radically different ways remains open to question. As we shall indicate in the next chapter, such uncertainties about the audience pose significant problems for the industry itself.

Notes

1 These months were selected in order to include one school holiday, during which the schedules are typically different from those during term time.
2 Blumler (1992); Davies and Corbett (1997).
3 The presentation of the data in the more recent BSC report is significantly more detailed than space will permit here. This report also uses BARB (Broadcasters' Audience Research Bureau) data, which were not available to us. On the other hand, we have also analysed programme formats, and correlated these data with a more detailed classification of content and country of origin, as well as considering these separately.
4 See Abrams (1956). This issue is discussed in more detail in Chapter Four.
5 The analysis was conducted by Chris Mottershead, who provides a useful discussion of the methodological difficulties: Blumler (1992), pp. 47–67.
6 For example, the category 'animation' is much more inclusive in the 1997 report than in the 1992 report, which makes it highly misleading to claim that the proportion of animation has risen between 1981 (analysed in the first report) and 1997 (analysed in the second): see Davies and Corbett (1997), p. 252. As we saw in the Introduction, it was this 'finding' that also provided the main focus for much of the press coverage.
7 Buckingham (1993), Chapter Six.
8 We would accept that these schedules are not always wholly reliable, for example in comparison with BARB data. In particular, the timings of programmes are only approximate, and do not account for advertising breaks, continuity links, and so forth.
9 Scannell (1996), p. 150.
10 As we have indicated (Chapter One), this explicit definition of the target audience became a significant point of contention during the late 1950s.
11 See Oswell (1995).
12 See Scannell (1996), pp. 150–1; Hill (1991).
13 The watershed seems to have emerged in a somewhat piecemeal fashion following the publication of the O'Conor Report in 1960. It was not finally fixed until 1962.
14 Sendall (1983), p. 356.
15 As we have noted, this was at least an aim of the BBC Children's Department in the early 1950s; although it was abandoned later in the decade in response to competition. Incidentally, this period also saw the first programme aimed at children with special needs, the art show for deaf children *Vision On*, which provided the title for this chapter.
16 See Oswell (1995).

17 See Staples (1997) for an extremely informative account of the history of children's cinema exhibition.
18 Home (1993), p. 171.
19 See Wagg (1992); Buckingham (1995b).
20 Given that we are relying on printed schedules rather than BARB data, all timings are approximate. Where necessary, times were rounded up to the nearest five minutes.
21 Although those working in children's departments themselves consistently called for children's programmes to be provided during school holidays.
22 Conversely, British pre-school specialists such as Ragdoll Productions have been very successful in exporting to North America.
23 For example, we were told that until recently there were only ever thirteen episodes of *Postman Pat*. Presumably it was assumed that neither children nor their parents would notice this – or that if children did, they would be unlikely to complain.
24 For discussions of this issue, see Hebdige (1988) and Webster (1991).
25 On the other hand, it could be pointed out that much 'American' animation is now manufactured in South East Asia.
26 These issues will be taken up in more detail in Buckingham (forthcoming a).
27 See Home (1993), pp. 80–6.
28 Again, see Home (1993), pp. 84–5.
29 It is worth noting that the second BSC report (Davies and Corbett, 1997) does not confirm Blumler's predictions about a decline in either factual programmes or drama between 1992 and 1996, although it does point out that ITV's record in these respects is rather worse than the BBC's.
30 See Buckingham (1997) for a discussion of how particular areas of content are typically defined as 'children's issues' in factual programmes.
31 See Bazalgette and Staples (1995).
32 Our findings here echo those of the second BSC report (Davies and Corbett, 1997), at least in respect of its conclusions about the period 1992–6.
33 See Buckingham (forthcoming a).
34 This is one finding of the BBC's time budget studies: see Scannell (1996), pp. 175–6.
35 This is apparent in the early findings of the 'Himmelweit 2' project, 'Children, Young People and the Changing Media Environment', currently under way at the London School of Economics.

4 Wise Up
The Functions and Practices of Audience Research

Definitions of the child audience clearly depend upon a whole range of psychological, moral and ideological assumptions. These assumptions have been addressed at various points in our account, and will be analysed more systematically in Chapter Five. Our concern in this chapter, however, is with the kinds of knowledge on which these different constructions of the child audience are based – and specifically with the knowledge derived from research conducted by the television industry itself. How do broadcasters come to know about their target audience? And what kinds of knowledge are seen as most valuable or significant in the increasingly commercial context of contemporary television?

Obviously, a good deal of broadcasters' knowledge about the child audience will be subjective or anecdotal. They will rely on their experiences with their own children, or those of their friends or relatives; or even on their own childhood memories. Research in programme production will often necessarily entail contact with children; and children are, of course, frequently involved in programme-making as actors or participants. Producers may also engage in comparatively 'informal' contacts with their target audience, for example through occasional visits to schools. Finally, there is the information that is gained through viewers' correspondence. Children's producers often boast of the high levels of response from their audience; and this is encouraged by the reading of viewers' letters, which is a routine aspect of continuity sequences between programmes, and of shows such as *Live and Kicking* and *Blue Peter*. Aside from the few ritualistic vehicles for complaint (such as the BBC's *Points of View* or Channel Four's *Right to Reply*), it is hard to think of parallels in 'adult' television – which may itself point to a significant difference in terms of how children's relationships with 'their' programmes are cultivated and defined. While academic researchers might question the validity or representativeness of this kind of data, it would be wrong to underestimate its value and influence. The BBC's *Grange Hill*, for example, has recently employed one persistent teenage letter-writer as a part-time script consultant, which may reflect the significance (and the difficulty) for such programmes of remaining 'authentic' to teenagers' experiences.

Nevertheless, broadcasting organisations also make use of an extensive apparatus of more formal research. Some of this work is conducted in-house, via audience research departments; while some is bought in on a regular contract basis or in the form of one-off projects. Very little of this research – even that which is funded by public money, in the case of the BBC – is made publicly available. Historically, it has been felt that to do so would be damaging to programme-makers; or alternatively, that it would lead to a confusion between research and public relations.[1] Yet the primary reason for secrecy, particularly in today's competitive commercial environment, is that information about the child audience is a very valuable commodity. Increasing amounts of money are being invested in these attempts to 'know' the audience – whether the ultimate aim is to serve it or simply to sell it to advertisers.

In this chapter, we describe and analyse this relatively hidden aspect of the television industry. Following a brief discussion of the functions of audience research, we look at the early history of such work, and the sometimes uneasy ways in which children were defined as appropriate objects of study. In particular, we analyse the debates surrounding the commissioning and publication of the book *Television and the Child* in the late 1950s,[2] as they reveal a great deal about the relationships between the industry, the academy and the audience. We then move on to consider the contemporary practice of audience research within the industry, in the form of ratings and market research, both quantitative and quali- tative. We attempt to explain the increasing significance of audience research, and how it is used in different sectors of the industry. Ratings are, of course, the most significant and influential of these forms of information; although they have been increasingly condemned as unreliable. In the final section of this chapter, we therefore look at what ratings can and cannot tell us about the distinctiveness and diversity of the contemporary child audience.

Hunting wild savages?

Our approach here is partly descriptive, but it is also critical. We do not regard research (whether it is conducted by academics or by market researchers) as a straightforward source of scientific knowledge. On the contrary, we analyse research as a form of *discursive practice* – as something which constitutes and defines its 'objects' (in this case, 'children' and 'television') in particular ways, for particular social, institutional and ideological purposes. This is not to suggest that such research is in any simple sense 'wrong', or insufficiently scientific, simply that it is inevitably *partial*. Like the broadcasters, policy-makers and regulators whose views we will be analysing in the following chapter, researchers also define children in particular ways, through the kinds of questions they ask, their choice of methods and their assumptions about what 'counts' as valid knowledge.

Ien Ang develops these arguments in her powerful academic critique of such research, *Desperately Seeking the Audience*.[3] Ang argues that the television industry is engaged in a desperate struggle to locate and control the audience – a struggle which it is ultimately bound to lose. Particularly with the advent of video recorders and remote controls, she argues, the era of the 'streamlined audience' has passed. Despite the use of more sensitive technologies such as 'people meters', the ratings are inherently unreliable: it is no longer possible (if indeed it ever was) to know – and hence to manage – the audience's behaviour. Unlike Bentham's panopticon, which offered a similar promise of complete control, the technologies of audience measurement fail to transform audiences into 'docile bodies'.[4] The audience, according to Ang, is a 'wild savage' which the industry attempts to tame and colonise, but which it will never succeed in capturing.

In this context, Ang argues, the discourse of television ratings provides a kind of symbolic reassurance, a scientistic rhetoric that attempts to impose patterns of stability and predictability by gathering audience members into 'taxonomic collectives'. While the 'knowledge' provided by ratings may thus be epistemologically problematic, it is nevertheless institutionally enabling. Indeed, the denial of the diverse realities of audiences is necessary for the activity of television production to be sustained. Ratings become a means of reducing uncertainty, of overcoming the fear of risk. At the same time, Ang suggests, there is a sense in which broadcasters actively do not *want* to know too much about the audience, because to do so would disturb the certainty they so urgently seek.

Ang's analysis may be particularly relevant to children, who are arguably one of the least 'knowable' of audiences.[5] As we have indicated, the struggle to control the audience has been particularly acute in relation to children, whose desire to watch material which adults deem unsuitable for them has created some of the industry's most significant public dilemmas. What the *Daily Mail* in 1996 termed 'The Scandal of the View-As-You-Like Generation'[6] has always been with us: children have always been more interested in 'adult' television than in children's television, and they have always resisted being addressed as 'children' – at least as soon as they reach middle childhood.[7] In this context, the findings of audience research – however limited they may be – have sometimes been decidedly double-edged, both for the industry and for its critics. The ultimate problem with children, it would seem, is their unwillingness to *be* children – at least as defined by adults.

Nevertheless, Ang's suggestion that there is growing uncertainty in the industry about the validity of ratings may be overstated. It was hard to detect much epistemological anxiety among the researchers we interviewed; and while industry researchers acknowledge the limitations of ratings methodology, they implicitly accept these as reasonable margins of error, as we shall see below. In retrospect, it is hard to agree with Ang's assessment of zapping and timeshifting as 'the revolt of the viewer', particularly as viewers have gradually adapted to these new technologies. The advent of the remote control, for example, may have initially led to several frenzied years of minute-by-minute channel-changing, although some of the researchers we interviewed suggested that this had now levelled off.[8] Certainly, a great deal of viewer behaviour can still be predicted on the basis of scheduling: time-honoured practices such as 'inheritance' (leading an audience from one programme to the next on the same channel) and 'hammocking' (scheduling a weaker programme between two stronger ones) continue to be effective.

Ultimately, there is a kind of romanticism about Ang's separation between the discursively constructed audience and the 'actual social worlds' of real audiences – and particularly about the notion that real audiences are somehow infinitely diverse, wild and anarchic, and that they automatically resist the institution's attempts at control. As we have implied, the predictability of audience behaviour – and hence the ease with which it can be controlled – depends very much on the historical context, and on the pace of technological change. There may be moments (for example, in the late 1950s or the early 1990s in Britain) where a significant gap opens up between the project of broadcasters and the behaviour of viewers. Yet for most of the time, we would argue that audience behaviour is actually rather more orderly and conventional than Ang's analysis would suggest. Even in the impending future of digital television, when audiences may appear to be faced with a bewildering range of choices, they may eventually come to follow quite predictable routines.

Discovering the child audience

As Ien Ang points out, public service broadcasters have traditionally seen the audience as a public rather than a market.[9] Their concern has been with what the audience 'needs' rather than what it 'wants'.[10] As a result, public service channels have not historically regarded audience measurement as a priority; although the UK was in fact ahead of most other European countries in this respect.[11] Even here, however, researchers insisted that the *size* of the audience should not be seen as the most significant criterion of success.[12] The paternalistic ethos of public service broadcasting, with its emphasis on the cultural 'uplift' of the audience, necessarily required more qualitative measures of effectiveness; although in practice such measures have been fairly limited.

Against the opposition of Lord Reith – for whom audience research was tantamount to pandering to the lowest common denominator[13] – research on the BBC's listening public began in the 1930s and grew steadily during wartime. Children, however, were absent from these early samples, and were only 'discovered' in the initial surveys of television viewing in 1949–50. Even here, it was apparent that children did not only like programmes explicitly intended for them: as we have noted, Robert Silvey, head of the BBC's ARD, was startled by the interest in 'cabaret' among children – even if they displayed little enthusiasm for opera and instrumental recitals.[14] The first large-scale survey of the younger audience was undertaken in 1955, although there was still considerable doubt about the reliability of children as interviewees; and it was not until 1960 that children became a regular fixture in the mainstream daily survey of listening and viewing – despite the fact that ownership of sets was significantly higher in households with children than in those without. This uncertainty about researching the child audience clearly reflects the broader uncertainty which characterised the period, discussed in Chapter One.

Predictably, age and gender were key variables at this point; although these early studies also placed a central emphasis on social class – a factor which steadily disappears from view in subsequent studies of the child audience. As we have indicated in Chapter One, social class was systematically related to differences in taste; although its significance was complex. Mark Abrams, in an article based on the 1955 'Minors' study, noted that middle-class parents were more likely to acquire a television set, and only marginally more likely to restrict their children's viewing. At the same time, age combined with class to bring about a widespread rejection of children's television among older children. Commenting upon the

BBC's children's programmes, Abrams notes: 'About most of them there is the atmosphere of a kindly middle-class nursery with a devoted sensible "nannie" in the background. Presumably most modern children have outgrown this by the time they have reached 14.'[15] As this implies, the majority of children much preferred 'adult' evening programmes, while a substantial percentage ignored children's television altogether. There were significant overlaps between children's and adults' preferences; and a large proportion of children were still watching after 9 o'clock in the evening. Children, it seemed, were already refusing to view in the manner adults had prescribed to be good for them.

Predictably, the findings of this kind of research became increasingly significant in the context of competition. As we noted in Chapter One, the BBC Children's Department was regularly criticised at weekly management meetings in the late 1950s because of their low audience share, particularly among working-class children. Nevertheless, even at this stage, a distinction began to emerge between the kinds of research that were valued by producers and those that were valued by executives and policy-makers – although this distinction itself changed somewhat over time.

Himmelweit and after: the first view-as-you-like generation?

The spectre of the uncontrollable child audience was to loom large in the debates surrounding the first substantial British study of the child audience, Hilde Himmelweit et al.'s *Television and the Child*. These debates also reveal a great deal about the awkward relations between the broadcasters and their public, and the emerging distinctions between different *kinds* of research.

In offering his support to this research, Robert Silvey felt it was appropriate to look at children separately from adults, on the following grounds:

> Public concern about the former was a good deal greater and consisted principally of misgivings in the face of the evident enthusiasm of children for television and the scarifying accounts of child-addiction which were reaching this country from the USA.[16]

Silvey himself was sceptical about such claims, and regarded the effects of television as primarily a matter of reinforcement. But it would clearly not be persuasive for broadcasters to protest their own innocence. Bearing in mind the scale of the task, and particularly its 'contentious' nature, he therefore recommended that it should be conducted 'under wholly independent auspices'.[17] The Nuffield Foundation was duly persuaded to fund the study, which was undertaken by a team based at the London School of Economics. From the perspective of a group of British academics, the study offered an opportunity to establish a presence in a field that had hitherto been dominated by US researchers. As in the case of the violence studies that were to become so prevalent in the 1960s, the funding of research was therefore driven both by the political tensions surrounding the regulation of broadcasting and by attempts to establish the legitimacy of new academic fields of study.[18] As we shall see, these tensions came to the fore in the debates that followed the publication of the report.

Television and the Child is a substantial and diverse collection of research studies, and it is not our intention to summarise its findings here. Instead, we would like to identify three of its key concerns, all of which seem remarkably contemporary. First, in terms of its discussion of the *effects* of television, the book is strikingly lacking in the 'scarifying' tone identified by Silvey. Indeed, it points to the way in which new media often give rise to disproportionate fears, and argues that television should not be made a scapegoat for symptoms that in fact derive from other causes.[19] Despite its concern about the consequences of 'television addiction', its main message is that the medium's effects are neither massively negative nor positive. Thus, for example, the study concludes that television has displaced some 'functionally similar' activities (notably radio listening), but it largely seems to fill children's time by default – in other words, because they lack alternative options. Likewise, it finds little evidence that the viewing of violent incidents contributes to aggressive behaviour, and seems more concerned with the extent to which children might be 'disturbed' by such material; and in this area, it recommends that a system of advisory certification for 'unsuitable' material be published in the television listings magazines.

In fact, the study is rather more concerned with the effects of television on *values and beliefs:* for example, in analysing its impact on children's stereotyped views of occupations or of 'foreigners'. Indeed, its concern about television violence (at least in the form of crime fiction) is also defined primarily in terms of its potential effects on children's *attitudes* – for example, on the belief that all problems can be solved through violence – rather than on 'copycat' behaviour. Himmelweit's central preoccupation, then, is with social values and representations; and in this respect, she even goes so far as to suggest that there should be more programmes specifically targeted at girls – a suggestion which seems strikingly ahead of its time, and which caused the Independent Television Companies' Association (ITCA) to complain of the dangers of 'heroine worship' in its response to the report.[20] As in its discussion of behavioural effects, however, the study emphasises that the influence of television on children's attitudes will not be uniform, and that it should be seen in the context of other factors in their lives.

Finally, *Television and the Child* is also very much concerned with questions of diversity and 'balance' in television programming, in a manner which prefigures the concerns of contemporary lobby groups discussed in earlier chapters. Like the 'Minors' study mentioned above,[21] Himmelweit finds that children tend to prefer 'adult' programmes; and while there was some evidence from other studies that this was more prevalent among lower social classes,[22] Himmelweit argues that the most significant variable, aside from age and gender, was that of educational attainment rather than class. While much of the fieldwork for the study was conducted in 1954–5, prior to the advent of ITV, Himmelweit is critical of the potential impact of competition. She argues that a second channel makes it easier for children to avoid children's or educational programming. She also notes that much of the content that provokes concern – whether in terms of its 'suitability' or in terms of its representation of social groups – is more prevalent on the commercial channel: ITV is directly criticised for its reliance on Westerns, crime and adventure dramas, particularly in prime time. However, Himmelweit also points out that children's tastes are quite diverse: they enjoy factual programmes, for example, even if they do not actively seek them out. Nevertheless, she fears that the advent of competition will lead to a narrowing of taste, because children will find it easier to limit themselves to their favourite types of programme. In consequence, she recommends that the BBC and ITV should agree to a kind of 'truce', during which they would both transmit 'instructive' programmes in order to discourage children from switching over.

The debates that followed the publication of Himmelweit's study addressed these concerns very selectively. The BBC and the ITA convened a joint committee, the O'Conor Committee, to inquire into the study's recommendations. The Committee, which reported in 1960, was caught between the imperatives of the broadcasting institutions and the pressures of public debate.[23] The former undoubtedly led to most of Himmelweit's more concrete recommendations being summarily dismissed. For example, the notion of targeting programming specifically at girls was rejected on the grounds that it might alienate boys; the proposal for an educational 'truce' was seen to raise problems of definition, and would inhibit scheduling; while the call to certificate potentially 'unsuitable' material was resisted on the grounds that it would hold out the promise of 'forbidden fruit', and fail to reflect differences of context and the child's developmental level. In its submission to the Committee, the BBC asserted the adequacy of its existing procedures, noting that the primary aim of children's television was to provide 'entertainment' rather than 'education in the direct sense'.[24] The ITA's response was even more forthright, insisting on the primacy of the 'creative element' in television, and implicitly rejecting Himmelweit as out of date and 'sociological'. Both responses effectively insisted on the autonomy of the broadcasters from outside interference – an insistence which would obviously have been much more difficult to sustain if the BBC and ITA had undertaken the research themselves.

On the other hand, the O'Conor Report was bound to respond to what was perceived as growing public concern about television's influence on children – albeit that much of this concern was (as Silvey noted) imported from across the Atlantic. Thus, the Report places its central emphasis on what it takes to be 'the most important fact to emerge from *Television and the Child*', namely that children were watching substantial amounts of 'adult' programmes between 6 and 9 p.m. By contrast, children's programmes reached comparatively low audiences. Revealingly, the Report notes 'the stigma apparently attached to programmes known by children to be intended for them'; and it observes that the BBC's audience share between 5 and 6 p.m. increased significantly when the generic title 'Children's Television' was dropped (see Chapter One).

While children's enthusiasm for 'adult' television was scarcely a new finding even at the time (as we have noted above), its ability to generate concern seems to pass unabated from one generation to the next. Increasing the number of channels inevitably means that children can select what they want – and what they want is often not what adults perceive to be good for them. The Report accurately pinpoints the dilemma of the broadcasters here: how to acknowledge the presence of children in the audience without having to 'dilute' or 'emasculate' programmes in order to make them suitable for the family audience. If the BBC is to remain 'the national broadcasting organisation', it has to retain a certain level of audience share; and yet, the Report argues, 'programmes designed for the largest audience depend on material which is unsuitable for children' (p. 3).

The Report's response to this situation is surprisingly censorious, at least in comparison with the comparatively mild tone of Himmelweit. It supports Himmelweit's argument that children should be offered 'balanced' and 'varied' programming, and that this should include 'serious and informative' material; but it goes on to spend much of its energy attacking the use of 'double entendres' in comedy, the 'drivel' and 'degraded attitude to sex' in pop lyrics and the emphasis on the 'sordid aspects of life' in television drama. Many of these judgments about the 'suitability' of such material, or about what is 'injurious to children mentally, morally, or physically', do not seem to be based on Himmelweit's research, but simply on opinion (p.10ff).

Even in this area, however, the Report is ultimately toothless. It questions the value of written codes of practice, preferring to rely on 'the development within the television organisations of a climate of opinion in which it would become inevitable in producing programmes to consider the special needs of the family audience';[25] and it prefers to rely on a 'machinery' of special advisers and committees. Reading between the lines, one can detect very clear signs of dispute on this issue. The BBC and ITA's joint preface to the Report, for example, states firmly that they 'do not believe that the needs of children should be allowed to determine the nature of all television output up to 9.0 p.m.'[26] On the other hand, the ITCA's argument in its submission that parents (rather than broadcasters) should be responsible for their children's viewing, and for ensuring that they are 'critical and selective', is strongly rejected in the text of the Report itself.

As this implies, the O'Conor Report was the focus of a struggle for autonomy; and this struggle was also reflected in broadcasters' subsequent responses to its recommendations. Broadly speaking, the broadcasters resisted attempts at *external* control – for example, by rejecting the Committee's recommendation that educational advisers be involved in the production of children's programmes. On the contrary, they sought to assuage or deflect 'public' concern by producing *internal* codes of practice: for example, on the treatment of violence. Such codes became very much the favoured response of broadcasters in the decades that followed.

Nevertheless, in the wake of Himmelweit, the spectre of the uncontrollable child audience continued to generate anxiety. One year after the O'Conor Report, the ITV regional company Granada Television published a brief update on Himmelweit, designed 'to supply descriptive information rather than a definitive solution to present day controversy'.[27] This study acknowledged that there had been an increase in children's viewing hours since *Television and the Child*, and that children were watching substantial amounts of 'adult' programmes, particularly on ITV, which at the time was enjoying a 78 per cent audience share. However, it sought to calm fears about unsupervised viewing: children, it argued, were predominantly watching in the company of family members, and they were making discriminating choices about what they watched. Very few children were being forced to watch adult programmes, nor were they simply watching out of habit.

What can be concluded from this brief account of the 'moment' of Himmelweit? Clearly, the manner in which the report was commissioned and then debated and used depended very much on the contemporary political tensions between broadcasters and would-be regulators. The aim for the broadcasters was essentially to deflect public criticism, to retain their autonomy and to sustain the size of their audiences. To support independent academic research might be useful, not least in so far as it provided evidence that they were taking their responsibilities seriously; but if its conclusions were too awkward, they could be condemned as unworkable and idealistic.

Himmelweit is often described as 'influential', and some of its criticisms of ITV were clearly echoed in the Pilkington Report, published in 1962. Yet aside from the codes of practice relating to violence, it is frankly hard to detect signs of any direct influence within the broadcasting institutions, such was the resistance it generated. In the academy, by contrast, it is regarded (although perhaps not sufficiently recognised) as a cornerstone in the establishment of media research. In some respects, though, it also represents a parting of the ways between the academy and the industry. It is certainly remarkable that no British study of similar scope was funded until the 'Himmelweit 2' project began some forty years later (it is currently under way at the LSE) – although in this case it may be symptomatic that its primary support comes from the BSC, rather than from the industry itself. This is not to suggest that broadcasters have not supported or learned from academic research: in addition to the BSC, the IBA and its successor the ITC have a strong track record in this field. Nevertheless, the moment of Himmelweit is one in which a certain division of labour was instituted between the industry and the academy. In this respect, it is revealing that Robert Silvey concludes his discussion of Himmelweit and the Knight Committee's report, *Television and the Family*, published two years later, by observing that, with these studies completed, 'our work in the field of the social – as distinct from the broadcasting-centred – effects of viewing was for the time thankfully left on one side.'[28]

Institutionalising the audience

In the decades following Himmelweit, research within the broadcasting institutions – which is our central concern in this chapter – became much more narrowly driven by institutional imperatives. What Silvey terms 'broadcasting-centred' research became the order of the day, and questions about 'social effects' were largely left to academics or regulators.[29] A full history of audience research within broadcasting is beyond the scope of this book, although some broad shifts should be noted before we move on to our account of contemporary practice.

Ien Ang[30] argues that in the Reithian era, public service broadcasters did not really need audience research: their work was based on the conviction that they already knew what was good for the audience, and hence how it should be addressed. In fact, this may be something of an overstatement: there was a fair amount of research conducted prior to the advent of competition, at least some of which was motivated by a genuine curiosity – and indeed uncertainty – about how broadcasts were received and understood. However, this conviction was more seriously eroded by the advent of commercial competition; and in the 1960s, Reithian paternalism was gradually abandoned in favour of a view of broadcasting as a 'mirror' for the diversity of social lives – no longer leading the audience but *representing* it.[31] In this context, broadcasting became 'professionalised': it was an activity undertaken by an enclosed elite, with internal criteria for judgment and a routinised relationship with its client group. In the process, the relation between broadcasters and their audience was loosened. The audience became a kind of abstraction. Ien Ang and Tom Burns[32] describe how, in this context, audience research quickly became bureaucratised in the form of audience *measurement*. As Burns[33] argues, the relationship between the broadcaster and the audience was 'taken care of' by means of ratings, a procedure which 'reduces awareness of the public to the safe dimensions of percentages'. Audience measurement, he argues, is not a bridge between broadcasters and the public but a barricade between them, which allows broadcasters to 'cultivate their own professionalism in a decent privacy'. In the process, he suggests, 'communication with audiences is reduced to the common *gestalt* of a programme "stream" ... public issues are translated into methods of programme construction, moral problems into professional judgements.'[34]

On one level, this analysis clearly does apply to broadcasters' relationships with the child audience, at least during the era of the regulated duopoly. As we have noted, children were now routinely included within adult viewing panels, although studies of 'public opinion' (for example, in BBC reports on 'The Public's Use of Television in 1974/5' or 'Aspects of Public Opinion about Television') seemed to exclude children from their definition of 'the public'. 'Special' audience research studies were narrowly programme-specific, to the extent that broader implications for production practice were often neglected. A typical BBC Audience Research Report on *John Craven's Newsround*, conducted in 1976, for example, meticulously calibrated the presenter's popularity against the hosts of other children's programmes; but its finding that children seemed to recall very little of what they watched did not lead to any more fundamental reflection on the effectiveness of news programming for children. Despite their more qualitative dimensions, the primary concern throughout these studies is with questions of audience size, and how it might be maximised.

Nevertheless, ratings were generally a less pressing issue for children's broadcasters at this time than they had been in the late 1950s and early 1960s. As we have indicated, children's television under the regulated duopoly was characterised by some comparatively settled assumptions about the nature of its audience. During the 1970s, producers were relatively confident that they could follow and conduct a dialogue with the changing tastes of children. On the other hand, 'moral problems' of the kind mentioned by Burns were never far from the top of the agenda for children's broadcasters, and grew in importance as the decade progressed. As we shall indicate in Chapter Five, these problems became much more acute as children's interests (for example, in popular music) began to develop into a new, commercially driven, sexually charged youth culture.

During this period, the concerns about negative effects which informed the setting up of the Himmelweit study gave way to a more developmentalist preoccupation with the child's 'place in the world'; although Himmelweit's concern with social representation resurfaced strongly in the 1980s, most notably in the Department of Education and Science Report, *Popular Television and Schoolchildren*.[35] Nevertheless, public controversies about the moral 'effects' of television continued to pose occasional problems for broadcasters. For example, *Children as Viewers and Listeners*, a 1974 report by the BBC for its General Advisory Council, draws on research to counter parental concerns about the negative effects of its programmes.[36] Yet again, it notes the popularity of 'adult' programmes with children, and the substantial percentages of five- to fourteen-year-olds watching after the 9 o'clock watershed; and again it argues that it will never be possible to control children's viewing completely. Likewise, in response to complaints, it notes that the popularity of many disc jockeys and children's presenters derives precisely from the fact that they are *not* parental or teacherly, and that an unduly 'stuffy' approach would alienate their audience. Here again, it would seem, children were still failing to conform to adults' criteria of suitability.

The emergence of the child consumer

Despite these underlying fears about the uncontrollable nature of the child audience, industry research soon placed its major emphasis on the reassuring business of collecting ratings information. The systematic, routine nature of this kind of enquiry suggests a relatively stable relationship between broadcasters, programme-makers and 'the child': there was, broadly speaking, a shared understanding about the nature of children and how best to serve them.

As we indicated in Chapter Two, the emergence of new media technologies and the proliferation of media outlets which began in the 1980s led to a much more competitive, commercially oriented environment, in which these shared understandings were gradually disturbed. There was growing competition for advertising revenue, both within television and between television and other media; and the audience increasingly came to be regarded, not as homogenous, but as a collection of fragmented interest groups. In this context, children and young people began to be seen as an important and valuable niche market, but also as one that was difficult to reach. As one market research study noted:

> At a time when the media are faced with many challenges in adapting to the needs of new markets and maximising the opportunities offered by rapid developments in new technology, it is essential to keep abreast of the child and teenage consumer. The responses of this target audience ... are of vital importance to all involved in advertising and marketing.[37]

Of course, children have always had limited disposable income, gathered from pocket money, birthday gifts and sometimes from casual employment; and the marketing of toys, sticker collections and other children's products has a long history.[38] In the 1980s, however, this market began to expand dramatically, as children became a major new target in capitalism's restless search for fresh markets. Meanwhile, there was also a growing awareness of the influence children could have on household purchasing decisions – a 'discovery' that children are interested in programmes, advertisements or products that are not directly aimed at them. As we have seen, the fact that children have always preferred adult television programmes had been established since the 1950s, although this was often regarded as somewhat embarrassing, and (at least by some) as an indication of broader moral problems. In the context of an increasingly deregulated media market, however, it began to assume substantial *economic* significance.

Thus, in 1984 the Cocks Williamsons Associates Ltd (CWA) survey *Children and the Media* found that children's favourite television commercials included adverts for non-children's products; while the Association of Market Survey Organisations (AMSO) reported in 1988 that beer advertising was the second favourite category of advertising among eleven- to twelve-year-olds. While such findings (particularly the latter) generated predictable complaints, they also reflected the way in which the potential of 'pester power' was being actively reconsidered. Not only would children pester parents to buy things that they wanted for themselves, they could also pester them to buy this brand of car, or that brand of toilet paper.

As well as investigating children's economic influence on the household, market researchers also became interested in the Jesuitical notion of 'catching them young'. Appealing to children could be a way of establishing brand loyalty over the longer term. As the AMSO report suggested: 'They [children] are of prime significance, both since they represent one of the most volatile sectors in terms of commitment, and as they will become the adult audiences of the next decade.'[39] Perhaps most significantly, children are perceived to be at the cutting edge of technological change: 'All our experience demonstrates that it is this age group which is consistently ahead of technological developments and as such constitutes a powerful force within the family unit in terms of establishing ownership and usage patterns.'[40] As we have noted, it is partly children who are seen to drive domestic investment in media technologies; and in many cases, it seems that the establishment and success of any new medium is dependent on it being accepted by the child and youth market. Yet the practice of marketing specifically to *children* gives a particular inflection to the rhetoric. Many of the researchers we interviewed emphasised that children were a particularly 'fickle' audience. Children seem to be perceived as a kind of consumer *avant-garde*, which is unlike any other audience: they are volatile, unpredictable and hard to reach. Yet if they can be trained appropriately, they might develop into ideal consumers. It is no coincidence, in this respect, that advertising research has been particularly fond of developmentalist approaches, in which a neatly divided sequence of 'ages and stages' provides a powerful illusion of control.[41]

Nevertheless, the perceived unpredictability of children creates an urgent need for information. Children must be *known* in order that they can be targeted. As Youth TGI (Target Group Index), the leading British market research company in this field, proudly boast in their 1997 corporate hand-out:

> They [children] spend an increasing amount of money ... Yet there is, relatively speaking, very little information available on the youth market. With the advent of YOUTH TGI, advertisers, advertising agencies and media owners have, for the first time, access

to a single-source survey of the product and brand usage, media consumption and attitudes of those aged 7–19.

In the boom in consumer spending of the 1980s, the market was seen by some as a liberating and empowering force – at least for certain sectors of the adult population. Nevertheless, there was much more ambivalence surrounding children. The charge that children were being 'exploited' by unscrupulous commercial interests was one which could unite left-wing critics with those on the right who wished to return to a more traditional, protective conception of childhood. As we shall indicate in the following chapter, this uneasiness about the relationship between childhood and commerce has to some extent been managed through the discourse of media regulation. As in the case of the Himmelweit study, research has also been seen as a necessary response to such controversies – and, by the industry, as a way of guaranteeing their own social responsibility while helping to assuage public concern.

Thus, alongside the growth in market research focusing on children, the 1980s witnessed an eruption of studies about the influence of advertising on children. Regulatory bodies such as the IBA and the Advertising Standards Authority played a major role in funding such reports, although others were supported directly by industry – particularly in areas which had generated the most substantial public concern, such as nutrition and toys. The title of a 1994 report by the National Food Alliance seems to epitomise this double-edged approach: *Children: Advertisers' Dream – Nutrition Nightmare*.

Much of the debate here centred on children's ability to 'defend themselves' against potentially misleading advertising, and hence to make rational purchasing decisions. Researchers sought to refute the popular idea that children were merely vulnerable dupes, whose exposure to advertisements for sugared breakfast cereal would result in nutritional disaster. On the contrary, children were increasingly represented as discerning, sophisticated 'young adults' who were able to deconstruct the manipulative language and editing techniques of advertising at will. There exists (for us at least) an uneasy coincidence here between the discourse of industry research and the appearance of similar arguments in the academy. Cynically, one could argue that the emergence of research proving the existence of the 'media-literate' child served as a useful means for the industry to allay anxieties about commercialism, and to reject the charge that making money out of children was simply a form of exploitation.

The contemporary status of research

Contemporary changes in the media industries have thus had significant consequences for the status of audience research. The fundamental challenge for advertisers and marketers in an era of media fragmentation is how best to reach audiences when they can no longer be gathered together so easily. For example, there has been a significant growth in multi-set households, as TV sets have dropped in price relative to inflation; and these sets are now being used for a wider range of purposes (video, both rental and timeshift, and computer games, as well as broadcast TV). Hours of viewing are slightly declining, while the range of options presented to the consumer has dramatically increased, particularly for those with cable and satellite. This proliferation of channels and other outlets, and the growth in transmission hours on terrestrial TV, create significantly more opportunities to advertise: advertising time on terrestrial TV alone trebled during the 1980s.[42] New technological developments – such as the Internet – might offer greater opportunities for targeted marketing, but (like children) they are regarded as in many ways an unknowable force.

In this situation, there is bound to be increasing competition to attract advertisers and to convince them that you are 'delivering' the audience commodity. Global figures are difficult to obtain, but we were repeatedly told that the industry is now spending a great deal more money on audience research than in previous decades. Research is also being taken increasingly seriously by schedulers and programme-planners. Under the new structural arrangements of terrestrial broadcasting, programme-makers – and the more impressionistic kinds of research they tend to favour – have become correspondingly less influential.

In the process, the research itself is becoming significantly more detailed and intensive. There is an urgent search for more accurate measures of audience behaviour, in the form of ratings; and yet there is also a growing need for more in-depth information about attitudes and preferences, and the reasons for them. Market researchers want to be able to correlate measures of media use with indicators of purchasing behaviour, although at present this is regarded as difficult, because it places a significant burden on panel members and requires large samples.[43] The Orwellian scenario here is one in which information from 'passive people meters', which monitor who is watching in the home, is correlated with barcode information from supermarket purchases using 'loyalty cards'. Researchers are also increasingly interested in 'qualitative ratings' – that is, measures not just of audience size but of appreciation – on the grounds that the appeal or impact of programmes might influence viewers' susceptibility to the advertising placed within them.[44] Closer attention is being paid to establishing connections between programmes and brands which are thought to possess similar market profiles, not just through sponsorship but also through the placement of spot advertising. The less predictable audiences are perceived to be, the more investment is likely to be made in research.

However, audience research is driven by a variety of motivations, and takes a variety of forms. In the following sections, we offer a brief descriptive account of the range of contemporary forms of industry research, with examples focusing specifically on the child audience.

The supremacy of the ratings

For most people working in British television, the bottom line is always the BARB figures. BARB is a joint industry body funded by television companies and advertising agencies that is responsible for overseeing the collection and dissemination of quantitative (and some qualitative) information about viewing. Based on a representative sample of 4,700 households equipped with 'people meters', BARB audience data provide crude information about how many people are watching a channel or programme at any time, both in terms of numbers and audience share. These figures are then broken down to provide more nuanced information about the composition of the audience in terms of age, gender, social class and region. AGB, one of the two research companies that administer BARB, also provides additional information about the household composition of the sample and the number of television sets owned, which can then be cross-tabulated with viewing behaviour.[45]

Ratings are often described as the 'currency' of the television industry. They provide evidence for advertisers of the existence of the commodity – that is, the audience – which they are being 'sold'. Thus, BARB data are used by sales departments to set advertising rates when selling airtime. At the same time, ratings are also widely perceived as measures of 'success', even within the BBC. The data are used to analyse the performance of programmes or schedules, and thereby fed back into commissioning and programming decisions – a practice Tom Burns describes as 'rather like watching the whole practice of medicine being reduced to the use of the thermometer'.[46] There are research companies whose sole function is to use ratings information for this kind of strategic research and development; and individuals, for instance in BBC audience research, who specialise in using ratings to explain the behaviour of the child audience.

This kind of strategic planning is predicated on the time-based character of television and is therefore closely tied to scheduling. Researchers will talk about the 'needs of the schedule' as the most significant influence on commissioning decisions. Both the BBC and ITV have approximately two hours on weekday afternoons to fill with children's television, and each channel wants their schedule to be more appealing than their competitors' (including cable and satellite). Minute-by-minute ratings are therefore used to assess how the schedule is performing. So, for instance, if it is found that a significant proportion of the BBC children's audience turns over when *Rugrats* finishes to watch *Scooby Doo* on ITV, rather than staying on to watch *Record Breakers*, this information might be used to reassess the wisdom of scheduling *Record Breakers* against a popular, established animation show.

More nuanced analysis of the ratings is also used to target particular subsections of the audience. For instance, ratings show that as the afternoon progresses there are more ten- to twelve-year-olds in the audience; and therefore programmes with an appeal to older children will be scheduled around 5 p.m., when they are more likely to be available to view. Demographic breakdowns are also used to examine what kinds of programmes have a particular appeal to specific sections of the audience. For instance, ratings analysis shows that ITV's drama *The Ward* is more popular with girls, and it would therefore be sensible to broadcast this programme when it is not competing against another programme with female appeal, such as *Grange Hill*. As we have noted, this kind of demographic analysis of children's ratings focuses primarily on age and gender – unlike ratings analysis of adults, which is also concerned with region and social class. Such detailed breakdowns of the ratings are also used to assess how particular items within programmes perform. For instance, in a Saturday-morning magazine show it is possible to identify the most popular items by looking at who changes channels at what point: for example, it might be found that ten- to twelve-year old girls are switching over when the interview with a boy band finishes on BBC 1 to watch another current star on ITV.[47]

Researchers in this field confidently claim that the analysis of BARB data can, in most cases, explain *why* a programme performs well or badly in the ratings. In some cases, this is straightforward: a programme like *Blue Peter* always gets high ratings among children because it has no competition from children's ITV, which goes off the air at 5.10 p.m. Low ratings for a new drama might be explained by it being scheduled unfavourably after a low-rated show (perhaps one which is essential to meet regulatory requirements). In general, it is only in cases when no obvious explanation for a programme's failure to perform in the ratings can be found that more qualitative research will be employed. As one researcher put it:

> We're looking at what did they watch and who watched it and when did they stop watching it, and why. But the why may be explainable by things like opposition, or it may not be. And when it isn't – when you've gone through everything else . . . you might have to start from 'I don't know why they didn't watch it' and go and ask them.

Even where more qualitative methods are employed, however, researchers are very aware of the differences between what children say they want and what they actually watch. While children in a focus group might say how much they like a programme, one look at the ratings will often show that they didn't like it enough to watch it – although in this respect, they are no less reliable than adults. In the last analysis, it is the ratings that win the day: within the industry, the BARB 'overnights' are widely seen as the most crucial information about audiences, not only by executives and schedulers but also by producers themselves.

This kind of retrospective ratings research is of far more use to the mainstream terrestrial broadcasters than to their competitors in cable and satellite. The BARB survey was devised for the age of spectrum scarcity. The sample is comparatively small, and is notoriously bad at registering the fragmented audiences that are reached by specialist channels. Only 1,000 of the overall sample are four- to fifteen-year-olds, and only one-third of them would live in cable/satellite households. By the time the sample has been broken down into (say) four- to seven-year-old girls who have cable, the numbers are too small to be reliable. It is for this reason that the BARB figures have been criticised by, among others, the Cable Companies' Association – although for commercial reasons, they obviously would like to claim that their viewing figures are much higher than is suggested by the BARB system. Meanwhile, there is continuing uncertainty about what *counts* as 'viewing'. Observational research[48] has challenged the notion that being in the room while the set is on should necessarily be equated with viewing; although coincidental surveys (phoning to check) suggest that the margin of error is only around 6 per cent.[49] In this respect, Ang's assertion that there is widespread scepticism within the industry about the value of ratings would seem to be overstated.[50] Nevertheless, it would seem that the accurate measurement of audience size is becoming even more important in the multi-channel environment.

For all the criticisms of ratings, they remain the key determinant of decision-making within the television industry. Given that it is this view of the audience that dominates commissioning and scheduling, programmes that are believed to *guarantee* ratings will always find airtime. This is one of the reasons for the dominance of animation in the children's schedules, along with the more specifically economic arguments identified in Chapter Two. Generic animation rarely dominates the children's top ten, nor does it feature prominently in qualitative studies among children's favourite programmes. Compared to other kinds of programmes, it does not even achieve particularly high audience appreciation indices (see below). However, because animation has consistently commanded a respectable audience share, and is seen to have a broad-based appeal (to adults as well as children), the truism has developed that children will always watch animation. In this area, as in others, ratings could be said to have a highly conservative function within the television industry: they encourage broadcasters to err on the safe side, and to avoid taking too many risks.

Research as ammunition: Appreciation Indices, special reports and image tracking

While ratings are collected regularly and systematically, there are other sources of information about audience attitude, preference and behaviour that are available to broadcasters. The most widely used is the audience Appreciation Index (commonly known as AI), which is also administered by BARB. The AI is a crude measure of the extent to which an audience enjoyed a particular programme and is expressed as a mark out of ten. While a high AI is obviously satisfying to the producers of a programme on a creative level, AIs also have a commercial function, in that appreciative audiences are, in theory, more amenable to advertising than unappreciative audiences. The AI is collected via a panel, administered alongside the main BARB ratings. AIs are supposed to be confidential but, like ratings information, a high AI can be used as grounds for scheduling or recommissioning particular programmes. Of course, the AI score for any one programme can only reflect the opinions of people on the panel who actually watched it; and the fact that they are watching it in the first place suggests that they are less likely to dislike it. As a result, AIs always tend to be high; and distinctions are now increasingly made between AIs for all viewers and AIs for viewers who specifically chose to watch.

BARB also runs panels of viewers who are regularly or periodically asked more nuanced questions about their viewing behaviour. Thus, there is a panel comprising 1,500 four- to fifteen-year-olds known as the Young View Panel; and broadcasters can have additional questions inserted in the panel questionnaire in order to investigate a particular programme. For example, in 1995, the BBC Children's Department wanted to look more closely at audience responses to their new drama series *The Demon Headmaster*. Like AIs, this kind of information has a clear strategic function. Positive responses within the BBC to the first series provided justification enough to recommission it; and this decision was subsequently confirmed by its good ratings. However, if there was going to be a second series, it was felt that it would be worth finding out what particular aspects of the programme were popular or unpopular and with whom, in order to minimise the risk of failure. As ever with children's programmes, there is the added sensitivity around 'suitability' and the risk of incurring complaints (particularly at the BBC). A programme such as *The Demon Headmaster*, with its spooky imagery and suspenseful storyline, was a target for concerned complainants. For this reason, some of the questions to the Young View Panel focused on whether they found the series scary or disturbing: these findings could potentially be helpful both in responding to complaints and in modifying the second series. In addition, the series producer and executive producer conducted a small number of focus-group discussions in schools to evaluate responses to the first episode. Of course, it is hard to tell how this kind of information is used, although (as was the case here) producers will typically maintain that it merely confirms their creative 'hunches'.[51]

As well as the AIs and the Young View Panel, terrestrial broadcasters will commission special reports on particular programmes or parts of the schedule. This kind of research is occasional and usually undertaken to address a specific problem which cannot be explained by analysis of the ratings. One example of this was the report on *John Craven's Newsround* mentioned earlier. Contemporary examples have included reports focusing on the ITV Network's search for a Saturday-morning programme to compete with the BBC's *Live and Kicking*, or on Channel Four's development of the 'teen' soap *Hollyoaks*. This kind of research typically involves more detailed quantitative analysis than the BARB data, together with qualitative analysis of focus groups of children from the targeted age group, gender or region. It is usually commissioned from a specialist children's market research company (see below).

Strategic, competitive research such as this is primarily initiated by broadcasting executives rather than producers. Broadcasters, particularly in the commercial sector but increasingly in the BBC, are primarily concerned with servicing the 'needs of the schedule': they want programmes that will hold up well against the competition and deliver the right audiences. In this way, research is frequently used by executives and schedulers as a way of backing up hunches or minimising risk: when a programme is commissioned at a cost of £30,000 per half-hour, the investment can be justified if you have qualitative research with groups of ten- to twelve-year-old girls which shows that they loved it. Producers – both independents and those within the BBC or ITV companies – have a far more ambivalent relationship with this kind of qualitative research. It is often argued that research is antithetical to the creative process, and that producers will only be inhibited by focus groups and audience monitoring. This resistance to research may have something to do with the fact that it is generally commissioned by executives rather than producers; although some bigger production companies and producers understand that they too can benefit from such research, not least because it can be used as a way of selling their programmes. One producer explained how this can work: 'It [the programme] is a very odd project ... it's extremely risky. So we commissioned ... a very expensive piece of research to analyse whether it would have an appeal ... and that resulted in them actually commissioning it.'

As the industry moves away from in-house production and towards a commissioning or outsourcing model, this use of research is bound to become more common. Nevertheless, at least within terrestrial broadcasting, 'concept research' – that is, testing viewers' responses to *potential* programme ideas – is rarely undertaken, on the grounds that it is seen as unreliable; and there is as yet no UK equivalent to the US system of 'piloting' ideas on the basis of single episodes.[52] As in the case of *The Demon Headmaster*, research on existing programmes may be used to inform the development of new programmes or series; but research is almost always conducted on a *post hoc* basis. Nevertheless, as we shall see below, such research is likely to play a more significant role in programme development in the future.

Finally, research into the attitudes and opinions of the target audience is also increasingly used to track the image or brand of a certain broadcaster or channel. This is particularly necessary for the new cable and satellite companies who are keen to set out their commercial stall in this highly competitive market. For example, TCC's decision to spin off the new channel Trouble in 1996 (described in Chapter Two) resulted from research suggesting that they had more interest from teen audiences. Consequently, they ran an extensive advertising campaign emphasising the more street-smart or rebellious programmes in the TCC roster (for example, *Heartbreak High* rather than *Art Attack*). At every step of the campaign, storyboards and poster ideas were focus-tested to assess whether they had the right appeal to the target audience. In the increasingly bewildering world of the specialist channels, such research on children's responses to 'branding' and promotional strategies may well become just as important as research on actual programmes. Significantly, both the BBC and Nickelodeon also conduct annual surveys of parents: in the case of the BBC, this may well reflect a continuing sensitivity about parental complaints (discussed in Chapter Two), although in the case of Nickelodeon it also reflects the fact that it is ultimately parents, rather than children, who pay the subscription charge.

'Today's rapacious consumers ... tomorrow's lifetime brand choosers': market research and the quest for the child consumer

Children's habits and behaviour have been the subject of serious scrutiny for well over a hundred years. The need to find out about children's diet, leisure activities or emotional well-being has been a preoccupation for successive generations of policy-makers, educational psychologists and social workers. Each discipline provides its own definition of the object of study, 'the child'. From a Foucauldian perspective, these different strategies would all be seen as forms of surveillance, whose ultimate aim is the control of potentially recalcitrant populations – however much they may claim to derive from a concern with children's welfare.[53] Despite our more general scepticism about such arguments, they are hard to avoid when one encounters the operations of contemporary market research. It is not an exaggeration to say that there is now an industry devoted to investigating every aspect of children's lives. The major studies such as SMRC's Childwise or BMRB's Youth TGI are vast in scale and scope; while media companies like Nickelodeon, in their quest to be seen as the 'kid's friend', are engaged in an endless inquisitive courtship, involving a whole range of electronic means. This information is not employed to allocate healthcare or school places, as in the child welfare tradition:

it is used to get kids to buy things. As a somewhat hysterical article in *Business Week* proclaimed:

> Their [market researchers'] goal is to know more about children's preferences than even parents do. Researchers host online chats ... They hire toddlers to play with new toys and then watch from behind a two-way mirror ... Marketers now know more than ever about the child's psyche. That has helped them translate the urges and obsessions of different age groups into bigger sales.[54]

The most well-established and exhaustive British research into children as consumers is undertaken by BMRB's Youth TGI. As we have seen, children are regarded as an increasingly important market; and according to TGI, there are about nine million seven- to nineteen-year-olds in Britain, with an estimated total disposable income of £8 billion. The Youth TGI runs as an adjacent survey to the main TGI, which is concerned with describing the characteristics of particular targeted groups of consumers. It is based on an annual sample of 6,000 seven- to nineteen-year-olds, who are given an exhaustive survey asking them about everything from their favourite flavour crisps to how concerned they are about the environment. These data are broken down demographically and can be cross-tabulated to create consumer profiles. So, theoretically, one could identify a subgroup within the overall sample of ten-year-old girls who always buy valentine cards, wash their hair at least once a day and would answer 'agree strongly' to the statement, 'It's important to me to feel part of a group'. Similar surveys are run by SMRC (Childwise) and Carrick James Market Research (Childwatch).

This kind of information is primarily of interest to advertisers, marketers and media planners and is not directly used by broadcasters. Yet for commercial broadcasters, the kind of consumer information amassed by surveys like Youth TGI can be used in an effort to maintain a competitive edge. So, for instance, if nine-year-old boys who spend more than £5 a week on chocolate like watching ITV programmes, the ability to deliver that audience to Cadbury's adds value to Children's ITV airtime. At the same time, the reasoning behind such exhaustive surveys of children's behaviour and attitudes is based not only on children's own purchasing power but on the influence that children have on household expenditure in general.

The companies who undertake this kind of research also sell their information as a possible index of social and cultural change, and it is often reported in this way in the national press. The systematic and routine nature of their enquiries (annually for Youth TGI and Childwise, quarterly for Childwatch) enables the researchers to trace developing trends and changing patterns of social behaviour. Again, this kind of information can be strategically useful to broadcasters: for example, in informing editorial or production decisions about, say, which sport is up-and-coming or which kind of music is in decline.

This kind of research is symptomatic of the 'information economy'. The more accurate a company's knowledge is of who is going to buy what, where and why, the greater their competitive edge. At the same time, the research companies also have to sell themselves against their competitors, and so they have to offer ever new ways of segmenting, analysing and explaining the target consumers. Consequently, this information does not come cheap: subscribers to these surveys pay several hundred pounds for the basic service, and can then pay substantial additional fees for specialist analyses or for strategically inserted questions.

Nor is such research simply neutral. The endless quest to know more and more about the child consumer is, in itself, an intervention. Research does not simply reflect tastes; it also, subtly, shifts them. Inevitably, the questions children are asked in these surveys and the choices they are offered are limited by the economic interests of the subscribers. In the sixty-plus pages of the Youth TGI survey aimed at eleven- to fourteen-year-olds, for example, there are only four questions that do not directly relate to purchasing: two of these are clearly of commercial interest ('what charities do you give money to?' and a three-point attitudinal question about the environment); one of them, under the heading 'More About You' asks respondents to agree or disagree with statements about individual identity, which are primarily defined in terms of consumption (for example, 'I like to buy things my friends approve of' or 'You can judge a person by the car they drive'); and the other question asks respondents to choose from a list of twenty-one 'issues' they are concerned about. On one level, this could be seen as evidence that children's attitudes and perspectives on the world are being taken seriously. Yet ultimately, all that matters about children's attitudes and behaviour is whether they directly or indirectly relate to their individual consumption. Social 'issues' are only of interest in so far as they provide a means for more accurate targeting of the market.

'Getting the music right': research as product development

The final category of research that would seem to be in the ascendant is traditionally known as formative research – or, in the current climate, is more likely to be described as product testing. Just as, during the 1997 election campaign, the Labour Party is reputed to have tested every policy statement on hand-picked focus groups, increasingly broadcasters are looking to similar groups to fine-tune programme ideas. As yet, this is more common in the non-terrestrial sector, where stiff competition and small margins mean programmes are under more pressure to be instant hits.

Even the most ardent advocates of research draw the line at using groups of children to develop a script, accepting that there is some kind of professional distinction between producer and consumer. Researchers are keen to point out that, ultimately, creative decisions rest with the creative personnel and that research can sometimes be wrong. As one research executive put it: 'Creativity is what drives this whole business and, yes, it's crucial. Most of what kids suggest is not going to [work] – kids would never have suggested the theme for *Rugrats*.'

Nevertheless, research is increasingly at the heart of all decision-making in international companies like Disney or Nickelodeon. For example, Nickelodeon will bring in focus groups early on in the development process to gather audience feedback about characters, storylines or incidental music. As we shall indicate in the following chapter, Nickelodeon's kid-centred rhetoric conceives of research as a means of 'giving children a voice', a way of enabling them to express their opinions about what they want to watch. In practice, this means that every programme is product tested, whether it is an acquired animation or an original drama. So, for instance, if the focus groups don't like an animated character's voice, it might then be re-dubbed. Similarly, if a supporting character in a pilot drama is found to be more appealing than the lead, scripts will be altered and priorities shifted. This process starts before the pilot stage, with some programme ideas even being tested in storyboard form. Likewise, once a programme has been acquired, focus groups might be used to determine where it should be scheduled, via questions such as 'Is this for little kids?' or 'Would you watch it with your older brother?'

Likewise, in non-fiction genres, this kind of research might be used to select a presenter for a magazine programme or game show. Before contracts are signed, the prospective presenters will be analysed and assessed by children from the relevant target group. One example of this was Carlton's children's game show *Crazy Cottage*, where five possible front-people were tested on groups of children to find out who was the most appealing. In practice, however, these kinds of choices are necessarily narrow: the production team had already made most of the decisions about what kind of show it would be, and the children were simply given the choice between five presenters – all of them fresh from drama school, and all cast to seem 'emotionally childlike'. They were not given the option, for example, of an older presenter; and only one of the five was female. Again, research of this nature is primarily about minimising risk and having the ammunition to back up decisions. And as with all production decisions, the final choice of presenter will be just as influenced by factors such as the performer's fee or availability as by what the potential audience says it wants.

Research of this kind is not necessarily to be condemned as cynical or manipulative. The most exhaustively researched programme in the history of children's television, the Children's Television Workshop production *Sesame Street*, was effectively built through formative research of this nature; and this research has contributed a great deal to our broader understanding of the most effective programme formats, at least with pre-school children.[55] Nevertheless, research should not be mistaken for access or participation in programme-making – just as we have argued that 'consumer sovereignty' should not be confused with children's rights. Such research might appear to be a way of giving children what they want; but it only gets them what they want if they want what the industry is prepared to give them.

Consumer control?

The shift towards a more competitive, commercially oriented, multi-channel environment has undoubtedly raised the status of audience research. Whether it has raised the status of the audience itself is another matter. In some respects, as we have shown, the market may encourage a greater degree of responsiveness to consumers than a public service system. Even today, audience research seems to be much more significant in the commercial sector than in the BBC – not least in terms of the amount of money that is invested in it. Audience research within the BBC still appears to be a largely routine bureaucratic operation, whose main preoccupation remains with market share, and hence with justifying the main-tenance of the licence fee; although its fate in the wake of the restructuring and disaggregation of the Corporation seems uncertain. Partly because they are still building their audiences, the cable and satellite channels have adopted more inno-vative methods; and, as we have indicated, they have a stronger interest in 'brand tracking' and in formative research.

Nevertheless, market research should not be confused with accountability. Advocates of such research typically argue that it offers a means of 'giving the audience what it wants'; but as we have argued, the primary aim of such research is not to 'empower' the audience, but to ensure that it can be targeted more effectively. In the process, the audience is implicitly conceived as a mass of indi-vidual consumers; and it is invited to select 'what it wants' from a limited range of options. As a result, research can become an actively conservative force, militating against the kind of risk-taking which is necessary to ensure innovation and diver-sity. In this respect, research within the industry seems to have become steadily narrower in its approach, even as it has become more refined and methodologi-cally sophisticated. The broader social issues which were on the agenda at the time of Himmelweit have largely been left to academic researchers – and such research often generates considerable suspicion, and sometimes hostility, from the broad-casters themselves. The potential for research to give a voice to the audience, and to enable it to contribute to a wider debate about the social and cultural purposes of broadcasting, is one which the industry has largely neglected.

The distinctiveness of the child audience

Our primary emphasis in this chapter has been on the functions and practices of audience research within the television industry. We have not sought to summarise its findings, not least because we do not regard 'findings' as somehow self-evident or objectively given. However, we would like to conclude by consider-ing what the available data – and particularly the ratings – can tell us about the child audience, at least in their own terms. For all the criticisms that have been made of them, the ratings clearly do provide a kind of 'knowledge' which is highly influential within the industry. Indeed, analysis of the most highly rated shows among children can be used to explore whether children are indeed a 'special' audience for television. Do they have distinct tastes and preferences that mark them off from the general audience, and if so what do such preferences suggest? Are there differences *within* this audience – for example, in terms of age, social class or gender – which should cause us to question attempts to talk about 'children' as though they were a unitary or homogeneous group?

We attempted to examine these questions by comparing the programmes most watched by children (aged four to fifteen) with those most watched by the general audience, and with the most-watched children's programmes (children's programmes are defined by BARB as a distinct genre like drama). The most recent year for which full figures were available at the time of writing was 1995. There are marked differences between the three charts, which cast an interesting light on children's apparent preference for 'adult' television. At the same time, analysis of the figures also points to the significance of scheduling in determining audience size. In both respects, the figures suggest that children may be rather more predictable, and hence more easily controllable, than the 'wild savages' described by Ien Ang.

The most highly rated programme among all individuals in 1995 was the *Panorama* special interview with Princess Diana. This does not feature at all in the list of the most-watched programmes for four- to fifteen-year-olds. Given the scheduling of this programme after the 9 o'clock watershed, this is not particularly surprising. Similarly, the top programme among children – the TV premiere of the US movie *Home Alone* – is only twenty-fourth on the list of the most highly rated programmes for adults. *Home Alone* could be seen as a film which takes a child's point of view, and hence one which would have a distinct appeal for children.

Apart from *Home Alone*, only five other programmes are common to both the children's and the general charts. These are *The National Lottery Live*, *EastEnders*, *Casualty*, *Coronation Street* and *International Gladiators*. The popular drama serial or soap is an obvious area of overlap between general and child tastes, although there are some interesting anomalies. While *Coronation Street* is the second most-watched programme in general, it is only twenty-fifth among children. *EastEnders* has a larger constituency among young viewers: it is eighth in the children's chart and numbers nine, ten and twelve among all individuals. Interestingly, the episode of *EastEnders* with the highest viewing figures in general is not the same as the episode most popular among children. This is also true of *Coronation Street*, which would suggest not only that children have somewhat different tastes in pro-grammes but also that they are actively discriminating between particular storylines within those programmes.

The clearest difference between general taste and children's taste for drama serials is in the popularity of Australian soaps. *Neighbours* is number four in the children's chart (the most highly rated non-film drama) and does not feature at all for the general audience. Of course, this could partly be accounted for by scheduling (*Neighbours* is transmitted at 5.35 p.m., when many adults would not be available to view), but it may also reflect the greater emphasis on younger char-acters in these serials, and their subject matter and tone.

The other kind of programme common to both charts is the 'event'-style light entertainment game show as represented by *Gladiators* and *The National Lottery*. The Lottery's popularity for both children and adults needs no explanation – although it is interesting to note that it is slightly higher in the children's chart, despite the fact that children are not legally allowed to buy Lottery tickets. *International Gladiators*, the second-highest-rated show among children, only just makes it into the general top thirty at number thirty. With its cartoon-style, chore-ographed combat and its marketing tie-ins, *Gladiators* is arguably a programme with a deliberate and distinct 'kid-appeal'. Both these shows are also scheduled in what might be termed the 'kidult' ghetto of early Saturday evenings (see Chapter Three), which has historically been a site for particular kinds of child-oriented general programmes (such as *Doctor Who*), and has always attracted high ratings among children.

Programmes which appear in the top thirty for children but not for adults are

Gladiators (domestic rather than international), *Noel's House Party* and *The New Adventures of Superman*, all of which are scheduled in the same Saturday slot; *Wallace and Gromit*, *Neighbours* and four *Mr Bean* specials; and the TV screenings of the films *Beethoven*, *The Goonies*, *Hook*, *Santa Claus: The Movie* and *Who Framed Roger Rabbit?*

The popularity of movies with children is distinctive: only one film makes it into the general chart, namely *Home Alone* – and this is probably accounted for by the high numbers of children in the audience (it is top of the children's chart). This preponderance of movies can be explained in a number of ways. First, children have less access to theatrical showings of films, and therefore TV is their primary distribution medium. Given the publicity surrounding big US film releases and the high level of media convergence – through tie-ins with magazines, advertising and merchandising, as well as TV programmes which review movies – films have a high recognition factor among children. Second, film premieres are often scheduled during holidays and at weekends, times when overall viewing increases and children are more likely to be able to stay up late. For example, *Beethoven* (number six in the children's chart) and *Hook* (number eighteen) were premiered on Boxing Day and Christmas Day respectively. Third, if we consider the subject matter and content of the films which are popular with children, it is not too hard to identify a distinctive 'kid-appeal': they feature children as heroes (*Home Alone, Hook, Goonies*); they depict recognisable familial situations (*Beethoven, Home Alone*); or they have strong visual and fantasy elements (*Hook, Santa Claus, Who Framed Roger Rabbit?*).

While children's taste in drama is for Hollywood 'family' films, this contrasts strongly with the most highly rated drama in general. Leaving aside soaps, the most highly rated dramas for adults include *Inspector Morse, Heartbeat, Soldier, Soldier, A Touch of Frost* and *Peak Practice* – all of them resolutely British, broadly realist and entirely concerned with the behaviour of adults. Indeed, while the general top thirty is made up almost exclusively of British-produced programmes, imported material is much more prominent in the children's chart. As we noted in Chapter One, there is a long history of young audiences' preference for US material, which suggests that appreciation of programmes like *The New Adventures of Superman* is also distinctive of children's tastes.

Differences would also seem to exist between the children's and the general audience's taste in comedy. The most highly rated comedy programmes overall are *One Foot in the Grave* (number eight) and *Keeping Up Appearances* (number thirteen), both about elderly people. While both were Christmas specials – when presumably children would also be available to view – neither programme appears in the children's top thirty. The all-conquering comedy programme in the children's chart is Mr Bean in *Curse of Mr Bean* (number nine), *Do It Yourself Mr Bean* (number eleven), *Mind the Baby Mr Bean* (number nineteen), *Trouble with Mr Bean* (number twenty-one) and *Goodnight Mr Bean* (number twenty-seven). Despite being broadcast in prime time, Rowan Atkinson's alter ego is absent from the overall top thirty. The popularity of Mr Bean is undoubtedly a topic for extensive in-depth research; but we would suggest that it may have something to do with children's pleasure in feeling superior to adult idiocy.

Given the differences that exist between children and adults, it is instructive to look in more detail at the scheduling of these programmes. For example, *Do It Yourself Mr Bean* was shown on ITV on 7 January 1995 at 8.15 p.m., between *Blind Date* and *The News*. Overall, the programme got a 48 per cent share of the audience (although the live viewing figure was only 24 per cent, which means that half of its viewers watched it on video). It was scheduled against a documentary, *Keepers of the Kingdom*, on Channel Four and a series about the early days of cinema, *The Last Machine*, on BBC 2 (neither of which would have a particularly strong child-appeal). On BBC 1, however, it was up against the film *Star Trek VI*, which one might expect to provide more competition. During the half-hour it was screened, 40 per cent of all children were watching television: 28 per cent (TVR) of all of them were watching *Mr Bean*, compared to 24 per cent (TVR) of all adults. These figures switch around from the previous programme *Blind Date*, which had a TVR among adults of 26 and only 19 for children. So we can deduce that 9 per cent of children switched over to ITV specifically for Mr Bean. As we have noted, the Saturday-evening schedules have always been popular with the child audience, and *Do It Yourself Mr Bean* was expertly scheduled to maximise its appeal.

Another example of a Saturday-evening programme popular with children that is worth examining is the light entertainment show *Noel's House Party*. The most-watched edition of this programme was broadcast on Saturday 4 March 1995 between 7.00 and 7.50 p.m. on BBC 1. Scheduled against it were *The News* (BBC 2), *A Week in Politics* (Channel Four) and *Blind Date* (ITV). Among the whole population, *Blind Date* actually got more viewers than *Noel's House Party*, but only 14 per cent of children (out of a possible 43 per cent watching television) tuned into *Blind Date*, and 27 per cent, over half of all children watching, switched on *House Party*. Adult viewers were split far more evenly between the two programmes. Here again, the audience figures would indicate that children's interests – in the knockabout comedy of Mr Blobby rather than the intricacies of dating – are comparatively predictable.

These indications of the distinctiveness of children's tastes are reinforced if we consider programmes made specifically for them. Of course, scheduling and availability to view are crucial factors here too: there are simply far fewer adults available to watch television on weekday afternoons. Even so, the viewing behaviour of those adults who are watching television at this time is markedly different from that of children. An example of this might be the BBC drama serial *The Queen's Nose*. The most highly rated episode of this drama was shown on Wednesday 20 December 1995 between 4.35 and 5.00 p.m. At this time, 35 per cent of all children were watching television, compared to 20 per cent of all adults. Roughly two-thirds of the children were tuned into *The Queen's Nose* (TVR 25), compared to only one-seventh of adults (TVR 3). The over-fifteens watching television at this time split much more evenly between channels – although this means that there are still significant numbers of adults watching children's programmes, at least on terrestrial television, and they frequently outnumber children. Nevertheless, depending on the options, those children who watch television in the afternoon slot (and they are a minority) actively prefer to watch children's programmes. The figures for *The Queen's Nose* are also suggestive of children's genre preferences. Only 8 per cent of children chose to watch the rival show on Children's ITV, the US animation *The Incredible Hulk*. Despite the commonsense wisdom that children will always watch animation, this may be partly a response to the available alternatives.

As this analysis suggests, children do have distinctive preferences when compared with adults. While they do watch 'adult' programmes, they select particular *types* of adult programmes which are not necessarily very popular with adults themselves. As we shall indicate below, crude ratings of this kind do not tell us about the behaviour of particular subsections of the child audience – for example, in terms of gender or social class; and even in terms of age, the category 'four to fifteen' obviously disguises some significant differences. The question for broadcasters, however, is whether these differences are actually significant in terms of audience size. What is very clear is that the preferences of children as a whole are comparatively predictable; and that their behaviour as viewers can be largely understood – and hence controlled – on the basis of scheduling. In this respect at least, fears about the 'uncontrollable' nature of the child audience may say rather more about the adults who hold those fears than they do about children themselves.

Hardware and technology

A further aspect of children's distinctiveness as an audience is their comparatively high level of access to particular kinds of technology and media-delivery systems.[56] Children under fifteen make up 22 per cent of all individuals in TV households, and they are more likely to live in households with two or more television sets than any other age group. Children's bedrooms seem to be the most prevalent choice for locating new or second sets. Just under 80 per cent of households with TV sets in rooms other than the main living room have sets in a child's bedroom. Likewise, as we indicated in Chapter Two, children are key subscription drivers in the take-up of cable and satellite packages. While households with children constitute only 29 per cent of all households, children are present in 43 per cent of cable and satellite homes. Furthermore, 67 per cent of children live in homes that have either a computer or a computer games console, far more than any other group. The rate at which such households are investing in new hardware far outstrips those without children. For example, households of young families (two parents with children under twelve) and single parents have recorded more than 50 per cent increase in computer ownership since 1993, compared to the overall increase of 23 per cent.

The availability of hardware has predictable implications in terms of usage. Thus, young families constitute just over 16 per cent of all cable and satellite viewing, a figure beaten only by retired couples (18 per cent). If you add the figures for older families, mixed families and single parents, over 40 per cent of all satellite and cable viewing takes place in households with children. As we noted in Chapter Two, audiences for the BBC and ITV are declining among children in cable and satellite homes, while the viewing of dedicated children's channels is steadily increasing among those who have the option. In the first three months of 1996, children's channels took just over one-fifth of children's viewing (in cable homes), up from one-seventh in the same period of 1995.

In fact, the presence of children in the household is much more significant in these respects than factors such as social class. For example, AB households make up 18 per cent of the population, and also make up 18 per cent of cable/satellite homes; similarly C1 households comprise 27 per cent of all homes and 28 per cent of cable and satellite homes. The biggest difference appears in the E category – people on low, fixed income – who make up 21 per cent of all households but only 10 per cent of households with access to cable and satellite.

Children are also a significant market in terms of video sales and rentals.[57] Children's videos accounted for 26.5 per cent of all video sales in 1995 (although this is down on the 1994 figure of 30 per cent). Of the top ten video sales overall, four of them are specifically children's films (*The Lion King*, *The Aristocats*, *The Fox and the Hound* and *Pinocchio*, all produced by Disney) and a further two have a distinct child-appeal (*Star Wars* and *The Mask*). Pre-school videos also represent a significant market, accounting for approximately 60 per cent of non-Disney children's video sales. It is illuminating to look at the demographic breakdown of who is buying videos – particularly children's videos. In general, women buy slightly more videos than men – 54 per cent to 46 per cent. However, this gap is even wider for children's videos, with women accounting for 65 per cent of sales. While overall, 22 per cent of videos are bought by socio-economic group AB and 29 per cent by C1, sales to ABs account for only 7 per cent of children's videos compared to 39 per cent of C1s and 27 per cent of C2s. It would seem, then, that buying videos for children is not a middle-class activity. Interestingly, this discrepancy is far less marked when it comes to video rental: ABs account for 15 per cent of children's video rental compared to 21 per cent for C1s and 33 per cent for C2s.

Distinctiveness and diversity: beyond 'the child audience'

While there are some significant (and perhaps surprising) social differences here, the presence of children in a household does appear to be a strong predictor of patterns of media behaviour and preference, independent of other factors. Nevertheless, it is much harder to find evidence of diversity *within* the children's/family audience, at least from publicly available figures. The BARB weekly reports, for example, divide audiences into men, women, 'housewives' and children, and then by region. There is no subdivision within these categories. While there are some intriguing regional differences – audiences for children's programmes in Ulster, for example, are consistently lower than in the rest of the UK – these are clearly of most interest to regional ITV companies, which is presumably why they are included. While BARB and the BVA do break down the adult population by social class, gender and region, these reports only seem to define children in terms of age. Even with adult samples, there is surprisingly little cross-tabulation between categories, unless one is prepared to invest in further analysis of the kind undertaken by specialist companies within the industry. In some ways, the lack of public information about how these factors relate to children is revealing in itself.

In fact, as we have shown, industry researchers are able to make fine distinctions between different age groups, and between girls and boys. The researchers we interviewed used ratings which were broken down into four age bands, and would sometimes refer to the typical viewer of a given programme as 'ten-year-old boys' or 'eight-year-old girls'. The 'needs of the schedule' were typically defined in this way, as demographic gaps in the market which needed to be filled. It was recognised that certain programmes – most notably action-adventure cartoons – were heavily 'gendered', particularly in terms of AIs. Nevertheless, both researchers and programme-makers recognised that the actual audience composition for programmes was much less narrowly defined; and they were particularly keen to refute the suggestion that programmes were explicitly *targeted* at girls or boys. Interestingly, social class differences were hardly ever referred to here, which contrasts with their significance in early research, although the BARB sample can be broken down in this way also. In practice, age was apparently regarded as by far the most significant defining variable – a fact which points to the continuing significance of developmentalist explanations of childhood.

Here again, the categories and variables researchers choose to employ cannot be seen as merely neutral or descriptive. While sociologists have increasingly challenged the unitary concept of 'the child', and emphasised the social and cultural diversity of children's experiences (see Introduction), it may not be in the interests of the media industries – or of the researchers who serve them – to recognise this. If the distinctiveness of the 'child audience' appears to be much more significant than its diversity, this may be partly because of its relatively small size and its continuing lack of economic importance compared with other, more valuable target audiences. While the logic of contemporary media may be moving towards increasing audience fragmentation, it could be some time before the 'child audience' is broken down into a series of smaller niche markets – and this will in turn depend primarily upon how valuable those niche markets are seen to be to advertisers. Of course, it may be that these other differences between children are not nearly as significant as what they have in common. Yet there is something of a circular argument here. At least for the moment, the maintenance of a 'children's culture' that appears to transcend differences of social class, gender and ethnicity remains very much in the interests of the industry.

Notes

1 See Silvey (1974).
2 Himmelweit, Oppenheim and Vince (1958).
3 Ang (1991).
4 See Foucault (1979).
5 Cf. Rose (1984).
6 *Daily Mail*, 20 June 1996.
7 As we have indicated, it is important to make distinctions within the broad category of 'children' in these respects: see pages 144–5.
8 This claim was made by researchers from Paradigm, the company that conducts ratings research for the ITV network (interview with the authors, 1997).
9 Ang (1991).
10 This distinction will be pursued in some detail in the following two chapters.
11 Gane (1994).

12 Silvey (1974).
13 Pegg (1983).
14 Silvey (1974), p. 161.
15 Abrams (1956), p. 36.
16 Silvey (1974), p. 167.
17 Ibid., p. 168.
18 This is apparent in Rowland's (1983) account of the violence research.
19 Himmelweit et al. (1958), p. 49.
20 See BBC/ITA (1960).
21 Abrams (1956).
22 For example, Associated Rediffusion (1963).
23 BBC/ITA (1960).
24 Ibid., p. 28.
25 Ibid., p. 17.
26 Ibid., p. 2.
27 Abrams (1961), p. 1
28 Silvey (1974), p. 173.
29 Perhaps the most significant exception to this in the case of the BBC has been the series of time budget studies entitled 'Daily Life' – although this research has not been widely used outside the Corporation.
30 Ang (1991).
31 This is Ang's (1991) formulation.
32 Burns (1977).
33 Burns (1977), p. 134.
34 Ibid., pp. 143–4.
35 Department of Education and Science (1983).
36 BBC (1974).
37 Association of Market Survey Organisations (1988), pp. 46–7.
38 See Kline (1993); Fleming (1996).
39 Association of Market Survey Organisations (1988), pp. 46–7.
40 Ibid.
41 Cf. Young (1990).
42 Sharot (1994).
43 Kent (1994).
44 Ang (1991); Kent (1994).
45 See Barwise and Ehrenberg (1988); Kent (1994).
46 Burns (1977), p. 141.
47 This view of the child audience as incorrigible 'zappers', restlessly flicking between channels, was very much shared by the producers of such programmes.
48 For example, Collett and Lamb (1986).
49 Gane (1994).
50 Ang (1991).
51 The series producer, Roger Singleton-Turner, told us that 'nothing emerged [from the research] that made modification of the series necessary, although we all "felt" the second series should move on from the first in some way'.
52 For an analysis of this practice, see Gitlin (1983).
53 See, for example, Foucault (1979).
54 David Leonhardt and Kathleen Kerwin, 'Hey kids, buy this!', *Business Week*, 30 June 1997.
55 See Fisch (1998).
56 All figures here are taken from the BARB Annual Report 1996.
57 All figures here are taken from the BVA Annual Report 1996.

5 Look Who's Talking
How Media Producers Define the Child Audience

Institutional history, political economy, scheduling, research – the topics we have so far considered all, in a strong sense, reflect the relationship between children's television and its audience. Tracking these topics across time, and through different contexts, has revealed something of the variability of this relationship. We have seen how conflicts over departmental structures, fears about the effects of the market-driven expansion of children's television and the basic techniques of scheduling and the paradigms of research have all involved, at least implicitly, some conceptualisation of the child audience – and, indeed, of childhood itself. In this chapter we examine these conceptualisations in more detail, by exploring the ways in which the child audience is discussed by those who work in children's television.

The material we analyse here was mostly gathered from interviews – about forty of them – with people responsible in some way for producing, distributing or regulating television for children. Between them, our interviewees covered the whole range of children's television – script-writing, direction, production, research and marketing; they worked for the BBC, for independent production or research companies, for regulatory bodies and in cable and satellite broadcasting. Historically, their experience extended from the earliest days of the BBC/ITV duopoly to the contemporary multi-channel marketplace. In the interviews, we tried to explore two central questions. The first concerned the ways in which people understood the *specificity* of the child audience and its needs and interests. The second focused on how these ideas about the special nature of the audience translated into decisions about the form and content of 'media products' (we use this term, rather than simply 'television programmes', because some of what we discussed went well beyond questions of programme-making and extended into areas of branding, merchandising and so on).

Answers to these questions were, of course, entangled with the particular positions and interests of the interviewees. Those involved directly in programme-making, for instance, talked about their audience in terms that stressed 'engagement', 'reaching out' and 'breaking through the screen'. Those with a more distant commissioning or regulatory role were more inclined to dwell on issues of 'range' and 'diversity'. Similarly, 'need' meant different things to people working in different, age-related sectors of television: an involvement with the pre-school audience tended to produce a very different account of 'need' from that developed in the course of making television for older children. Our interviewees were aware of the specificities of their own position; yet they inevitably tended to generalise from this, and to develop an overall account of television's relation to children's needs and interests.

The presence of such differences suggests perhaps that the interviews disclose more about the particularities of specific institutional roles than about any general trends in children's television. This is a possibility which we've considered, and made some allowance for, but in overall terms rejected. On the basis of the interviews, we think it is possible to trace clear connections between changes in the organisational and economic structures of children's television and the discourses of the people whom we will very loosely call 'media producers'. These connections apply – though in varying ways – to the prevailing discourses in all sectors of children's television, whether age-specific or inclusive; and among bearers of all its functions – production, commissioning and scheduling, marketing, research and regulation.

By 'discourse' we mean, most simply, a 'domain of language use unified by common assumptions'.[1] Identifying discourses is not a precise science. As Volosinov long ago suggested, language is 'an atmosphere made up of multifarious speech performances that engulf and wash over all persistent kinds of ideological creativity'.[2] This multifariousness is given some shape by the play of social interests and the existence of situations that are shared by members of a social group. On the basis of these interests and situations – which are never fully stable – a tendency emerges to 'fix' meanings, and to identify certain topics as central. It is the existence of these processes of fixing and prioritising which allows us to speak of *a* discourse, even if the fixing of meaning is temporary and the prioritising is contested. To speak, then, of 'media industry discourse' is not to impute to our interviewees some entirely coherent paradigm. It is rather to suggest that the interviews offer evidence of a common area of language use, whose boundaries are not well defined but whose existence can be determined by persistent resemblances in linguistic patterns.

The interviews encode convictions, emotions, beliefs, ideas embedded in everyday work habits, interpretations of history, guesses about the future. In doing so, they involve a particular construction of childhood, and of the 'moment' of broadcasting in the late 1990s: from the vast range of child behaviour and the experience of television production, and from all the complex and conflicting interpretations of them, our interviewees *select* particular characteristics they regard as salient, and offer an account of the child audience in those terms. Thus, for instance, all are agreed that the audience has special characteristics which distinguish it from adult audiences, and to which broadcasters must respond. What is controversial is whether these characteristics are best understood as *needs* or *wants*: that is, as requirements which children may not consciously or even willingly possess, but which can legitimately be ascribed to them by broadcasters determined to promote their welfare; or alternatively as consumer demands which are directly signalled by children, and which should form the cornerstone of broadcasting policy. Differences over such issues mean that discussions of children's television are 'multi-accentual': they necessarily invoke diverse and conflicting assumptions about the meaning of contemporary childhood.

Within the overall field, then, we can identify four broad subcategories of producer discourse about the child audience. The first of these centres on the idea of the 'vulnerable child' – the child threatened by the bad effects of television or seductively interpellated by consumer culture, and for both reasons in need of protection. The second is a 'child-centred' discourse, in which ideas about children's essential nature, the stages of children's development and their consequent needs and wants are used to justify particular kinds of scheduling and programme-making. The third and fourth types of discourse involve an assumption that children are articulate 'social actors'. They are similar in that they stress the primacy of children's preferences and draw attention to children's social capabilities. They differ in so far as they inflect this socially active child in conceptually distinct – though in practice overlapping – ways: the child is understood here either as a *consumer* or as a potential *citizen*.

At first glance, the story of post-war broadcasting might suggest a chronological development of these models. The early years of the BBC would in this account embody the paternalistic view of the audience as vulnerable; while its 1970s 'golden age' might represent the heyday of child-centred discourse. 'The child as social actor' (especially in his/her consumer guise) could then be understood as the discourse most characteristic of our own period, the zenith of a commercial culture of childhood which treats its consumers with the enthusiastic seriousness it thinks they deserve.

Such a chronological interpretation – involving a move from a paternalism based on the notion of 'needs' to an unequivocal approval of children's 'wants' as consumers – has something to commend it. It certainly identifies a rough general tendency in children's television, and plausibly predicts its future development. But what it cannot capture is what might be called the 'sedimented' nature of discourse. In contemporary children's television, all these definitions of the child audience – although they developed at different historical moments – are in fact simultaneously present. Nor are the discursive positions they embody divided by uncrossable frontiers. Different historical contexts give rise to different combinations or articulations of discourses. Thus, protectionism and child-centredness, which once confronted each other largely as opposites, now share a concern with the cultural particularities of childhood which, in their view, market forces tend to destroy. In other contexts, it is often hard to distinguish where 'child-centredness' ends and notions of the child as consumer or 'active citizen' begin. As a result of this (constant) process of combination and recontextualisation, discourses are modified. Thus, while the 'protectionism' of the 1990s employs some of the tropes familiar from earlier decades, in other respects, as we shall show, its themes are more novel.

But if these discourses are simultaneously present, it is not in any simple form: they are not equal in power, nor are they all at a similar stage in their development. Protectionism – as we suggested in Chapter Two – still has considerable influence as a public discourse about television; but as an occupational ideology it occupies a less commanding position. Though child-centredness remains central, but it is losing the secure institutional basis on which it once flourished, and now depends for its survival on a fraught and unceasing negotiation with the pressures of the marketplace. Meanwhile, the third discourse – the model of the child as active consumer – is now being driven by the force of commercial expansion into every corner of children's television.

To capture both the unequal relations between discourses, and their various origins, their rise and decline and continuing bases of support, we can make use of some ideas developed more than twenty years ago by Raymond Williams.[3] Williams argued that cultures can be understood as combinations of 'dominant', 'residual' and 'emergent' elements. By 'dominant' Williams means 'the central [and] effective system of values' – values which are 'not merely abstract but ... organised and lived'. The 'residual' element comprises 'experiences, meanings and values which cannot' – certainly not in their totality – 'be verified or expressed in terms of the dominant culture', but which can either serve as a rallying point for opposition to dominant cultures, or can at least in part be incorporated within it. 'Emergent' cultures are those 'new meanings and values, new practices, new significances and experiences' which are continually being created, and which may be incorporated within the dominant culture, or may remain outside, offering a substantial challenge to it.

We can adapt Williams's ideas – which in their scope are intended to address a vast process of societal change – to the smaller world of media discourse. The category of 'residual' can be applied, we think, to protectionist discourse. This is not to say that it has been completely marginalised. Those involved in children's television agree that questions of 'effect' remain important, and draw on protectionist discourses to discuss the issue. Moreover, protectionism still provides a public language in which to discuss television policy and criticise television practice. But this is not the same as saying that it provides the central reference point in debates about television's future, or the most useful intellectual resources with which to discuss it. Contemporary debates centre much more frequently and intricately upon the challenge to a dominant, child-centred discourse from an emergent culture of an exceptionally forceful kind. Generated by the competitive drive of cable and satellite television, flourishing in the climate of the global marketisation of television that has now spread to include the BBC, and feeding from a range of ideas about childhood that extends beyond television into educational, political and academic contexts, the emergent discourse of 'the child as consumer' is vying to become the most important source of meaning and value in thinking about children's television.

The major question raised by these developments concerns the fate of child-centredness. For the past three decades, the discourse of child-centredness has provided the main principles by which television professionals have, in Williams's phrase, 'organised and lived' their work. In one way or another, implicitly or explicitly, those whom we interviewed acknowledged that the conditions in which they worked had changed to the point where the resources afforded by a child-centred discourse were no longer enough to provide a rationale and a direction for their practice. Where they differed was in their evaluation of the completeness of this process: for some, the marketisation of television necessitated a new way of thinking about children which emphasised above all their power as consumers; for others, values and institutional arrangements based on child-centredness could, with some repositioning, continue to form the basis of their work.

Of course, the new emergent position itself presents not just an illustration of

Williams's argument but an especially provocative challenge to it. In Williams's thinking, 'emergent' cultures had a progressive status, though – unlike in some left-wing formulations – their eventual success was never assured. Representing the militant vitality of subordinate groups, they stood not for the extension of market principles but in most important respects for their suppression, in the name of democratic principle, social solidarity and the realisation of human needs. The emergent culture of children's television is very different. Though it accommodates ideas about children's rights, its focal point is not democracy or public service, but the market. It is founded not upon the suppression of market principles – but upon their further development. It involves a belief that competition raises standards, promotes innovation, discovers needs and in doing so develops the capacities and satisfies the desires of audiences. Through the benign workings of the market, wants not previously recognised, or even appreciated by those in whom they are generated, can be identified and provided for. From the vantage point provided by the emergent discourse, older positions appear limited, paternalistic and static; their emphasis on predetermined ideas of 'what children need' neglects or undervalues the capacities of their audience.

However, consumer sovereignty is not the only language in which the newly emergent understandings of children are expressed. Child-centredness has also been qualified and to some extent challenged by the fourth discourse, which emphasises children's agency and their capacities for choice and social action. This is a discourse which draws more from the political sphere of ideas of participation and citizenship than it does from the economic sphere of consumption. This discourse is not necessarily sustained by market forces, and in fact is often hostile to them.[4] Nevertheless, as we suggest towards the end of this chapter, it has had some influence on how the relationship of children to television has been rethought in professional discourse, and it provides resources which are valuable to the overall reshaping of television policy. In some respects, it provides an alternative form of the emergent discourse, though – like all the discursive forms we analyse – it is always combined or articulated in complex ways with other discourses.

In the sections that follow we explore and analyse some of the main features of these four discourses. In doing so, we dwell far more on substantive than methodological issues: we present the words of our interviewees as if they represented consistent and context-free positions, without explicitly considering whether and how the interview situation itself was responsible for 'producing' the utterances we have diligently transcribed. Thus, it is as well to register here something of the context of the interviews.

Like everyone else, our interviewees had positions to defend, interests to safeguard. We – academic researchers, outsiders to the business of television, often ignorant of its subtler politics – were not the most formidable of interrogators. Nevertheless, particularly in our intention to publish our research, we were connected to the public domain – the domain in which television professionals have to make their pitch, justify their choices, defend their company, their role, their job. As a result, we often felt like the audience before whom public presentations were rehearsed. For the purposes of this chapter, this was not a problem – public discourse is discourse nonetheless, the presentations were often vivid and cogent, and we do not believe that we were told anything fundamentally at variance either with broadcasters' published utterances or with their everyday working practice. Nevertheless, when executives in cable/satellite companies with a very small market share talked of their companies as a major challenge to the BBC, or when schedulers stressed the wholesome social motivations that lay behind their choice of programmes, we could not avoid noting that their statements had a rhetorical, rather than a merely descriptive, function.

The following discourses have thus at least a triple context: the immediate encounter of the interview and the wider background of the debates both about contemporary childhood and about television practice. In our account it is the latter two contexts which are most salient. We aim to suggest the conditions which make possible these particular professional discourses; we try to indicate their coherence and suggest both where they overlap and their limitations. We begin with perhaps the most familiar figure in the discourse of children's television – the vulnerable child.

Protectionism

At the heart of many debates about television is the child who needs protection. This is a principle which entire schedules have silently accepted. As we have noted, before 1957, television was not broadcast between 6 and 7p.m. This blank zone was meant to insulate children from the stories of 'rape', 'abortion' and 'capital punishment' which might occupy the news bulletin.[5] The 'toddlers' truce', briefly observed by both the BBC and ITV, has gone, but the principle which underlies it in part remains. The 9 o'clock watershed, gradually introduced in the early 1960s, is intended to provide a signal to parents that a point has been reached after which programmes may be unsuitable for family viewing. Nor are protective attitudes just a feature of scheduling. Arguments about childhood have also been deployed in order to justify regulatory approaches to television. The Pilkington Report of 1962, for instance, criticised and called for changes in ITV programming policy partly on the grounds that it was having adverse effects on children, 'who are normally protected from outside influences and therefore especially vulnerable'.[6] In Pilkington's version of protectionism, the commercialism of ITV was in broadcasting terms the main enemy of the child.

Changes in the structure of broadcasting – and in family life – have since made aspects of the paternalistic position less tenable. As one producer pointed out – though somewhat exaggerating the differences between present and past – children are no longer dependent or controlled viewers:

> When you had a paternal scheduler . . . I mean, they assumed in the 1950s that Mummy was at home and that you would put children's television on at teatime and they would sit down and that would be it, and they wouldn't watch beyond whatever. You can't schedule in that paternalistic way any longer. You've got cable and satellite and video and all the rest.

In this contemporary situation, the regulated schedule takes on what is in some respects a merely formal character. 'It seems bizarre', a lobbyist remarked, 'that at the same time as you've got children's programmes at 5 o'clock, you have Oprah

Winfrey or something on the other two channels.' Likewise, though less reflectively, a children's producer at the BBC explained to us the seriousness with which her department adhered to regulative guidelines, and yet went on to say that what children watched outside of scheduled children's time was no part of her responsibility.

These infringements of regulated boundaries have increased in the 1990s; but they have not eliminated the vulnerable child from the everyday working imagination of producers. While at one level they are keen to entice the audience, at another they are just as aware as their counterparts in the 1950s of the necessarily protectionist element in children's television. In particular, many of our interviewees spoke in Pilkingtonian terms of the threat of commercial influence. And they likewise combined, quite in the manner of an Owen Reed, resistance to the idea that television in any direct way influences the behaviour of children with a sense of the limits of what should be represented. Even producers who are noted for their embrace of controversial issues made clear distinctions of this kind:

> There are practical things, physical things I won't do. The big no-no is glue sniffing ... The research shows that if you are someone with a particular kind of metabolism, one smell will react with you and cause serious damage, even death ... With twelve million people watching, that's just too big a risk.

Thus strong traces of earlier attitudes remain. But in contemporary discourse they take on a new and more intense meaning. As long ago as 1958, Hilde Himmelweit and her colleagues expressed concern about the effects of competition: 'once there is a choice of channels, with programmes as at present distributed, those with educational value or those which have been especially made for children are most likely to suffer.'[7] Market pressures are incomparably stronger now; and public service discourses are on the defensive. Childhood itself, as we suggested in the Introduction, is a site of constant worry and contention. In these circumstances, protectionist fears become more acute and more complex. The result is the mingling of two conflicting and contradictory ideas about vulnerability. On the one hand, there is a fear that the child may obtain *too much* knowledge, particularly of a sexual kind. On the other, the child is regarded as a target for commercial interests, possessing *too little* experience or knowledge to resist them. Thus, it is argued, children need to be protected both from the consequences of their premature knowledge and from those that stem from their prolonged state of ignorance. For many broadcasters, particularly those with a background in public service television, both dangers are carried on the winds of market forces.

The threat of the new

More than one of our interviewees offered us a potted history of children's television. In most cases, the history described an increasingly fraught experience, of the kind elaborated in this classically ambivalent account provided by one former BBC producer:

153

[In the past] I think it would be true to say that neither controller gave a fig about children's programmes ... It was a ghetto in the sense that nobody from the bigger world ever went there ... They just handed it over and knew nothing about it, probably cared even less. And it was all just in the hands of children's programmes. That was OK. You got strong people who'd got very clear ideas about what they were doing ... But then things changed. As the environment became more competitive and every single slot became an issue for competition, at least in terms of ensuring reach if not share, it meant that every corner of the schedule was being opened up ... There were inevitably then questions starting to be asked by people who had never previously looked or asked about what they were doing: why were they doing it? how were they doing it? was it successful? – and successful clearly meant, you know, bums on seats. That is a reality people prefer not to discuss too much ... Certain things disappeared – for instance, *Jackanory*. Certain other things started to appear more frequently, viz. cartoons ... In children's programming, as in every other area, increased competition took various faltering steps as people struggled over what was the appropriate response to that competitive threat.

In this narrative, children's television is dragged from its 'ghetto' (or haven) into the clear and competitive light of day. Some things are lost, and the influence of 'strong', committed people declines: the moral and cultural principles of protectionism seem to be undermined by the forces of competition. But at the same time, children's television encounters 'reality', and in the process begins a process of 'faltering' change.

Other interviewees were less equivocal. 'There is a lot of nervousness,' one ITV executive told us, 'there is a lot of uncertainty. There is a lot of worry about the future.' She went on to underline the key term in this discourse of increasing danger: 'my job is a constant battle to preserve my time slots, *preserve the quality*.' Quality for this interviewee, as to several others, entailed not just a set of production values but a sense of 'responsibility' to the child audience. 'Responsibility' – 'a frightening role' – in turn is grounded not just on adherence to particular professional norms but on a recognition and an honouring of wider social practices and values, in which nation and family both play a part. As this executive observed:

> ITV and the BBC have a role to play which is ... preserving quality, preserving information, preserving cultural identity. 'Cultural identity' – what the hell does it mean without – to me it means, somehow, English voices, regional voices, not everything that's American. It's about how we live in this country and the pressures that are put upon us. It's not cloud-cuckoo-land – you know, *Clarissa*.

'How we live in this country', she went on, may not be particularly 'hip and cool'. Attending to it may be 'old-fashioned' and 'patronising', but it involves nonetheless a necessary descent from such a 'cloud-cuckoo-land' – the safe, suburban world of the Nickelodeon sitcom *Clarissa Explains It All* – in which (it is implied) wealth, style and teenage autonomy are indiscriminately celebrated. In contrast, our interviewee argued, we must begin to recognise certain domestic values and necessities. 'Where's the family? You know, where's the family?' she demanded, rhetorically, of cable and satellite companies, 'the terrestrial base where you are happy to sit with your mum and watch television?'

In this strongly self-justifying account, protectionism has both a cultural and a moral dimension. Public service traditions serve as the upholder of 'regional' life against commercial tendencies which both homogenise what is offered to children ('at the end of the day', the same executive told us, 'everything will look just the same') and promote a fashionable but unrepresentative metropolitan experience as the core lifestyle for children. Simultaneously, the argument extends beyond the issue of representativeness into the area of morality: one of the things that is wrong with a metropolitan bias is that it exposes children to knowledge and attitudes that they would be better off without:

> At the end of the day, a child in the Midlands or a child in Border of twelve is not the same as a child of twelve in London. And I think this is the dilemma for everybody ... It's London where the huge battle is going on: that's where satellite will take its toll and continue to take its toll. In the rest of the country where maybe children, you know, are allowed to be children ... in certain parts of the country where children do have a family life – look at the ratings, it's fascinating to see – it says something about class, it says something about ethnic balance ... You find a very, very strong metropolitan division and particularly a London experience. And I think that's the dilemma for children's television ... There's a show called *Moesha* [on satellite] ... which is actually quite fearsome in its attitude to sex ... It is indicative of the trendiness and – of London. And I think in a way *Moesha* goes one step again – pushes the boundaries yet again for kids who will watch it ... I mean there are scenes in it where the step-mum – there's a joke about the fact that she pushes condoms in Moesha's handbag on her sixteenth birthday, and it's all part of the frivolity ... I suspect that if you look at where *Moesha* will do best, it will inevitably do better in London than anywhere else.

The shifts and turns in the argument here are worth close attention. Questions of popularity and ratings are interwoven with those of regional, class and ethnic difference. Outside London, it is argued, there remains a strong audience for the BBC and ITV. Competition between terrestrial and cable/satellite companies is fiercest in the cities, where class and ethnic diversity provide favourable cultural conditions for the growth of a channel like Nickelodeon. Its growth both feeds from and contributes to a pattern of changing taste and cultural attitude whose consequences are considered alarming. Market competition and lightly regulated television bring with them an undesirable knowledge: 'the London experience' – an experience which incorporates a strong black element (*Moesha* is a sitcom featuring African-American teenagers) – undermines the moral certainties of 'regional life'.

By contrast, for other producers the problem has more to do with the way in which such competition contributes to cultural tendencies towards ignorance. Several of our interviewees, especially those with a BBC background, contrasted the 'needs-oriented' past of the BBC with a 'wants-oriented' present. The sense they had developed of the needs – and the vulnerability – of their audience stemmed from their experience as programme-makers. The BBC's traditional way of seeing children, claimed one long-standing producer, encouraged programme-makers to 'personalise' the audience, and thus to sensitise themselves to the potential effects of their work:

> The attitude to children was 'we have an audience, and the audience isn't six million or five million or whatever, it's the six-year-old sitting at home perhaps on his own, perhaps on her own'. And there was a kind of awareness of how the programme would be viewed.

By conceptualising the audience as a body made up of individual children, producers were able – they claimed – to develop a sense of those children's all-round needs, which included education as much as entertainment. They were also resistant to children's immediate wants. If children have a desire for instant gratification, that desire must not necessarily be satisfied. 'You don't give children what they want all the time,' the same interviewee told us, elaborating on the kind of dietary metaphor which recurred several times in our interviews. 'You don't give them Mars bars all the time. You don't give them sweets all the time. You make sure they have something substantial.'

But because contemporary television is constantly in search of the largest possible audience, the argument follows that it has discarded this sometimes unobliging sense of audience need in favour of collusion in some of the least attractive features of contemporary culture. According to some of our interviewees, the failures of contemporary parenting are compounded by television's willingness to accept and exploit the situation that this failure creates. As the same long-standing BBC producer put it:

> Parents don't read to their children like they used to. Children who seem to enjoy *Jackanory*...seem to be the children who have parents who read to them a lot. That tradition is changing or dying somewhat ... and I think *Jackanory* is about to lose out ... I think there's an attention span problem ... I don't think parents even sit down with their children and watch children's programmes, quite honestly.

From this perspective, the duty of the programme-maker is to swim against the current. Children need to be led away from the compulsions of the marketplace, even though the tendency of television is now to sweep them ever more directly towards it. But this is a daunting task. As one entertainment producer at the BBC told us, 'Children of six are being seen as consumers rather than viewers.' The logic of the market – in the context of an abundance of airtime – is for producers to seek out a particular audience, and to give it a great deal of what it wants, so as to command its continuing attention. As this producer told us, whole sections of weekend television are devoted to the minute-by-minute pursuit, or placating, of what is deemed to be a fickle but demanding audience:

> Now, because they've also got the chance to determine themselves that something else is coming along by hitting that remote control, we've got to make sure they don't. We want them to stay with us ... we want them to stay with us ... we want them to be part of the aura that the programme is producing, and it's a case of trying to say, 'this is good, the thing after is better, the thing after that is even better than that'.

In the process, some producers feel, the range and variety that are the hallmarks of public service television for children are in danger of disappearing. Instead, children are most exposed to what can most easily manipulate them. 'Are there particular groups within the audience that you think are more vulnerable?' we asked one BBC executive. Yes, she answered. Her channel was committed to range and variety. It could not aim to satisfy fully the wants of every audience group. Yet cable and satellite could do just this, with visible effects on the behaviour of its (totally immersed and therefore manipulable) target audience:

Young boys ... will go to the Cartoon Network, and if you've ever sat in a room watching young boys watch the Cartoon Network it is one of the most frightening experiences I've ever seen. Because it is total ... I mean, they see a cartoon over and over again and they will pre-empt what's going to happen, but it's not like it's a – it's like an experience.

For those who employ or inhabit a protectionist discourse, then, the encounter between children's television and market forces involves both the exposure of children to undesirable, 'mature' knowledge and the manipulation of their immaturity. In this respect, a discourse whose origins lie in the earliest days of children's television has entered new times, and has been reshaped by them.

'Child-centred' television

In the rhetoric of social and cultural policy, the mid-twentieth century was the era of 'child-centredness'. Occupational discourses in a number of fields conceptualised the role of professionals as a matter of meeting the needs of children. Children were in turn credited with qualities which served to validate and render essential the particular ways of working developed by professionals. Education is perhaps the best example of this line of argument. Here it was claimed that young children learned best through activity rather than simply instruction, and that the pace of cognitive and affective development varied widely from one child to another. On this basis, educationalists argued for a break from the 'desk-bound' teaching of the past, and put forward a case for a school system based on a strong degree of professional autonomy in the design of curricula: since there was such a degree of variation among children, patterns of teaching and learning were best determined at classroom level.[8] Thus, particular conceptions of the child and of the teacher-as-expert were at one and the same time ratified: the child's uniqueness could be celebrated; the teacher's protection from governmental interference secured.

To some extent insulated from the wider world of television between the 1960s and the 1980s, professional discourse in children's television reproduced these arguments. It embodied definitions that guided everyday practice, and strategies that advanced producer interests. It made a case for a particular version of children's television in terms of general claims about the nature of the child audience, and indeed of childhood itself. Those who employed the discourse utilised these claims to justify their mission, and to defend themselves against sceptics – such as Stuart Hood – who doubted the need for a dedicated children's service. In this section, we want to distinguish between the various components of the discourse and to show how it has increasingly been undermined, both by institutional change and by the rise of other accounts of children's nature and needs.

We can identify five enduring features of child-centredness – that is, of an approach to scheduling and programme-making which proceeds from assertions about 'what children are like' and about their consequent needs. All have become part of the everyday working practice of producers, and are reflected in the intrinsic institutional arrangements of public service television. The first is the existence of something that several interviewees referred to as 'the children's own world', a world that is relatively distinct from adulthood. It is on this basis that children have to be addressed differently by television. Their needs cannot be met by allowing them, as it were, to look over the shoulders of adults; they must have programmes that relate to them in an appropriate, distinctive way. But although the television needs of children are in one way different from those of adults, in another they are similar – homologous. Children have whole personalities and all-round requirements, and thus need what one of our interviewees called 'a mini-channel with all the genres' – or what the BBC in 1974 referred to as a 'comprehensive television service of their own in which virtually every kind of programme ... is represented'.[9] This belief in 'comprehensive television' – or the 'mini-schedule' – we identify as the second feature of child-centredness. It is closely related to a third feature, the demarcation of children's television from *schools* television. Children, it would seem, cannot live by education alone: comprehensiveness involves recognising children's other needs – to relax and be entertained, and to have an area of their lives in which educational demands (though they have a place) do not come first.

Fourth, there is an assumption that needs are fundamentally age-related. 'Life is a process of growth,' claimed one of the key texts in the educational emergence of child-centredness, 'in which there are successive stages, each with its own character and needs.'[10] According to one former BBC executive, 'It doesn't matter whether they are three or thirteen, children have to be thought about in terms of their age.' From her perspective, one of the great fallacies upheld by opponents of the BBC Children's Department was that 'all children would like the same things'. Only a specific kind of professional expertise could rescue television from the consequences of this misapprehension: 'it's only when you have a dedicated children's department that you will have people thinking of what is appropriate for a five-year-old or an eleven-year-old.' In this respect, what was true in the 1970s continues to apply now. Conceptions of age-related difference shape quite fundamentally the approaches of programme-makers: children under seven (we were told by one producer) like 'surreal things'; while another executive mapped out a complete developmental sequence, in which six- to eight-year-olds were 'fresh', 'open' and 'inquisitive', nine- and ten-year-olds were fashion-conscious and tended to be 'jaded', and eleven- and twelve-year-olds responded to 'contemporary-based, issue-led soap'. For schedulers, the existence of such differences cannot be set aside, though it creates difficulties that need constant attention, as one executive explained:

> The requirement that we have from the ITC to cover all children, that's a very difficult job within a very constrained and very short time band, which is 3.30 to 5.10 p.m. ... At the end of the day, you cannot stop at nine-year-olds. At the end of the day, I could say, 'I only want to take four- to nine-year-olds', because there's absolutely no doubt that the shows we are best at are shows for four- to nine-year-olds. But we are going up to eleven-year-olds.

Lastly, the child-centred discourse is also marked by a concern with children's welfare. In part, this concern is necessarily protectionist. It involves making decisions about suitable and unsuitable viewing material, based on the implicit fear that children are imitative, vulnerable, far from completely rational people. But it also has a place in child-centredness: a concern for the aesthetic, social and intellectual needs of children has historically been accompanied by a strong and minutely detailed commitment to their welfare. 'Was children's television a vocation?' we asked one producer. 'Absolutely, absolutely, absolutely', she replied, and elaborated her answer in two ways, both of which centred on the 'commitment and care' of producers. In the first instance, care entailed thinking about physical safety. 'I've drawn up a whole list of danger ... guidelines for children ... Things like you never show children in front of a fire without a fireguard, you don't see them crossing a road without an adult.' Yet in the second instance, the duty of care had broader implications, which were not merely protectionist: children were entitled to 'a television service of their own' which 'reflected' their lives; programme-makers committed to children's broader welfare had a duty to provide such a service – and in this sense caring for children involved a recognition of their autonomy as well as their vulnerability.

The nature of the child

So far, we have outlined the general features of child-centredness as a professional discourse, with particular emphasis on how these features have affected the overall design of public service television for children. We now want to discuss in more detail one particular aspect of the discourse – the way in which it imagines the nature of the child. In the course of this discussion, some of the differences between child-centredness and protectionism will become clear.

Child-centredness, as it has been used in television since the 1960s, rests in the first place upon a historical distinction. It offers a version of history which depicts the past as a time of protectiveness, which subjected children to an adult reading of their tastes and preferences and declared some of their most vital interests to be out of bounds. As we've already seen in Doreen Stephens's account from the mid-1960s (see Chapter One), this way of writing history demarcated the 'condescension', 'cushioned ignorance' and 'overprotectiveness' of the past from a present in which television promoted the 'natural growth and development of the mind'. From 1964 until the mid-1980s, this self-perception, with some variation, provided the central motif of producer discourse about childhood. It had two major components. The first of these could be described as a form of child-centredness based on a *universal*, socially abstract conception of the nature of children. Like the versions of progressive education circulating in the post-war years, it combined a certain romanticism with a particular sort of learning theory. The second component was a child-centredness of a more *social* kind, which stressed the specific cultures of children, often in class-related terms. Again, there are educational parallels here.

The discourse of 'universalist child-centredness' was developed particularly in the context of television made for very young children. Its themes were most clearly rendered by Monica Sims in 1971, describing the purposes of *Play School*, in terms which although already quoted are vivid enough to bear repeating here:

There is no directive to learn but constant encouragement to play – with games, rhymes, stories, songs, movement, sounds, painting and dressing-up. To find out, make, build, watch, enquire, listen and help. To experiment with water, shapes, textures, movement and sounds. To wonder, think and imagine.[11]

Here the child is a combination of engineer, scientist, artist and seer blest. Play and learning are intertwined, since education and entertainment, in the case of young children, are one and the same. The image which lies at the heart of public service television for children is thus that of the child as playful learner. It is this intrinsic linkage which has allowed BBC producers to insist for so long on both the enjoyability and the unforced educativeness of their programmes: it was this, for instance, that enabled a producer of *Teletubbies* to describe her programme as educative in as much as it was 'an extension of imaginative play'.

A theory of learning as play and of play (broadly understood) as learning provides in the first instance a justification for programme-making for the under-fives. But it also finds echoes in accounts of television made for older age groups, where the elision of education and play distinguishes children's programmes from those produced for schools. Thus, in the 1970s, the value of the magazine programme *Blue Peter* was seen to lie in its ability to stimulate its viewers into activity in a way that was both educational and useful. It set out 'to encourage individual thought and action on the part of the audience'. It prompted children 'to send in some 4,000 letters every week' and 'invited them to join in helping others less fortunate'.[12] Children's drama – an art that was seen to unite pleasure and learning – was also justified in this way. Like the novels on which its adaptations were based, it served as a form of emotional education, an encounter with a particular literary tradition, which was also a means of promoting the growth of central human faculties – empathy, sensibility, moral awareness and judgment. Owen Reed's account of the developmental purposes of children's drama, quoted in Chapter One, was echoed in the 1960s and 1970s by similar claims; and the struggle of producers to recapture drama for the Children's Department only takes on its full meaning against this conceptual background – of childhood understood as a process of natural growth that could be fostered through the provision by wise broadcasters of opportunities to watch, enquire, learn and imagine.

As in education, universalist child-centredness contains a strong normative dimension, so much so that an uncanny similarity often emerges between the needs of childhood and the historic mission of public service television: the nature of children is such that children have a need to be educated and informed as well as entertained, and it so happens that this is what Reithian television is about. But to see child-centredness as just protectionism in a new guise – as a way of ascribing characteristics to the child audience in order to confine it more effectively within the limits of traditional public service practice – would be to overlook the broader aspects of the discourse. Child-centredness has also encouraged a certain alertness to the tastes and preferences of children. It has accepted that children's cultures are in a state of constant change and has thus continually made an issue of television's ability to track and respond to these changes. At this point, universalist child-centredness becomes something more specific, and producers have to develop conceptions of need that grow out of audience preoccupation as much as from broadcasters' ascriptions. Ideas about the fundamental nature of children are not abandoned, but they are qualified by cultural judgments. Some of these judgments relate to historical change and proceed from the recognition that children are not what they were. Others relate to *social* differences among the audience. Monica Sims, for instance, defending the specificity of British television against US imports, invoked the radical theories of the educationalist Basil Bernstein:

> We should start knowing that the social experience the child already possesses is valid and significant, and that his social experience should be reflected back to him as being valid and significant. It can only be reflected back to him if it is part of the texture of the learning experience we create.[13]

Sims's invocation of 'social experience' was not wholly matched by the actual practice of children's television at the time. Nevertheless, it both indicates the openness of child-centred discourse to a more culturally specific inflection and prefigures developments of the later 1970s, when the abstract universalism of earlier conceptions of the child was supplemented by a greater awareness of social difference, in which politically accented notions of 'experience' and 'relevance' acquired prominence. *Grange Hill,* first shown in 1978, is particularly salient in this context.[14] It stressed 'issue-based' drama, rather than timeless universals, and its producers understood 'issues' in a novel way. The appeal of *Grange Hill,* one of its producers suggested, was that it was 'organic . . . coming from our own culture'. Another producer, justifying the *Grange Hill* project, argued that its appeal lay not in the didacticism of much topical drama for children, but in the close connection it made with concerns that its audience experienced as central:

> Issues are only issues because the audience as a body politic are interested in it. And because in some ways it affects their lives. Therefore it is legitimate for drama because it is touching people in their emotions and passions and feelings. And that applies to everything, whether it's kids or adults. Therefore, this thing about issues – we don't have a checklist or a shopping list of issues – you really have to keep plugging in all the time to see what people are concerned about – what are the issues of the moment, and if you do that the kids will come with you. They'll watch you.

Child-centredness at the crossroads

As we indicated in Chapter Two, the relatively protected occupational cultures of public service television are now exposed to the pressures of the marketplace. Audience numbers cease to be predictable, income is not guaranteed, working environments have become unsettled and insecure, creativity in programme-making is not enough to ensure survival. As one executive told us:

> Ultimately, the companies that will survive in children's programmes will be those who have equal skills at raising the money and running the programme as a business, and have creative ideas . . . We are going to have to become salesmen as well as programme creators and programme developers and we have to enthuse others with putting up the money.

But this new situation is not predominantly perceived in polarising terms of 'creativity' versus 'commerce': producers will become 'salesmen', without ceasing to be creators. Rather than condemning the market, or accepting it in some cynical spirit of necessity, public service broadcasters are now beginning to consider the possibility of a marriage between 'quality' and marketability. 'Creativity' from this perspective seems less the enemy of success than its guarantor; linked to an effective marketing strategy, it provides the path to the afterlife on which real profit depends. As the same executive suggested:

> We are very rarely cynically saying, 'well, we'll do this because it will get a slot'. We are tending to do what we think will work, what we think will work internationally, what we think will make money for us ... And as a company we are consciously avoiding the ephemeral ... Everything we do, we want it to have an afterlife ... We're looking for a long life – a long shelf life and spin-offs into books, merchandising and whatever.

Child-centredness, in such a context, is modified. In some respects, children's television becomes *more* child-centred: producers work with ever-greater ingenuity to discover and respond to children's needs. Yet at the same time, child-centredness is translated into something that is philosophically less central. It becomes a means – to commercial success – rather than (as some broadcasters in the 1970s might have put it) an end in itself. The survival of a television practice inspired by child-centredness now depends upon meeting criteria that do not stem directly from an invocation of the needs of children, but from market imperatives. This new tension is written into the basic structures of contemporary television discourse, even – or perhaps especially – where those who employ the discourse have a special commitment to child-centred positions.

Thus, one independent producer spoke eloquently of the 'paradox' of children's television. In programme-making terms, everything she did was devoted to a child-centred concept of her (pre-school) audience. Her work was alert to 'the different perceptions of little children'. Its formal innovations were based on a response to what she perceived as their needs: the absence of a presenter allowed children to 'lead themselves'; the frequent replacement of adult voices by those of children was one method she used to 'break through that glass screen and pull people in'. At the same time, as she was acutely aware, the viability of her work lay not only in its aesthetic vitality but in its ability to fill a niche in the market. She recognised that pre-school programmes 'if done right ... make a great deal of money for broadcasters'. This for her was the heart of the paradox. Something as seemingly distant from market values as the nurturing of young children had become a new heartland of commerce; and yet in the process of coping with this conjunction, she had discovered, counter-intuitively, and against the grain of her former belief, that there was something sustaining about it. The development of new markets – video sales, exports, merchandising – had raised the status of pre-school television and given her creativity a new scope. Yet the elated force of this perception was overshadowed by a sense of some compulsory Faustian pact: 'to some extent, you have to say that we are forced to trust market forces; not that I was ever a Mrs Thatcher fan, Lord forbid. It's the way it's going, and we can't stop it.' The only way to survive this unstoppable movement is to accept it – to compete and succeed on its terms, even if success entails a kind of passivity and subordination:

We are being forced to do two things. One is to establish a brand name, so that parents up there will recognise that whenever you see this sign it's a built-in guarantee of something, and so there has to be a consistency therefore in what we do. And the other is to have a global presence. Because unless we can sell our work internationally we won't survive.

Thus, pursuit of marketable quality involves developing a consistency of product that sells in many different national contexts; and it requires continuous expansion. At these points a contradiction arises: what if expansion and 'creativity' pull in opposite directions, and if the tension between them escalates?

We need to keep small in order to keep the creative part of the business focused, but we have to get big in order to get the finance that we need, because no [one] broadcaster now pays the price per minute that I need ... So it is getting harder to do it, really.

As we have implied, it may be that the forces which have afforded this producer her creative opportunities are also working to reduce the chance of anyone repeating her success in the future. Perhaps the meeting of child-centredness and market success was not something that typified the new possibilities of global television, so much as a single and unrepeatable event – the commercial utilisation of resources accumulated in a public service context whose institutional basis has now crumbled, and which are unlikely ever to be reassembled. 'What is possibly a danger,' this producer recognised, 'what is happening as broadcasting institutions have broken down ... is that there isn't a tradition any more, [and] once they go, there is a whole body of experience and expertise which it is much more difficult to pass on.' Poised at the crossroads, child-centredness is by no means certain whether its momentary success is being bought at too high and too damaging a price.

Wants and needs

The engagement with the market among broadcasters shaped by child-centredness – however successful – is also ambivalent and at least partly critical. Even among the most successful there is a sense of foreboding and of impending decline. No such doubts affect the discourse of the child as sovereign consumer. Carried forward on a wave of deregulated expansion, it is unequivocal in its belief that the interests of children are best served by market forces. It tends to dismiss older discourses associated with public service broadcasting as self-serving defences of adult interests, which denied children what they want in favour of restrictive conceptions of what they need.

We have already sketched some of the ways in which discursive conflicts around children's television have centred on this counterposition between wants and needs. The dichotomy is a long-established one. John Reith, first Director-General of the BBC, noted in the 1920s that 'It is occasionally indicated to us that we are apparently setting out to give the public what we think they need and not what they want – but few know what they want, and very few what they need.'[15] In 1950, the BBC's submission to the Beveridge Committee, which was examining commercial involvement in broadcasting, developed the argument further. Introducing competition for audiences into broadcasting, it argued, would lead to a lowering of programme standards. 'The good, in the long run, will inevitably be driven out by the bad.' Competition would 'descend to a fight for the greatest number of listeners', and in this conflict 'it would be the lower forms of mass appetite which would more and more be catered for in programmes'. The 'purpose, taste, cultural aims, range and general sense of responsibility of the broadcasting service as a whole' would be degraded.[16] And, as we have described, in 1958, Hugh Greene – soon to be Director-General – rounded on ITV's programming for children. It might give the audience what they wanted, but should that, he asked, be the whole story?[17]

Thus the history of argument around taste, popularity, values and standards is as long-standing as broadcasting itself; and in this argument 'wants' have been depicted in negative terms. Want is something base and bodily. It is evoked in metaphors which dwell on the literalness of 'consumption', from the 'mass appetites' whose consequences the BBC feared in 1950 to the 'Mars bars' and 'bubblegum' to which popular children's television has been compared in the 1990s.[18] It is something which must, emphatically, not be allowed to act as the prime criterion for the making of public service television.

'Needs', by contrast, belong to a different realm. At one level, to speak of audience needs is to make a point about diversity: because audiences vary so widely in their tastes and situations, broadcasting cannot legitimately afford to respond only to the preferences of the majority. At another level, the concept of 'needs' appeals to values and to ideas of the personality that exist on a higher plane than mere gratification. In the Reithian framework, audiences have a need for knowledge, information and culturally broadening entertainment, whether they consciously recognise that need or not. The fuller development of the personality, particularly in a society organised around mass consumption of commercial goods, requires public service broadcasting that keeps alive this wider vision of human possibility. Nowhere is this argument more clearly put than in relation to children's television: children are seen, *par excellence*, as a social group which does not know its own needs, and thus requires protection from the consequences of its search for gratification.

Needs-based arguments form the explicit framework of all post-war reports on broadcasting from Beveridge to Annan. They suffuse the BBC's own internal debates and public pronouncements; and after ITV's early, overtly commercialist years, came to affect independent companies as well. As we have seen, they continue to provide the basis of critical commentary on present trends in children's television, which confidently asserts the superiority of 'needs-based' over 'wants-based' television, of public service broadcasting over its commercial competitors.

Since the mid-1970s, however, within a social and economic discourse which extends well beyond television, 'wants' have been rehabilitated. As we will discuss in our conclusion, the rise of market forces as determinants of television practice has been accompanied by a confident restatement of classical arguments for a philosophy of individualism and for a defence of markets as a means of discovering and responding to the preferences of consumers. In the process, the expression of want has come to be seen as an extension of freedom and a contribution to an efficient and non-coercive social order; its satisfaction is viewed as an enlargement of the personality. In this way, the appetites derided by advocates of state or public service provision become dignified, and it is those who seek to deny them who appear as enemies of cultural progress. Consciously or not, it is this store of ideas on which the emergent discourse of children's television has come to draw.

The sovereign consumer

In an earlier part of this chapter, we quoted an improvised version of television history, which centred on depicting the burgeoning threat of competition. Those who are leading the market-based transformation of children's television tell the story differently. They offer a history which is not so much accurate in its details as vivid in its evocation of television's leap from a period of scarcity and regulation to one of choice and abundance. In this account, public service television is an anachronism; popular taste escapes it; some of its functionaries were, according to one cable/satellite executive, 'frozen to death in 1900', and possess only a 'narrow' view of the potential of children's broadcasting. Like the post-war welfare regime of which it is judged to be part, it belongs to a dying age of bureaucracy: history – namely, the explosion of market forces that provide the conditions for cultural complexity and rapidly changing patterns of taste – has outgrown it. As this executive argued:

> My understanding in a way – sociologically – it's almost like education or it's almost like a function that has been performed in a public service way for so many years, and suddenly realises that actually the society which it's performing to has changed. And that's what I think you're seeing in terms of almost a television revolution that's happening now. In fact, going back to the 1945 Welfare Act – if you look at the Welfare Act it did all sorts of extraordinary and truly wonderful things – and if you relate that to society today, it doesn't actually bear much relation to the society we live in now. And yet we still hang on to the premise that that should actually be part of our lives.

Our interviewees were often blunt about the nature of the forces that have brought about this transformation. 'Why do you think this has happened?' we asked one executive in cable/satellite television. 'Money,' she answered, 'money.' The huge increase in the volume of children's programming had as its basis the fact that 'the advertisers, the merchandisers and every single toy manufacturer can now see the virtue of putting money into children's programming'. Children had at last become powerful consumers, if not directly then at least through the buying power of their parents. The arrival in full force of the market was, she remarked, in some respects not a pretty sight. It was a process that involved no measured concern for quality or balanced scheduling. 'Our shareholders', she told us, 'are a company of equity gatherers – they are not programmers, they want a quick buck for their investment and . . . in programming, there isn't a chance in hell of getting a quick buck back.'

Yet at the same time, this search for the quick buck was seen to have unin-tended, beneficial, even liberating consequences. The market's hidden hand was a benign one, for, in searching after profit, companies were compelled to take more seriously than any previous broadcaster the issue of consumer choice. The tastes and demands of the child audience were explored and evaluated (and produced and shaped) as never before. We asked a researcher with Nickelodeon about their contact with audiences, at a time when the channel's overall potential British audience was three million. 'We get about 250,000 to 300,000 phone calls per week,' she told us. 'We've got people paid to answer our phone lines and we interview kids who call in as well. We talk to kids through our on-line service ... We do tours and we take people round on tours ... We go to schools ... We also get 2,000 letters a week.'

This impressive research and communication activity – particularly in relation to the overall size of the audience – is the practical side of a rhetoric of consumer sovereignty that makes enormous liberatory claims. Consumption, together with the voicing of consumer preference embodied both in the act of choosing and in the opportunity provided by research to discuss that choice, is in this account a form of empowerment. They offer the chance to speak and the certainty of being heard. No paternal organisation is present to judge the choice and the preferences that underlie it; and individuality is not collapsed into some overall conception of the public good:

> It's that whole philosophy that Nick is Kids, Nick is Number One, empowering kids, giving kids a voice. Giving kids the television that appeals to them and speaks to them is something that Nickelodeon is about ... We're getting better at it now because we're getting into being a global brand, but more importantly we're into being a locally relevant channel. Because kids are not generic. Kids are different in every marketplace.

This was the most committed and powerful argument we heard in simultaneous defence of market principles and individual empowerment, though even then it does not attain the axiomatic intensity of a slogan devised by one of Nickelodeon's US directors: 'What's good for kids is good for business.'

Other executives in cable/satellite television offered more nuanced, if ultimately just as uncompromising, accounts. They may acknowledge the 'danger' of 'everything being entertainment, as opposed to drama or factual', but at the same time they have no intention of reproducing the public service model. The following account, which manages in a few sentences both to praise the BBC and fundamentally to attack it, draws a sharp line between the old television and the new:

> There's a continual dichotomy between the commercial and the creative which I think is even more so these days. You know, the BBC is desperately fighting to keep their principles in terms of what they're making for children's programming; however, realising that in this commercial marketplace they're in they can't necessarily do just that. And this leads on to all sorts of questions about what the audience wants and what they're prepared to accept and – who is it who's watching BBC television? Is it parents who are watching – or is it the children who are watching? ... And given the choice that children have now, the interesting question is to go and ask the children. Because for me, that's the most important question – how children perceive what they're given as a service in this marketplace.

Here the BBC is first presented as a 'principled' organisation, fighting to retain its creativity in the new 'commercial' context. After that, the analysis becomes complex and critical, since the crisis that faces public service television is revealed as not just one of commercial difficulty but also of remoteness from its audience.

To understand fully the challenge this account presents to public service broadcasting, it needs to be situated in a broader context. The market is seen here as a place where old values are necessarily and productively tested. Older, public service models of creativity placed a primary emphasis on broadcasters' social role. They had the obligation not just of interpreting but of evaluating social trends. The first requirement was that they should have 'a proper sensitivity to the world around them'. The next was that they should interpret social trends, as it were, teleologically: they should judge and respond to them on the basis of how they related to the goal of a good society – hence the declaration of one Director-General that the BBC's work should recognise and give expression to 'the growing points of our society'.[19] It was on such a basis that Pilkington attacked ITV companies for arguing that television should be shaped by society. On the contrary, it asserted, 'what must figure very largely' in the shaping of television 'are the attitudes, convictions and motives of those who plan and produce on our TV screens'.[20] Broadcasters had the social, creative and intellectual responsibility of exploring the range of subject matter and worthwhile experience, and of shaping it for their public.[21] It is this conception of the professional's role – much more weakly present in the 1990s than at the time of Pilkington, but still a force in children's television – which our interviewee wants to set aside. Her focus settles not on the interpretive role of the producer as responsible intellectual, but on the self-perceived needs of the audience. Ultimately, there is no higher criterion for producers than this. And – as the corporate discourse of Nickelodeon maintains – it is a criterion which should not be hidden or made in any way implicit. It can be defended in terms of consumer sovereignty and attentiveness to children's lives. Children, not regulators, governments or producers, are the ultimate judges of what they want and need. That is why, according to one Nickelodeon executive, 'we do not provide now for children what adults think they want'.

This does not mean, however, that the appeal to choice and consumer sovereignty alone can provide an ideology sufficient to sustain the Nickelodeon project. In the case of children, especially, it becomes important to find ways of defending the weak flanks of a choice-centred argument: issues of moral protection, and thus of producer responsibility, necessarily re-enter the discursive frame, and the purity of the channel's original consumerism is in this way 'contaminated' by pragmatic considerations. Nickelodeon executives are keen to qualify their rhetoric of child-empowerment with an insistence that parents will find the channel 'safe' for their kids. In doing so, they borrow from elements of a classic developmental/therapeutic account of the value of children's literature:[22]

> I am so ... imbued with the public service ethos that I think I behave like a public servant all the time when it comes to kids' programmes, because I believe passionately that the provision for kids should be appropriate and should give added value to their lives, so it has to treat them as intelligent human beings and stretch that intelligence ... We are very predominantly storytelling, whether drama or animation ... However, the significant difference here is that a lot of the storytelling covers emotional areas, life skill, growing-up things which I don't think traditional television did as much of ... [The storytelling] has to have a sort of truth within it, in that its characters have to be

real, identifiable, believable characters ... I think it has to be appropriate to kids' lives, in that it reflects what they do ... A programme that doesn't patronise is a quality programme.

Even here, however, at the point where it most obviously acknowledges its debt to traditional claims about the value and purpose of cultural production for children, the discourse departs significantly from earlier models of childhood. The appeal to the child embodied in what this executive called 'perfectly executed crafted drama either from literature or fantasies based on play houses' is rejected. Nor is there any suggestion of the audience's collective, more broadly social concerns: the former BBC producer quoted earlier in this chapter spoke of his audience as a 'body politic', but this is not the emphasis of Nickelodeon. Instead, there is a stress on the consumer as someone who is not so much part of a social collective as someone who is involved in a network of one-to-one relationships, which provides a context for his/her growing maturity. The child is neither overprotected nor rebellious; s/he is in search of emotional truth, and resistant to being patronised. Nickelodeon's image of itself – 'Nick *is* Kids' – needs to be understood in the light of this construction of the consumer: it is a branding which rests on a particular set of assertions about its audience, and these assertions in turn aim to have a material effect – they do not so much describe the characteristics of the audience as seek to produce them.

Currently, Nickelodeon's efforts to gain a competitive edge on channels like Disney and Fox Kids seem to be taking it further in the direction of shaping the taste, and the wider culture, of its audience. According to the same executive:

> We believe in supporting kids ... we are becoming more of a lifestyle channel ... in that we get out into other areas of kids' lives, so that we hope to reach them even if they're not watching the telly. And that's an interesting development that I think you'll find the BBC will certainly have to do – and ITV ... You've got the on-lines, you've got the web sites, you've got the magazines, then you've got the outreach, you've got things that are there for kids whether or not they're involved in the telly – that will become very important for everybody.

Children as citizens

The figure of the child as sovereign consumer is gaining influence in the professional discourse of contemporary television. It does so not because of some inherent persuasive power, but because of its material rationality: it is grounded in the new competitive era, and gives expression to the urgent quest for the audience that characterises it. Thus, although it appears in its purest form in the discourse of cable/satellite broadcasters, it is not confined to that sector alone. Several public service producers whom we interviewed spoke of the invigorating effects of competition; and as we have seen, child-centred professionals increasingly emphasise what they take to be fundamentally positive about competition – namely, its demand that producers do not treat their public as fools, wards or ignoramuses.

In its emphasis on the good sense of the viewer, and its assertion that making good television involves trusting the viewer's capabilities and preferences, the emerging discourse draws from other systems of ideas. As always, there is an overlap. Emergent discourses make new use of earlier, now-residual forms. The still-powerful discourse of child-centredness is re-inflected in consumer-oriented ways. And it is also the case that contemporary television discourse finds room for other versions of the child that do not fit completely either into consumerist or child-centred models. Especially important in this respect is our fourth discourse, which conceives of the child as an actual or potential citizen. While it echoes aspects of child-centredness, and is not completely separate from the 'child as consumer', it nonetheless possesses an identifiable coherence of its own. Like other discourses, it stresses the capacities of children as social actors, but it differs from them in locating action in the public sphere of social and political debate.

A prerequisite of the children's entry into this arena is the sometimes qualified and ambivalent recognition that they have 'rights'. In a recent article, Annie Franklin and Bob Franklin disentangle the complexity of meanings which surrounds the slogan 'rights of the child'.[23] They distinguish between three phases of its development. The first phase, and socially the most radical, ran through the 1970s, and was 'characterised by claims for libertarian participation rights for children, especially ... in education', which was customarily represented as an obstacle to children's development. The concerns of the second phase were crystallised in 1979, the 'International Year of the Child'. Here the focus shifted 'from education rights to the welfare and social arena'; the objective was now not so much the winning of participation rights for children as the securing of a greater degree of protection for them. Institutional developments – the drafting of a United Nations Convention on the Rights of the Child, the establishment of a Children's Legal Centre and of telephone helplines for children facing abuse and bullying – raised the profile of issues of child protection, and helped to make possible, towards the end of the 1980s, a third phase – the 'renewed emphasis on the need for children's participation rights'. Compared with the movements of the 1970s, this new emphasis on participation was less radically critical of existing social structures. It tended to limit children's participation to certain aspects of welfare, where their voice was required as an additional means of preventing their maltreatment. As Franklin and Franklin suggest, in this case 'the acquisition of participation rights was the handmaiden of the protectionist agenda'. Nevertheless, the embodying of even limited participation rights in the Children Act 1989 had a legitimising effect: 'provision, protection, and participation' became handy slogans with which to define a political project.[24] 'Children's rights' has become a discourse of significant, if limited, power, which is linked to substantial change in the legal and social position of children. It is not, however, a dominant discourse: Franklin and Franklin point out how little purchase it has on educational debate, and how conservatively the meaning of rights is interpreted in the courts.

Across its different versions, the tendency of the discourse of children's rights is to admit children to the public sphere. It treats them in certain respects as citizens, who have – at least potentially – a voice in public affairs and a recognised place in the network of social communication. Thus, the UN Convention declares that 'children's views should be given due consideration in processes that affect their interests'.[25] This recognition of children as participants in social communication

169

extends beyond the sphere of welfare rights into that of the media: the Convention affirms the 'freedom' of 'children to seek, receive and impart information of all kinds ... either orally, in writing or in print, in the form of art, or through any other media of the child's choice'.[26] In this way, children come to be granted a certain autonomy: in principle, at least, they are people who can speak for themselves; they do not need to be spoken for. The Children's Television Charter of 1995, to be discussed below, draws on the Convention and endorses – sometimes ambivalently – many of these emphases.

Alongside these international debates on broad matters of principle, there has developed in the 1990s a genre of programmes – such as Channel Four's *Wise Up* and the BBC's *As Seen on TV* – which set out to give access to children's voices. As one exponent of this approach put it, such programmes are based on the principle that 'you ask a kid's opinion of something which affects them rather than always reporting on adults reporting on kids'. Around these programmes has grown up a rhetoric in which children figure as participating citizens. 'It is a voice for kids,' explains the producer of one such programme:

> Reports go into each show done by different children, ranging from dealing with divorcing parents to a twelve-year-old pondering why all his girlfriends leave him for his best friend ... Our audience set the agenda for our programme. They create its content ... They tend to be very good presenters ... because they've devised the subjects and therefore they care about it.

Contemporary television, then, has increased the prominence given to the concept of the child – at least the older child – as a *citizen*, who can speak on matters pertaining to the public sphere as well as the private. This stress is not entirely new. Participation in one form or another has always been a feature of children's television, from the child presenters of the early BBC, to the presence of children and young people on programmes such as *No. 73* and *Speakeasy* in the 1970s and 1980s. What distinguishes the contemporary emphasis on rights is both its stronger presence, facilitated by technological developments such as the portable video camera, and its new political inflection: the children performing good works favoured by *Blue Peter* in the 1970s stand at some distance from the socially critical, reflexive child presenters of *Wise Up*.

In the official discourse of charters, conventions, summits and award ceremonies, this figure of the child as citizen has an increasingly important role. Children, according to one fairly representative document, are 'lively, trenchant, sometimes ruthless critics'.[27] In this formal and public sense, the promotion of citizenship is a central characteristic of contemporary debates about children's television, even though programmes which offer voice and access to children are actually neither common nor especially popular with the child audience. It is not that television is intrinsically hostile to the child-citizen; it is more that in a system driven primarily by market forces, and by the intense effort to respond to the immediate interests of consumers, programmes that invoke a different definition of childhood tend to take on a more marginal status. Channel Four's week-long *Look Who's Talking* initiative, besides supplying us with the title of this chapter (albeit one borrowed from Hollywood), was notable for its emphasis on children's direct involvement in programme-making. It was not representative, though, of

Channel Four's overall output, in which (as we have shown) animation and bought-in US programmes are more prominent.

But this is not to say that contemporary television simply marginalises questions of children's participation in the public sphere. There are areas outside of documentary programmes where such participation is signalled – notably in drama, where a sea-change has taken place. Interestingly, the implicit model of the child-as-citizen that features here appears to have undergone a change in gender. The idealised childhood of children's rights activists in the 1970s was urban, working class and male.[28] The role of this type of model child – not least in children's drama at the time – was to challenge and outsmart teachers and other authority figures. In the 1990s, by contrast, a different model of the socially active child has developed. The emphasis on participation stresses consensus rather than confrontation, feisty responsibility rather than general rebelliousness. It seeks to recognise children's social and technological accomplishments, and their growing maturity. This new socially active child is increasingly represented as female.

For several of the producers whom we interviewed, there were profound differences between the male and female audience. Boys of all ages were seen in terms of their interest in 'action', of a sports or computer-based kind; they were 'genuinely much harder to appeal to than girls ... because they are not quite so emotionally developed'. Boys, as one producer described them, 'don't seem to view things in quite the same [mature] manner'.[29] Girls, on the other hand, as one cable/satellite executive assured us, 'want more information ... Pre-pubescent and teenage girls are desperate for information about their roles in life, about their problems, about their friendships, about everything.' In the same way, the emotionally astute, responsible child evoked by Nickelodeon producers is more often than not a girl. As one of its executives told us, 'Nickelodeon is a channel ... that values girls and actually says, "you have a right to have a voice" – and the role models that they portray are very strong, sassy girls who always come out on top.'

In representations of this type, the boundaries of public and private – and hence the traditional notion of 'citizenship' – become blurred. The female roles described by these producers are not in a conventional sense 'political'. Nevertheless, this discourse does invest girls with some of the qualities associated with citizenly behaviour: they are social beings, who value information as well as entertainment and have a strong desire for self-expression; they are credited with an interest, if not in general rights, then at least in their own advancement, often 'against the odds'. To this extent, the child – the older female child, at least – is recognised as a social and political actor, and represented as such.

The recognition of the child as citizen is also ambiguous in another way, however. There are points at which a consumer-centred rhetoric of empowerment begins to overlap with issues of 'social action', and where the discourse of children's rights is intertwined with one that derives from marketing strategies. The language of UN Conventions – 'voice', 'expression', 'rights' – becomes also the means by which Nickelodeon can brand itself. Likewise, the title of Nickelodeon's own access programme, *MeTV*, fuses questions of voice with the self-absorption of consumer discourse. Recognition of the child as a social actor has become not only a principle of cultural democracy but also a key to market success. In a way that illustrates the complex interlocking of discourses on children and television, the discourse of rights is elaborated here in terms which ultimately acknowledge the supremacy of the market.

In search of consensus

Throughout this chapter, we have referred to the uncertain boundaries of discourse, and to the ways in which those discourses we have provisionally identified as separate tend to combine to form new, and shifting, entities. Analysing these combinations demonstrates how 'new' attitudes merge with 'old', 'rights' with 'protection', 'consumption' with 'child-centredness'. This allows us to understand the tangle of interests, pressures and motivations which contribute to the formation of policy, and underpin everyday practice.

The Children's Television Charter, originally drawn up at the 1995 World Summit on Children and Television in Melbourne, illustrates some of these continuing overlaps and ambivalences in contemporary definitions of children's needs (see Figure 1). The initiative for the Charter came primarily from public broadcasters, and particularly from Anna Home, the recently retired Head of the BBC Children's Department. As such, it is largely driven by the desire to defend traditional public service principles. Quality, diversity and universal access are thus among its key concerns: programmes should be made to 'the highest possible standards'; they should be 'wide-ranging in genre and content'; and they should be 'aired in regular slots at times when children are available to view, and/or distributed via other widely accessible media or technologies'. At the same time, traces of each of the four discourses we have identified in this chapter can be found – both directly articulated and indirectly referred to – in its seven clauses. Thus, protectionism is apparent in the references to 'gratuitous scenes of violence and sex', and the need to protect children from programmes that might 'exploit' them. Child-centredness emerges most strongly in the notion that programmes should 'allow children to develop physically, mentally and socially to their fullest potential'.

---

1. Children should have programmes of high quality which are made specifically for them, and which do not exploit them. These programmes, in addition to entertaining, should allow children to develop physically, mentally and socially to their fullest potential.

2. Children should hear, see and express themselves, their culture, their languages and their life experiences, through television programmes which affirm their sense of community and place.

3. Children's programmes should promote an awareness and appreciation of other cultures in parallel with the child's own cultural background.

4. Children's programmes should be wide-ranging in genre and content, but should not include gratuitous scenes of violence and sex.

5. Children's programmes should be aired in regular slots at times when children are available to view, and/or distributed via other widely accessible media or technologies.

6. Sufficient funds must be made available to make these programmes to the highest possible standards.

7. Governments, production, distribution and funding organisations should recognise both the importance and vulnerability of indigenous children's television and take steps to support and protect it.

Figure 1: The Children's Television Charter

172

The hidden presence here, of course, is that of the market, and particularly of the dominance in that market of the US. In the context of global commercialisation, issues of social representation and cultural identity have become highly problematic. Thus, the Charter argues that programmes should 'affirm [children's] sense of community and place'; while simultaneously promoting 'an awareness and appreciation of other cultures in parallel with the child's own cultural background'. The economic dimension of this concern is only fully apparent in the Charter's final clause, which calls for governmental support and protection for 'indigenous' production. Of course, it remains to be seen whether such statements of good intent will have any status whatsoever in the competitive, market-driven environment we have described: the crucial question here, as Anna Home herself has recognised, is whether the 'fine ideals' embodied in the Charter can be made to 'stick'.[30]

In each of these respects, however, the Charter speaks on behalf of children from within the world of broadcasting; it does not propose any new institutional means of relating to the child audience. It thus suffers from the problem of all such documents: it ascribes views, needs and interests to children without organising the kind of dialogue which would allow these assigned needs to be informed by children's own perspectives. Nevertheless, in what is for us a key passage, the Charter urges producers, companies and governments to affirm that 'children should hear, see and *express themselves*, their culture, their languages and their life experiences'. It is at this point, in its emphasis on the right to expression alongside those of consumption, that the document most clearly admits the child to a kind of citizenship.

Ultimately, however, the Charter remains a fundamentally *defensive* document. Its very existence draws attention to the disturbance of older discursive patterns by the emergence in children's television of a discourse of consumer sovereignty. Though it finds its most committed expression only in the utterances of a small number of producers, working for minority cable and satellite channels, the influence of this discourse is becoming increasingly widespread. The existence of competitive pressure and of the necessities of attracting, satisfying and re-attracting a large child audience mean that even producers in the 'public service' mainstream are aware, most often critically, of the power exerted by the child consumer. In our next and final chapter, we ask whether these new pressures and necessities are likely to shape the entire future of children's television. And we consider whether it would be a bad thing if they did.

Notes

Unless otherwise indicated here, all quotations in this chapter are taken from interviews conducted by the authors between 1996 and 1998.

1 Abercrombie et al. (1988), p. 71.
2 Volosinov (1973), p. 19.
3 Williams (1980), pp. 38–42. The article was originally published in 1973.
4 Programmes like Channel Four's *Wise Up* which are informed by this conception of the child as potential citizen are frequently critical of aspects of commercial youth culture.
5 Owen Reed, unpublished interview with John Lane for the BBC Oral History Project 1977. Interview with a former member of the BBC's Secretariat, 1998.

6 Pilkington Committee (1962), p. 15.

7 Himmelweit, Oppenheim and Vince (1958), p. 15.

8 National Union of Teachers (1969).

9 BBC (1974), p. 5.

10 The Hadow Report ('Report of the Consultative Committee of the Board of Education'), excerpted in MacLure (1986), p. 191.

11 Monica Sims, '*Sesame Street*', paper given to the European Broadcasting Union, 14 October 1971 (WAC T47/113). These words are quoted several times in BBC documents of the period, both internal and public. They originated, according to Sims (*BBC Children's Programmes*, internal paper, June 1969; WAC T47/113), with 'a *Play School* producer'.

12 BBC (1974), p. 6.

13 Sims, '*Sesame Street*'. The quotation is attributed to Basil Bernstein. We cannot trace it verbatim in Bernstein's work, but it corresponds intellectually and in some of its phrasing to the argument of 'A critique of the concept of compensatory education', in Bernstein (1971). This article, in turn, is a reworking of Bernstein's 'Education cannot compensate for society', *New Society*, No. 387, 26 February 1970, pp. 344–7.

14 For a more extensive discussion of *Grange Hill*, see Buckingham (forthcoming a).

15 Quoted in Briggs (1961), pp. 238–9.

16 Quoted in Scannell and Cardiff (1991), p. 17.

17 Hugh Carleton Greene, 'Two threats to broadcasting: political and commercial control', 13 March 1958 (WAC T16/45/2). See Chapter One.

18 See, for example, the report from the *Guardian*, 16 February 1998, quoted in the Introduction; and the observations of Jocelyn Hay, quoted in Chapter Two.

19 Hugh Greene, quoted in Hood (1967), pp. 49–50; Kenneth Adam, quoted in Tracey and Morrison (1979), p. 45.

20 Pilkington Committee (1962), p. 68.

21 Ibid., p. 16.

22 Cf. Bettelheim (1975).

23 Franklin and Franklin (1996).

24 Ibid., pp. 96–9.

25 United Nations Convention on the Rights of the Child (1989), Article 12.

26 Ibid., Article 13.

27 John Richmond (1996), programme introduction to the 'Children on Screen' conference brochure, London, British Film Institute.

28 Although it is worth noting that Jessica Samuels, the leader of *Grange Hill*'s school rebellions in the late 1970s, was female, albeit heavily 'masculinised': see Buckingham (forthcoming a).

29 Stephen Andrew, current producer of *Grange Hill*, speaking at 'Beyond the Square Window', a conference held at the London College of Printing and Distributive Trades, June 1996.

30 Anna Home, quoted in Lisosky (1998, p. 359).

6 Conclusion

In this chapter we want to respond more directly to the issues and problems which we have set out – at various times descriptively, analytically or polemically – at earlier points in the book. We claimed in our Introduction that the future of children's television is debated now in terms of two wider themes – the changing nature of childhood and the post-1980 revolution in broadcasting. We suggested that anxieties stemming from these changes saturated public discussion about children's television; and in subsequent chapters we traced their impact on different aspects of television practice. In outlining the policy-related conclusions of the book, we try to maintain this dual focus: some of what we say relates to broadcasting policy, some to a wider 'politics of childhood'. Both aspects, however, need to be understood against a wider, complex background of economic, social and political transformation.

Between 1979 and 1997, British Conservative governments preached with increasing fervour the necessity of global, deregulating economic change. As many commentators have noted, their commitment to economic liberalism sat uneasily beside a nation-centred social authoritarianism. The Conservatives' New Labour successors have accepted with even greater clarity the logic of the new world order. 'Globalisation', wrote Tony Blair in 1995, 'is changing the nature of the nation state as power becomes more diffuse and borders more porous. Technological change is reducing the capacity of government to control a domestic economy free from external influence.'[1] Blair's government has accordingly shed much of the nationalist and traditionalist inhibition which compromised the Conservative endorsement of change, particularly where issues of culture were at stake.

Yet in other respects, notably in social and educational policy, it has a different emphasis. Here, the work ethic prevails. In Blair's words, 'education, education, education' is the priority. His preoccupation is 'not to slow down the pace of change and so get off the world, but to educate and retrain for the next technologies, to prepare our country for new global competition'.[2] Thus the young unemployed are to be integrated into a (low-cost) workforce, and schooling policy is increasingly based not on a 1960s rhetoric of creative freedom, but on achievement targets defined in terms of a narrow and still-traditional curriculum; it imagines the child as a future adult who must be prepared now for that heavy responsibility. Whereas the media industries, reshaped by globalisation and deeply involved in exploring the newly identified consumer needs of children, emphasise pleasure, entertainment and the satisfaction of 'wants', education moves on a different plane. If television increasingly treats children as consumers to be pleasured, then government policy views them as economic resources to be augmented or as social problems who require a stronger disciplinary regime.

Both the changes identified by Blair and the policies his government promotes create difficulties for children's television. The first of these difficulties is economic. Blair's claims about the extent and inexorable power of globalisation have been challenged as exaggerated by several critics, who argue that such accounts needlessly concede the impossibility of political control of the new economic order.[3] But however overstated his claims about globalisation may be at a general level, Blair's analysis is much more closely pertinent to television. A sizeable part of 'British broadcasting' has no British base and has escaped national control. At the same time, the competitive proliferation of channels and systems of delivery, coupled with the permanent squeeze on public financing that arises from governments' determination to provide business with low-tax, low-inflation environments, means that the BBC has experienced strong pressures to drive down costs and to seek new sources of income from international co-production, co-transmission and marketing. In the process, its character as a national public sector broadcaster has been substantially modified. Thus, in several ways, the structures of children's television disregard national boundaries, to the point where sketching some kind of policy project may begin to seem like an exercise in fantasy. How can forces operating on such a global scale, with such rapid momentum, in the context of international institutional frameworks which heavily favour the workings of free enterprise, be at all affected by policies deriving from a national context and formed on the basis of an appeal to relatively weak institutions of government?

The second difficulty – less intractable, but equally noteworthy – is social. Broadly speaking, children now experience a growing contradiction between two cultural worlds. The first world is that of leisure, which for young children remains largely centred on television viewing. Television as a medium is pervasive, expanding and entertainment-centred; it is increasingly linked to film and computer products, and is the basis for an ever-broadening range of merchandising. This is also an unequal world: children from different social classes have varying levels of access to television and television-related products. Children's second world is school-based. Here, the emphases of curricula and policy fall on a print-centred literacy, and on traditional kinds of cultural value. In and around this second world, the influence of television on children is – as we saw in the Introduction – regularly decried by policy-makers; and the study of television and other media has yet to establish an important place in a heavily regulated curriculum. There is inequality here too. Despite the standardised nature of this curriculum, socially based differentials in attainment have not decreased; and there is an argument that a curriculum based so firmly on traditional definitions of what is educationally valuable may have a further, exclusionary effect on children from non-privileged backgrounds.[4]

A policy for children's television needs to take account of this world beyond production. Questions of access, and of the development of a broader, better-informed, more technologically capable audience should be central to it. These dimensions are not heavily stressed in current policy debate. Certainly, New Labour's double emphasis – on the necessities of both global economic change and disciplined, social cohesion – would appear to promote the worst of both worlds. It seems content to tolerate a market-driven expansion of television while neglecting the development in children of the capacities to understand and respond to it.

Public service versus the market?

Policies are not formed in an intellectual vacuum, but in argument with other positions. In earlier parts of this book, we have described two such positions – those of market-based and public service provision – and we return to them now, in a more open and critical encounter. Our position here is a dissatisfied one. In evaluating arguments between the 'old' television and the 'new', we find ourselves fully sympathetic to neither. 'Old' arguments identify the problems of the market (albeit sometimes in exaggerated ways), but rest on an outmoded and unduly narrow conception of childhood. 'New' arguments expose some of the paternalism of the old, but appear to promote an equally restricted conception of childhood, as something that begins and ends in the act of consumption. For different reasons and in different ways, neither position seems capable of addressing the full diversity and the changing nature of contemporary childhoods.

The best argument for organising television on a market basis is Rupert Murdoch's Edinburgh lecture of 1989 – an intervention memorable especially for the way it harnessed democratic themes to an anti-elitist cultural polemic, and then deftly proceeded to recruit both 'political freedom' and 'popular culture' to the cause of deregulation. Murdoch attacked the assumption of governments that 'the people could not be trusted to watch what they wanted to watch, so that [television] had to be controlled by like-minded people who knew what was good for us'.[5] In this assumption, governments were morally wrong and technologically outdated. New technologies of broadcasting meant that the case for governmental regulation of a limited resource – spectrum scarcity – had collapsed. The era which lay ahead, he predicted, would be one of 'freedom and choice rather than regulation and scarcity'. In such conditions, the market could come into its own, as what John Keane, explicating Murdoch, describes as an 'unsurpassed mechanism for discovering by trial and error what consumers want, how these tastes can be supplied at least cost, and whether new and challenging ideas and tastes will catch their eye'.[6] In addition to attributing to the market this intrinsic passion for innovation and quality, Murdoch added another claim: he placed himself in the great tradition of campaigners for freedom of expression, standing in a line of descent from those who fought in the seventeenth and eighteenth centuries against the 'regulations and censorship' enforced by church and state.[7] Achieving freedom in broadcasting, he concluded, was part of the unfinished agenda of democratic revolution in Britain. It would strike a blow against the power of cultural elites; it would end the dominance of a narrow set of cultural values; it would remove television from bureaucratic control and place it in the hands of 'the people'.[8]

We described in Chapter Five how these arguments have entered the bloodstream of some who work in television, providing them with a means of criticising the protective elitism embedded in public service working practice. Certainly, the positions of public service broadcasters have often provided an easy target for this kind of assault. Cecil McGivern's early objections to dance bands, BBC producers' distaste for the 'boom, boom, boom' of popular children's television, the later urge to protect children from representations of chip-eating and sexuality, and the unease felt by some contemporary media professionals at the growth of children's consumer culture – in their attitude to the child audience, these positions amount to a persisting history of distrust. Historically, public service professionals have acted as the gate-keepers who have turned away particular kinds of popular culture at the door. Aspects of children's lives which fail to meet with moral approval, which diverge from the cultural mainstream, which offend established notions of good taste and cultural value – which fail, in other words, to conform to worthy, paternalistic constructions of childhood – have largely remained on the margins. Children have had few opportunities to represent themselves, or to exercise any control in the making of programmes or broadcasting policy. And in the absence of strong structures of accountability, professional cultures have been insufficiently open to arguments for change.[9]

To recognise the force of Murdoch's attack, however, does not amount to accepting the positions from which it is launched; and to note the vulnerability of public service professionalism is not to see it as a completely exhausted tradition. We do not accept that markets in any long-term way deliver the popular freedom and wide-ranging choice that Murdoch claims. As Keane points out, in at least two essential ways markets inhibit freedom and choice: first, because they produce tendencies towards merger and monopoly; second, because the entry costs for participation in a global, high-tech market are discouragingly high.[10] Our analysis of the new children's cable and satellite providers in Chapter Two amply illustrates these points. But our research has also unearthed other factors. Subscription television does not offer universal access. It is not required, nor in principle committed, to providing a comprehensive range of programmes. To be sure, the advent of these new channels has brought novel styles of programming to British screens – albeit wholly from the US. Yet – to adopt Graham Murdock's argument – it is doubtful whether their programming policy will significantly extend 'the overall diversity of provision' over the longer term.[11]

As we suggested in Chapter Four, there is a wide gap between the rhetoric of market-centred broadcasters and the reality of their programming policies and research strategies: a discourse of consumer empowerment is accompanied by a practice which addresses only some sections of the potential audience about a limited range of issues. Even when the market exposes the weaknesses of public service television by addressing neglected audiences (ethnic minority audiences, in particular), its achievement is a contingent one, which offers no guarantees of continuing or systematic provision. This contingency is an effect of something which Murdoch, like other free-market advocates, regards as the central virtue of the private sector: that what it produces is not in any strong sense the outcome of public argument, but rather the result of producers' anticipation of, or response to, the aggregate of thousands of individual choices. The absence of any other form of public influence or normative control is one of the components of what Murdoch calls 'freedom'.

By contrast, public service broadcasting is justified by an idea that is in essence both normative and debatable – that of the public good. This is not to say that the idea has in practice been the subject of much public debate or public accountability. On the contrary, as we showed in Chapter One, broadcasters have been happy to arrogate to themselves the power to determine it. Nevertheless, the idea is still a productive one. It suggests that choices about broadcasting have to be related to wider social ends; and it implicitly addresses viewers as actors in the public sphere, rather than merely consumers. It thus enables arguments about policy to be conducted in terms that go beyond the assumption that somewhere, in the broadcasting marketplace, consumers will find something that matches their preferences and appeals to their taste. And it continues to have particular institutional features, whose ultimate justification lies in arguments about equity and citizenship: universal access; the screening – in the case of children's television – of programmes at a time when the audience is available to view; and a commitment to a range of programming that is educational and informative as well as entertaining.

There are two great problems with the 'public good', however – problems which weaken its position and the persuasive force of its argument in current broadcasting debates. First, it has never been a focus for non-professional argument: there is no culture of popular involvement in matters of broadcasting policy. Second, the definition of the 'public' with which broadcasters have operated has been a restricted one: some groups do not figure among the public at all; while others are granted only a minor place. Children are, of course, one of the most neglected audiences in this respect. Broadcasters have largely taken it upon themselves to define children's 'needs' – and in the process, to define what *counts* as 'range' or 'quality', or indeed as 'education' or 'entertainment' – rather than attempting to discover the ways in which children themselves might define or perceive them. As we indicated in Chapter Four, the market is now increasingly driven by the desire to gather information about children's *wants* – an investigation which throws into stark relief the relative failure of public broadcasters to explore or assess the validity of their own assumptions about children's *needs*.

In what follows, we suggest ways in which these weaknesses might be redressed. In doing so, our concern is partly to make proposals about structures of television provision; but more importantly perhaps, it involves suggestions for strengthening the public sphere that surrounds broadcasting, particularly as it relates to children. We want to help bring about a situation in which children's roles as critical consumers and active participants in this broader 'media culture' are recognised and responded to. To achieve this, we will suggest, involves changes that go well beyond the immediate concerns of television producers: it means attending more closely than before to the social and cultural capacities and experiences of television audiences.[12]

New forms of regulation?

Like others before us, we centre our alternatives to existing policies around ideas of *diversity* and *democracy*. In formulating them, we have responded to what on the one hand we see as the weaknesses of the present system, and on the other to what, in the current political and economic climate, we perceive as the furthest concrete possibilities of change. Thus, for example, we do not repeat Raymond Williams's call of the 1960s and 1970s for the means of communication to pass into public ownership, from where it would be franchised out to groups of producers.[13] We avoid this route, not because we think that Williams's policy is irredeemably flawed, but because in the 'moment' of the 1990s – unlike the 1960s – there is no chance that such a policy could be taken up by forces who could make any kind of difference to present arrangements. 'Commercial' television is an incomparably stronger force than in Williams's time. Class politics – the recognition of which sustained the whole of Williams's work – is in decline. In addition, the various educational and cultural movements whose work could illustrate what Williams's goal of a 'common culture' might mean in practice are largely gone, overwhelmed by the market or constrained by a managerial state. Williams's proposals, then, have in our terms passed beyond the realm of present possibility. Working for democratic goals, reducing inequalities, promoting diversity and strengthening popular involvement in the field of television now require a different approach, necessarily more incremental, and informed by the international scale of the problems it seeks to address.

We begin, then, from two convictions about children's television: that it should represent and encourage cultural diversity; and that, in common with other kinds of television, it should be both accountable and open to public participation. In outlining our arguments in this area, we need to say something about the differences between what we are suggesting here and other current approaches. Contemporary debates about media policy are dominated by new schemes for regulation. Richard Collins and Cristina Murroni, for example, provide what has been widely regarded as a kind of blueprint for New Labour policy.[14] Their proposals are based on a general definition of the public good – involving principles of security, opportunity, democracy and fairness – which we would broadly share. The prime strength of their approach lies in a realisation that the pace and scope of global media change have outstripped the ability of existing regulatory agencies to cope. The genie of channel proliferation is out of the bottle, and it is not possible – or desirable – to force it back in again. What is possible, they argue, is to regulate the industry in positive and accountable ways: regulation should not only be seen as a means of curbing the excesses of the market but also as a positive force for raising levels of quality. It can maintain universal access to some services; it can ensure that the cost of others is affordable; and it can work to make broadcasters more accountable.

The BBC is central to this conception of regulation: as a strong competitor in the marketplace, it 'provides an important benchmark of standards below which competitors' standards fall at their peril'.[15] To allow it to operate in this way, Collins and Murroni suggest, its various parts should be disaggregated, so that its public service functions can be separated from its commercial operations and from the pressures of the marketplace.[16] This strengthening of public service obligations should be accompanied by an overhaul of regulatory agencies. There should be a single regulatory body for all types of media and communications, which should promote competition and oppose monopoly. It should facilitate redress against misrepresentation; and it should (lightly) draw up guidelines to regulate media content.[17]

Collins and Murroni propose a concrete and to some extent persuasive set of policies. They seem to us, however, to involve several kinds of weakness – economic, political and cultural. In economic-political terms, their proposals rest on too sanguine an evaluation of the effects of markets. They see regulation as a means of 'translating the benefits of innovation, efficiency and a thriving industrial sector ... into fuller entitlements to participate in social, economic and political life for all citizens'.[18] Yet this is not an easy translation. One of the strong messages that emerges from our interviews with television professionals is that market arrangements, in driving down costs and pursuing efficiency, tend to undermine sustained, as opposed to episodic, efforts to achieve the kind of objectives championed by Collins and Murroni. Programme-makers have to think in terms of maximising audiences; production companies have to plan for the short term; and the drive to build on success by thinking in terms of international production and marketing is in tension with the need to maintain creative momentum.[19] Nor is it easy to see what interest cable and satellite companies – or indeed ITV franchise-holders – would have in promoting other objectives that might flow from the principles on which Collins and Murroni ground their work. In relation, say, to securing wider access to television production facilities or in promoting a stronger regional dimension to programme-making, the economics of the industry exert a negative pull towards a uniformity of content and an increasing distance between programme origin and the location of audiences. To counteract these tendencies is likely to require stronger regulatory powers than Collins and Murroni are prepared to advocate – and with the exercise of those powers comes the likelihood of sharp political conflict, a likelihood which their book serenely avoids.

Similar difficulties arise in their treatment of the BBC. Collins and Murroni are critical of the Corporation's tendency to paternalism and non-accountability, and argue that it cannot match the record of the private sector in providing a voice for interests and identities that have traditionally been ignored.[20] Their response to this problem is to advocate changes in the way BBC's governors are appointed, so that they more explicitly represent the public interest. Alongside such a change, they recommend new institutional forms – such as citizens' juries and a consumer council – that would strengthen formal and informal influence over the governors' performance.[21]

These proposals go some way towards addressing the democratic deficit that characterises broadcasting, but they are insufficient on their own. As in many other areas of social policy, such mechanisms for public accountability and participation are at risk of becoming citizenly duties that will only be performed by a small minority. They must be connected to a much broader public culture in which the whole range of people's media experiences can be addressed and debated. At this point, there is a striking absence in Collins's and Murroni's account – a developed sense of the *audience* (or indeed the public) in whose names these reforms are demanded.

We shall return to these questions of institutional reform in due course. Our key emphasis, however, is that the democratisation of television will only be partly a matter of institutional changes like these. It must also depend on a number of other factors to do with the relationship between the media and the wider public sphere – with what we have termed the 'media culture'. In other words, democratisation is an issue that involves both the internal organisation or 'micro-politics' of media organisations and a macro-level relationship between different social institutions and sectors. The discussion, we would argue, needs to begin where Collins and Murroni (and much New Labour policy-making) effectively leave off – that is, with the *audience*.

Changing media cultures

Our first proposals, then, lie outside the immediate area of media organisation. To some extent, they also lie outside the immediate realm of policy – if by policy we mean a programme that is reliant on government or corporate initiative for its realisation. What we have to propose is something much looser; one which relies, to some extent, upon government intervention, but which emphasises just as strongly other sorts of agency, including the influence of children. More than that, it has a discursive element: it attempts to alter the ways in which children's television is talked about, so that questions of purpose, quality and audience needs can be more productively discussed.

As we have suggested at several points in this book, traditional definitions of childhood no longer provide adequate resources for understanding the nature of children's experiences in the contemporary world. The ways in which children are commonly represented and regulated underestimate their capacities for cultural and social action, and mistakenly recognise creative energies as evidence of irrationality or consumer enslavement. One of the most pressing needs of children's television is for new accounts of childhood – its needs and wants, its diversity and complexity – to emerge into the public domain. Academic work has some part to play here. The rapid growth of historical and sociological writing about childhood is not just a reflection of the social changes which we sketched in our introduction but also itself a potential contributor to new kinds of popular thinking that more fully recognise children's situations and capacities. Sociologists of childhood have shown how differently the world appears once official accounts – of labour, of poverty, of health – are revised to include the experience of children.[22] Such revisionism can sometimes become the basis for new, widely shared ways of seeing. Likewise, it is possible to imagine how we can use the accumulated evidence of contemporary research into children's viewing to challenge fixed ideas. In this light, for example, children's preference for 'adult' media – for soap operas or indeed for horror movies – could be seen not as a sign of irrationality or corruptibility but as a demand to be addressed in ways that more fully recognise their maturity.[23]

These developments are as yet inadequately reflected in public – and particularly journalistic – debates about children's relationship with the media. As academics, we might perhaps be expected to criticise the triviality and superficiality of journalism in our field; yet there is now an extraordinary discrepancy between the vast scope and significance of media activity and the very limited grasp of it displayed within both popular and 'quality' journalism. As we have suggested, debates about children and television are all too often forced into an either/or logic, in which the medium is seen to be inherently 'good' or (much more frequently) 'bad' for children, irrespective of its content or of the ways in which it is used and interpreted. For many critics, such debates provide a convenient vehicle for laments about cultural decline that are based on little more than nostalgic fantasies about an illusory bygone age.

Changing children's media cultures, then, involves reshaping the discourses through which children are represented. It also requires transforming those powerful institutions outside broadcasting which regulate children's activities and attempt to shape their identities. Centrally important in this respect is the school. We began this chapter by sketching some of the problems of contemporary education policy – namely, its failure to address continuing inequalities, and the anxieties about children's performance and behaviour which underpin its narrow curricular approaches. It is beyond our scope here to suggest detailed ways in which these weaknesses can be addressed. What we do maintain is that, however globalised the media have become, it remains within the capacities of national governments to take measures to counteract cultural polarisation and to contribute to the creation of a new kind of child audience.

Increased education spending and the channelling of resources – including information and communication technologies – towards disadvantaged schools would begin to address these continuing inequalities. Yet the 'wiring up' of schools should not be seen as an end in itself. The gap between the 'information rich' and the 'information poor' is not simply a matter of access to equipment; nor indeed is it simply a matter of 'information'. Measures to redress inequalities of economic or technological capital must be accompanied by attempts to address *cultural* capital as well. Amid the hype that surrounds current government policy on information and communication technologies, far too little attention has been paid to the ways in which such technologies might be used, and the learning contexts in which this might occur. Much more should undoubtedly be invested in teacher education; but we also need a more fundamental rethinking of the curriculum.

As we approach the millennium, it seems quite extraordinary that the school curriculum should continue to neglect the forms of culture and communication that have so thoroughly dominated this century. Over the past two decades, a rigorous and coherent model of media education has emerged in Britain that combines the critical analysis of media texts and institutions with creative media production; yet, media education has largely remained on the margins of formal schooling. If children are to become critical consumers and participants in the media culture that surrounds them, they urgently need a curriculum that addresses these experiences in their full diversity and complexity. Apart from its broader social and cultural benefits, such a curriculum would encourage children to have high expectations of the media themselves.[24]

To create such an educational culture seems to us a highly desirable social objective. It would not, though, be primarily a creation of young people themselves, however much it facilitated their ability to become social actors. It would need to be complemented by policies that support the development of a sort of 'public sphere of the young', that go some way to fostering children's development as autonomous *citizens* who possess genuine social and cultural rights and responsibilities.

Episodically, during the period from 1968 to roughly 1994 (the year of the Criminal Justice Act), youth movements had a significant political and cultural presence, expressed in community unrest, protests against Youth Training and more or less organised discontent with education. More persistently, as Chris Richards has suggested, throughout this period youth music cultures were (and continue to be now) bearers of significant social meanings, which either went unrecognised or were perceived as threatening by the wider culture.[25] It is arguable that this activity, though to a large extent located not among children but among 16- to 24-year-olds, had an important, if indirect, effect on children's television. Without ever being fully acknowledged and represented, it helped to establish what we called in Chapter Five a 'social' version of child-centredness as an important element in public service broadcasting.

Strengthening such activity is not something that can be achieved in any regulatory manner – quite the opposite. But a policy that provides resources, tolerates dissent and lessens financial pressures on the young is much more likely to create the conditions for a productive media culture than one which emphasises conformity with restrictive and pre-set educational goals, enforces low-paid involvement in the workforce and rations social resources. Again, new information and communication technologies would appear to have some potential here, but they also pose certain dangers. Some enthusiasts have argued that the Internet will become exactly the kind of 'children's public sphere' that we have called for here – although at present it is of course confined to a relatively small elite.[26] Yet, like television, its potential in this respect will partly depend upon the extent to which it can develop independently of commercial influences and of attempts at moral regulation – both of which are currently directed at the young.

These ideas are, of course, merely indicative of the ways in which children's involvement in a wider 'media culture' might be extended and encouraged.[27] Realising children's rights of access to cultural expression inevitably has implications for their civil and political rights; and such moves would therefore need to be part of a more general 'enfranchisement' of young people. The more widely such a critical and participatory culture could be established, the more its diversity would become plain, and the more it would be able to act as a concrete reminder to broadcasters of the range of interests and capabilities possessed by their audience.

Changing institutions

Thus far, we have focused on changes in the cultures of children and young people – on creating a new kind of audience. We now move on to discuss potential changes in television institutions – changes which would both *respond* to the new kinds of demand we would expect to see emerging from the wider media culture and also serve to *strengthen* elements in that culture. We should stress that we do not see these two kinds of developments as opposed, but rather as complementary. The emphasis we place on democratisation, participation and accountability is often regarded as incompatible with producer autonomy. We feel that this is a false polarity. What the Pilkington Committee said in the 1960s remains true: good broadcasting is a question of practice, not prescription. It is not something that can be laid down by regulators, think-tanks or researchers. Yet good practice, in its turn, is not simply a product of the creative efforts of individuals: it requires a context of debate, a level of security, an everyday working climate and above all *a relationship with an audience* that will foster creativity and innovation.

The 'external' or 'audience-centred' approach to media policy we have outlined should be complemented by specific 'internal' measures. Here, the major issues are those of accountability, access, the nature of 'producer cultures' and the character of television output. These four issues need to be addressed across the range of television – public service and commercial, terrestrial and cable/satellite.

Accountability in children's television is a difficult issue. As we indicated in Chapters One and Two, there have always been pressure groups which seek to define the interests of children and to speak for them, insisting that broadcasters are sensitive to their demands and critiques. The views of these groups cannot and should not be set aside; but there is a strong need to establish means by which children themselves can speak more directly, collectively and loudly to broadcasters and regulators. Citizens' juries and a consumer council – the institutions in which Collins and Murroni try to concretise the idea of accountability – are not models which can usefully apply to the child audience. This is not so much because children are immature, as because their status as students – as people involved in a process of organised learning – enables them, potentially, to develop a deeper understanding of media issues than could ever be achieved in the brief meetings of a jury or in the small space that an adult-dominated consumer council would allow. A regular series of regional conferences, organised by the regulatory body, preceded by website debates and linked to the media education curriculum of primary and secondary schools would give children the opportunities to make a well-prepared, persistent contribution to debates about media policy. In the process, it would encourage children to think of themselves as citizens, and afford adults the chance to re-evaluate their view of children's capacities.

The remaining three questions – of access, producer cultures and output – need to be dealt with in the same framework of institutional provision. The fundamental issue for children's television is how the opportunities offered by the ever-greater abundance of channels can be utilised in a way that promotes greater access and diverse kinds of representation, while at the same time sustaining innovative and reasonably secure producer cultures.

The BBC remains a key institution in this respect. We believe that adequate public funding of the BBC is vital to ensure that it continues to be the major force in the national television market. The BBC has to be in a position to serve the public – and particular minority groups within that public – in ways that no other organisation can or would do. The BBC's Charter currently contains no specific commitment to children's television; and any renewal of the Charter – or any new regulatory regime – should rectify this omission. We would also argue that the principle of accountability and openness should be extended to the BBC's commercial activities, specifically in respect of children's television. While the BBC's initiatives in new media – such as children's websites or digital media channels – are broadly to be welcomed, these should not be at the expense of investment in the two main, free-to-air channels. The BBC should be reminded that its primary audience for children's programming is the majority of children in Britain – not parents concerned about their children's achievement at school or international buyers at trade fairs.

As we have indicated, the BBC can succeed in this new global market by capitalising on its reputation for 'quality'; but in the process, the definition of 'quality' may be narrowed, and certain genres of programming may stand to lose out. There is a particular threat posed here to genres such as contemporary 'realist' drama; but paradoxically, it may also apply to programmes that fail to meet traditional adult criteria of 'quality' and 'good taste', such as children's comedies or game shows. In principle, it should be the task of regulation to ensure that both the BBC and the commercial terrestrial channels provide the full range of genres – the 'mini-schedule' – that has historically characterised children's television. Nevertheless, as we have shown, genres are inevitably subject to historical change; and this kind of balance between genres is not one that can meaningfully be specified in the abstract. On the contrary, such regulation should proceed on the basis of a much more thoroughgoing consultation with the audience, that moves well beyond the limitations of market research.

In some ways, however, it is a mistake to place the BBC – even a reformed BBC – at the centre of future broadcasting policy. One of our major themes in this book has concerned the way in which the BBC has been prodded into innovation by various competitive challenges – from ITV in the late 1950s to Nickelodeon in the late 1990s. These observations would imply that one way to ensure productive change at the BBC is to improve the quality of its competition. We would propose at least four measures here.

The first is to emphasise, and make provision for funding, Channel Four's responsibility to screen experimental and innovative programmes for minority audiences of children. Channel Four's children's programmes should not be driven – as they mostly appear to be at present – by the need to find the largest possible audience. On the contrary, its children's schedule should serve as a breeding ground for new talent and ideas, and should be offering material that is substantially different from that of the BBC and ITV.

Our second proposal is to revise ITV's statutory commitment to children's television, so that it is expressed in terms of a budget share, rather than a set number of hours. Providing the share was set high enough, this would have the effect of creating opportunities for more original, domestic production within ITV's children's schedule; and it might also ensure that programmes were marketed and promoted more effectively than they are at present.

The third proposal is to use the opportunities offered by cable/satellite and digital television to create children's channels that involve high degrees of access, participation and local programming – in other words, to create conditions in which audiences became to some extent producers. This might build upon the approach of Channel Four's *Wise Up* and *Look Who's Talking* or the BBC's *As Seen on TV*; although we would hope to see children much more centrally involved in production and editorial decision-making than is often the case here. We recognise that such initiatives can result in a form of 'ghettoising', despite the best intentions of broadcasters or programme-makers; and it is important to find ways of avoiding this, both by providing appropriate levels of investment and by careful scheduling. Yet from the point of view of such channels, programmes of this kind would provide a fairly inexpensive way of generating original, domestically produced material – material which, in our view, they should be positively required to provide.

Finally, we would propose that separate funding should be provided from outside the industry – as it is in many other countries – to finance innovative production both for and by children. This approach might develop – and learn from – the experience of the 'workshops' that emerged in the early days of Channel Four, in which programme production was part of a broader set of educational initiatives, whose outcomes were not only directed at broadcasting.

None of these measures could be achieved without regulation, or indeed legislation; none could be defended simply on market grounds; and some would undoubtedly meet opposition from the owners and shareholders of commercial channels. They would therefore require political will to enforce. Nevertheless, we would argue that all these proposals are concrete and feasible; and that none is outside the power of a national government to achieve.

Change of this sort, especially when linked to the wider cultural shifts we sketched earlier, would alter the climate in which BBC children's television operated. Alongside the pressures of a new kind of regulation, it would probably strengthen tendencies towards innovation, in the way that Channel Four, in its early days, encouraged the reshaping of BBC 2. It would, in other words, amount to competition of a benign sort. Nevertheless – as some of the producers we interviewed in Chapter Five made clear – any strongly competitive regime in television, however benignly intended, creates a permanent state of turbulence in which job security and productive working conditions are both threatened. Programme producers become programme salespeople; production companies must expand to survive, and in expanding lose the traditions of creative working practice which brought them success in the first place. Specialist training is undoubtedly necessary for programme-makers who work for an audience that is by definition very different from themselves; and yet it is precisely this kind of training that seems bound to suffer in the uncertain new regime of contemporary television.

The issue of training and of 'producer cultures' therefore needs to be specifically addressed. This could be done in several ways. The BBC's market-mimicking regime of Producer Choice has to be modified so that it is compelled to make most of its programmes in-house, and thus to preserve the core of the Children's Department. Similar protection should be given to the children's departments of the larger independent companies, which (like the BBC) have historically served as the major means of specialist training for children's producers. We would also argue that commercial broadcasting should be levied to pay for a training and development fund that would ensure a continuing supply of expertise in this field. Funding prizes and awards, as well as one-off prestige productions in the *Film on Four* or *Screen Two* mould, would also help to raise the status of children's production within the industry as a whole, and hence attract the talented individuals who are vital to its success.

We have concluded, then, by suggesting some ways in which productive cultures of broadcasting can be sustained by the industry itself. But such cultures cannot survive on the old basis. A new, more democratic relationship with the audience needs to be established, one which is founded on principles of accountability and participation.

We began Chapter One with Owen Reed's evocative account of two middle-aged men, steeped in the culture of pre-war Middle England, aiming to settle the future of children's television over a stiff drink. They failed. Now as then, the future of children's television as a creative social and cultural force will depend not merely on the tactics of professionals, old or new, but on the boldness with which it lets its audience be heard and responds to their clamour.

Notes

1 Tony Blair, 'The Power of the message', *New Statesman*, 29 September 1995.
2. Ibid.
3 See, for example, Hirst and Thompson (1996).
4 Hatcher (1996).
5 Murdoch (1989), p. 2.
6 Keane (1991), p. 58.
7 Murdoch (1989), p. 3.
8 Ibid., p. 10.
9 See the critiques of Hall (1993) and Murdock (1990).
10 Keane (1991), p. 89.
11 Murdock (1990), p. 83.
12 See Cunningham (1992) for a discussion of the broader policy implications of this 'turn to the audience'.
13 Williams (1962, revised 1968, 1976).
14 Collins and Murroni (1996).
15 Ibid., p. 144.
16 Ibid., p. 148.
17 Ibid., Chapter Eight.
18 Ibid., p. 182.
19 See Chapter Five.
20 Collins and Murroni (1996), p. 5.
21 Ibid., pp. 152–4, 178–9.
22 See, for example, James, Jenks and Prout (1998).
23 See, for example, Buckingham (1993, 1996).
24 For an introductory account of media education, see Bazalgette (1992); and for an analysis of practice, see Buckingham and Sefton-Green (1994).
25 Richards (1998).
26 See, for example, Katz (1997) and Tapscott (1998).
27 These arguments will be developed more fully in Buckingham (forthcoming b).

Bibliography

Abercrombie, N., Hill, S. and Turner, B. S. (1988) *The Penguin Dictionary of Sociology*, Harmondsworth, Penguin.

Abrams, M. (1956) 'Child audiences for television in Great Britain', *Journalism Quarterly*, Vol. 33 No. 1, pp. 35–41.

Abrams, M. (1959) *The Teenage Consumer*, London, London Press Exchange.

Abrams, M. (1961) *What Children Watch*, Manchester, Granada Television.

Adams, M. (1950) 'Programmes for the young viewer', *BBC Quarterly*, Vol. 5 No. 9, pp. 81–9.

Ang, I. (1991) *Desperately Seeking the Audience*, London, Routledge.

Annan Committee (1977) *Report of the Committee on the Future of Broadcasting*, London, HMSO.

Associated Rediffusion (1963) *Children's Viewing of Children's Television Programmes*, London, Associated Rediffusion.

Association of Market Survey Organisations (1988) *Children's Television Choices*, London, AMSO

Australian Children's Television Foundation (1995) *Report of the World Summit on Children and Television*, Melbourne, ACTF.

Balio, T. (ed.) (1976) *The American Film Industry*, Madison, University of Wisconsin Press.

Barwise, P. and Ehrenberg, A. (1988) *Television and its Audience*, London, Sage.

Bazalgette, C. (1992) *Media Education*, London, Hodder & Stoughton.

Bazalgette, C. and Staples, T. (1995) 'Unshrinking the kids: children's cinema and the family film', in C. Bazalgette and D. Buckingham (eds), *In Front of the Children: Screen Entertainment and Young Audiences*, London, British Film Institute.

BBC (1957) *Programmes for Children: Report of the General Advisory Committee*, London, BBC.

BBC (1974) *Children as Viewers and Listeners: A Study by the BBC for its General Advisory Council*, London, BBC.

BBC/ITA (1960) *Children and Television Programmes* (O'Conor Report), London, BBC/ITA.

Bernstein, B. (1971) *Class, Codes and Control: Volume 1*, London, Routledge & Kegan Paul.

Bettelheim, B. (1975) *The Uses of Enchantment: The Meaning and Importance of Fairy Tales*, London, Thames and Hudson.

Beveridge Committee (1951) *Report of the Broadcasting Committee* Cmd 8116 HMSO, quoted in P. Scannell, 'Public service broadcasting: the history of a concept', in A. Goodwin and G. Whannel (eds) (1990), *Understanding Television*, London, Routledge.

Blumler, J. (1992) *The Future of Children's Television in Britain: An Enquiry for the Broadcasting Standards Council*, Research Working Paper VIII, London, Broadcasting Standards Council.

Blumler, J. and Biltereyst, D. (1998) *The Integrity and Erosion of Public Television for Children: A Pan-European Survey*, London, Broadcasting Standards Commission.

Briggs, A. (1961) *The History of Broadcasting in the United Kingdom. Volume I: The Birth of Broadcasting*, Oxford, Oxford University Press.

Briggs, A. (1995) *The History of Broadcasting in the United Kingdom. Volume V: Competition*, Oxford, Oxford University Press.

Brunsdon, C. (1990) 'Problems with quality', *Screen*, Vol. 31 No. 1, pp. 67–90.

Buckingham, D. (1993) *Children Talking Television: The Making of Television Literacy*, London, Falmer.

Buckingham, D. (1995a) 'The commercialisation of childhood? The place of the market in children's media culture', *Changing English*, Vol. 2 No. 2, pp. 17–41.

Buckingham, D. (1995b) 'On the impossibility of children's television: the case of Timmy Mallet', in C. Bazalgette and D. Buckingham (eds), *In Front of the Children: Screen Entertainment and Young Audiences*, London, British Film Institute.

Buckingham, D. (1996) *Moving Images: Understanding Children's Emotional Responses to Television*, Manchester, Manchester University Press.

Buckingham, D. (1997) 'The making of citizens: pedagogy and address in children's television news', *Journal of Educational Media*, Vol. 23 No. 2/3, pp. 119–39.

Buckingham, D. (1998) 'Telly trouble', *English and Media Magazine*, No. 39, pp. 14–18.

Buckingham, D. (ed.) (in preparation) *Television for Children: Texts and Genres*, London, British Film Institute.

Buckingham, D. (forthcoming a) *After the Death of Childhood: Growing Up in the Age of Electronic Media*, Cambridge, Polity.

Buckingham, D. and Sefton-Green, J. (1994) *Cultural Studies Goes to School: Reading and Teaching Popular Media*, London, Taylor & Francis.

Buckingham, D. and Sefton-Green, J. (1997) 'From regulation to education', *English and Media Magazine*, No. 36, pp. 28–32.

Burman, E. (1994) *Deconstructing Developmental Psychology*, London, Routledge.

Burns, T. (1977) *The BBC: Public Institution and Private World*, London, Macmillan.

Capon, N. (1952) 'The child and the dragon', *BBC Quarterly*, Vol. 6 No. 5, pp. 27–9.

Collett, P. and Lamb, R. (1986) *Watching People Watching Television*, report to the Independent Broadcasting Authority, London, IBA.

Collins, R. and Murroni, C. (1996) *New Media: New Policies*, Cambridge, Polity.

Connell, I. (1983) 'Commercial broadcasting and the British left', *Screen*, Vol. 24 No. 6, pp. 70–80.

Corner, J., Harvey, S. and Lury, C. (1995) 'Culture, quality and choice: the re-regulation of TV 1989–91', in S. Hood (ed.), *Behind the Screen*, London, Lawrence & Wishart.

Cunningham, S. (1992) *Framing Culture: Criticism and Policy in Australia*, Sydney, Allen & Unwin.

Curran, J. and Seaton, J. (1997) *Power without Responsibility: The Press and Broadcasting in Britain* (sixth edition), London, Routledge.

Davies, H., Buckingham, D. and Kelley, P. (1999) 'Kids' time: childhood, television and the regulation of time', *Journal of Educational Media*, Vol. 24 No. 1.

Davies, H., Buckingham, D. and Kelley, P. (forthcoming b) 'In the worst possible taste: children, television and cultural value', MS submitted for publication.

Davies, M. M. and Corbett, B. (1997) *The Provision of Children's Television in Britain: 1992–1996*, London, Broadcasting Standards Commission.

Davin, A. (1996) *Growing Up Poor*, London, Rivers Oram Press.

de Cordova, R. (1994) 'The Mickey in Macy's window: childhood, consumerism and Disney', in E. Smoodin (ed.), *Disney Discourse*, London, British Film Institute.

Department of Education and Science (1983) *Popular Television and Schoolchildren*, London, DES.

Dorfman, A. and Mattelart, A. (1975) *How to Read Donald Duck: Imperialist Ideology in the Disney Comic*, New York, International General.

Engelhardt, T. (1986) 'Children's television: the shortcake strategy', in T. Gitlin (ed.), *Watching Television*, New York, Pantheon.

Fisch, S. M. (1998) 'Children's Television Workshop: the experiment continues', in M. E. Price and R. G. Noll (eds), *Communications Cornucopia: Markle Readings in Information and Communication Policy*, New York, Brookings Institution Press.

Fish, S. (1980) *Is There a Text in This Class?*, Boston, Harvard University Press.

Fleming, D. (1996) *Powerplay: Toys as Popular Culture*, Manchester, Manchester University Press.

Foucault, M. (1979) *Discipline and Punish*, Harmondsworth, Peregrine.

Franklin, A. and Franklin, B. (1996) 'Growing pains: the developing children's rights movement in the United Kingdom', in J. Pilcher and S. Wagg (eds), *Thatcher's Children? Politics, Childhood and Society in the 1980s and 1990s*, London, Falmer.

Gane, R. (1994) 'Television audience measurement systems in Europe: a review and comparison', in R. Kent (ed.), *Measuring Media Audiences*, London, Routledge.

Garnham, N. (1983) 'Public service versus the market', *Screen*, Vol. 24 No. 1, pp. 6–27.

Garnham, N. (1990) *Capitalism and Communication: Global Culture and the Economics of Information*, London, Sage.

Gitlin, T. (1983) *Inside Prime Time*, New York, Pantheon.

Goodhardt, G., Ehrenberg, A. and Collins, M. (1975) *The Television Audience: Patterns of Viewing*, Farnborough, Saxon House.

Goodwin, P. (1992) 'Did the ITC save British public service broadcasting?', *Media, Culture and Society*, Vol. 14 No. 4, pp. 653–61.

Granada Television (1960) *Children's Television Viewing*, Manchester, Granada Television.

Hadow Committee (1931) *Report of the Consultative Committee of the Board of Education*, excerpted in S. MacLure, *Educational Documents: England and Wales 1816 to the Present Day*, London, Methuen.

Hall, S. (1993) 'Which public, whose service?', in W. Stevenson (ed.), *All Our Futures: The Changing Role and Purpose of the BBC*, London, British Film Institute.

Halsey, A. H. (ed.) (1972) *Educational Priority: EPA Problems and Policies. Volume 1*, London, HMSO.

Hatcher, R. (1996) 'The limitations of the new social democratic agendas: class, equality and agency', in K. Jones and R. Hatcher (eds), *Education After the Conservatives: The Response to the New Agenda of Reform*, Stoke-on-Trent, Trentham Books.

Hebdige, D. (1988) 'Towards a cartography of taste 1935–1962', in D. Hebdige, *Hiding in the Light*, London, Routledge.

Hendrick, H. (1997) *Children, Childhood and English Society. 1880–1990*, Cambridge, Cambridge University Press.

Hill, J. (1991) 'Television and pop: the case of the 1950s', in J. Corner (ed.), *Popular Television in Britain*, London, British Film Institute.

Himmelweit, H. T., Oppenheim, A. N. and Vince, P. (1958) *Television and the Child*, Oxford, Oxford University Press.

Hirst, P. and Thompson, G. (1996) *Globalisation in Question*, Cambridge, Polity.

Hollins, T. (1984) *Beyond Broadcasting: Into the Cable Age*, London, British Film Institute.

Home, A. (1993) *Into the Box of Delights: A History of Children's Television*, London, BBC Books.

Home, A. (1995) 'The public television view', *Metro Education*, No. 5, Special World Summit Edition, Spring 1995, pp. 21–9.

Hood, S. (1967) *A Survey of Broadcasting*, London, Heinemann.

James, A., Jenks, C. and Prout, A. (1998) *Theorizing Childhood*, Cambridge, Polity.

Jenks, C. (1996) *Childhood*, London, Routledge.

Johnson, R. W. (1998) Review of Ross McKibbin, *Class and Culture in England 1918–1951*, *London Review of Books*, 21 May.

Katz, J. (1997) *Virtuous Reality*, New York, Random House.

Keane, J. (1991) *The Media and Democracy*, Cambridge, Polity.

Kelley, P., Buckingham, D. and Davies, H. (1999) 'Talking dirty: children, sexual knowledge and television', *Childhood*, Vol 6 No 2.

Kent, R. (ed.) (1994) *Measuring Media Audiences*, London, Routledge.

Kinder, M. (1991) *Playing with Power in Movies, Television and Video Games: From Muppet Babies to Teenage Mutant Ninja Turtles*, Berkeley, University of California Press.

Kline, S. (1993) *Out of the Garden: Toys and Children's Culture in the Age of TV Marketing*, London, Verso.

Kunkel, D. (1993) 'Policy and the future of children's television', in G. Berry and J. Asamen (eds), *Children and Television*, London, Sage.

Kunkel, D. and Watkins, B. (1987) 'Evolution of children's television regulatory policy', *Journal of Broadcasting and Electronic Media*, Vol. 31 No. 4, pp. 367–89.

Leavis, F. R. (1948) *The Great Tradition*, London, Chatto & Windus.

Liebes, T. and Katz, E. (1990) *The Export of Meaning: Cross-Cultural Readings of Dallas*, New York, Oxford University Press.

Lingstrom, F. (1953) 'Children and television', *BBC Quarterly*, Vol. 8 No. 7, pp. 96–102.

Lisosky, J. M. (1998) 'The Children's Television Charter: assessing the feasibility of global consensus for television policy', in U. Carlsson and C. von Feilitzen (eds), *Children and Media Violence*, Goteborg, Sweden, UNESCO International Clearinghouse on Children and Violence on the Screen.

Lowe, R. (1988) *Schooling in the Post War Years*, London, Routledge.

MacLure, S. (1986) *Educational Documents: England and Wales 1816 to the Present Day*, London, Methuen.

Mandel, E. (1974) *An Introduction to Marxist Economic Theory*, New York, Pathfinder Press.

Melody, W. (1973) *Children's Television: The Economics of Exploitation*, New Haven, Yale University Press.

Meyrowitz, J. (1985) *No Sense of Place: The Impact of Electronic Media on Social Behaviour*, Oxford, Oxford University Press.

Murdoch, R. (1989) 'Freedom in broadcasting', MacTaggart Lecture, Edinburgh International Television Festival.

Murdock, G. (1990) 'Television and citizenship: in defence of public broadcasting', in A. Tomlinson (ed.), *Consumption, Identity and Style: Marketing Meanings and the Packaging of Pleasure*, London, Routledge.

Murdock, G. and Golding, P. (1989) 'Information poverty and political inequality: citizenship in the age of privatised communications', *Journal of Communication*, Vol. 39 No. 3, pp. 180–95.

National Union of Teachers (1969) *Into the Seventies: Towards a Policy for a New Education Act*, London, NUT.

Neuman, W. R. (1991) *The Future of the Mass Audience*, New York, Cambridge University Press.

Newburn, T. (1996) 'Back to the future? Youth crime, youth justice and the rediscovery of "authoritarian populism" ', in J. Pilcher and S. Wagg (eds), *Thatcher's Children? Politics, Childhood and Society in the 1980s and 1990s*, London, Falmer.

Nixon, H. (1998) 'Fun and games are serious business', in J. Sefton-Green (ed.), *Digital Diversions: Youth Culture in the Age of Multimedia*, London, University College London Press.

Ohmae, K. (1995) *The End of the Nation State*, New York, Harper Collins.

Oswell, D. (1995) *Watching with Mother: A Genealogy of the Child Television Audience*, unpublished PhD thesis, Open University.

Palmer, E. (1988) *Children in the Cradle of Television*, Lexington, MA, Lexington Books.

Pegg, M. (1983) *Broadcasting and Society 1918–1939*, London, Croom Helm.

Pilcher, J. and Wagg, S. (eds) (1996) *Thatcher's Children? Politics, Childhood and Society in the 1980s and 1990s*, London, Falmer.

Pilkington Committee (1962) *Report of the Committee on Broadcasting*, London, HMSO.

Postman, N. (1983) *The Disappearance of Childhood*, London, W. H. Allen.

Richards, C. (1998) *Teen Spirits: Music and Identity in Media Education*, London, University College London Press.

Rose, J. (1984) *The Case of Peter Pan: Or the Impossibility of Children's Fiction*, London, Macmillan.

Rowland, W. (1983) *The Politics of TV Violence: Policy Uses of Communication Research*, Beverly Hills, CA, Sage.

Rushkoff, D. (1996) *Playing the Future: How Kids' Culture Can Teach Us to Thrive in an Age of Chaos*, New York, Harper Collins.

Sanders, B. (1995) *A is for Ox*, New York, Vintage.

Scannell, P. (1996) *Radio, Television and Modern Life*, Oxford, Blackwell.

Scannell, P. and Cardiff, D. (1991) *A Social History of British Broadcasting 1922–1939: Serving the Nation*, Oxford, Blackwell.

Schneider, C. (1987) *Children's Television: The Art, the Business and How It Works*, Lincolnwood, IL, NTC Business Books.

Scraton, P. (ed.) (1997) *'Childhood' in 'Crisis'?*, London, University College London Press.

Seiter, E. (1993) *Sold Separately: Parents and Children in Consumer Culture*, New Brunswick, Rutgers University Press.

Sendall, B. (1982) *Independent Television in Britain. Volume 1: Origins and Foundations*, London, Macmillan.

Sharot, T. (1994) 'Measuring television audiences in the UK', in R. Kent (ed.), *Measuring Media Audiences*, London, Routledge.

Silvey, R. (1974) *Who's Listening?: The Story of BBC Audience Research*, London, Allen & Unwin.

Smythe, D. (1981) *Dependency Road*, Norwood, New Jersey, Ablex.

Staples, T. (1997) *All Pals Together: The Story of Children's Cinema*, Edinburgh, Edinburgh University Press.

Stephens, D. (1966) *Television for Children*, BBC lunchtime lectures, fifth series, London, BBC.

Tapscott, D. (1998) *Growing Up Digital: The Rise of the Net Generation*, New York, McGraw Hill.

Tomlinson, J. (1991) *Cultural Imperialism: A Critical Introduction*, Baltimore, MD, Johns Hopkins University Press.

Tracey, M. and Morrison, D. (1979) *Whitehouse*, London, Macmillan.

Tuman, M. (1992) *Word Perfect: Literacy in the Computer Age*, London, Falmer.

Turow, J. (1981) *Entertainment, Education and the Hard Sell*, New York, Praeger.

UN Convention on the Rights of the Child (1989) United Nations, New York (http://www.unicef.org/crc/conven.htm).

Varlaam, C. et al. (1990) *Skill Search: Television, Film and Video Industry Employment Patterns and Training Needs*, Brighton, The Institute of Manpower Studies.

Volosinov, V. N. (1973) *Marxism and the Philosophy of Language*, New York, Seminar Press.

Wagg, S. (1992) 'One I made earlier: media, popular culture and the politics of childhood', in D. Strinati and S. Wagg (eds), *Come on Down? Popular Media Culture in Post-War Britain*, London, Routledge.

Walkerdine, V. and Lucey, H. (1989) *Democracy in the Kitchen: Regulating Mothers and Socialising Daughters*, London, Virago.

Ward, C. (1994) 'Opportunities for childhoods in late twentieth century Britain', in B. Mayall (ed.), *Children's Childhoods Observed and Experienced*, London, Falmer.

Wartella, E. (1993) 'Producing children's television programs', in J. Ettema and D. Whitney (eds), *Audiencemaking: How the Media Create the Audience*, London, Sage.

Wartella, E., Heintz, K. E., Aidman, A. J. and Mazzarella, S. R. (1990) 'Television and beyond: children's video media in one community', *Communications Research*, Vol. 17 No. 1, pp. 45–64.

Webster, D. (1991) *Looka Yonder*, London, Comedia.

Williams, R. (1974) *Television, Technology and Cultural Form*, Glasgow, Fontana.

Williams, R. (1976) *Communications*, Harmondsworth, Penguin.

Williams, R. (1980) 'Base and superstructure in Marxist cultural theory', in R. Williams, *Problems in Materialism and Culture*, London, Verso.

Young, B. (1990) *Children and Television Advertising*, Oxford, Oxford University Press.

Index

References in italics refer to figures and tables